D0094497

ANCIENT-FUTURE
FAITH

*Rethinking Evangelicalism
for a Postmodern World*

ROBERT WEBBER

A Bridgepoint Book

Baker Books
A Division of Baker Book House Co
Grand Rapids, Michigan 49516

Published by Baker Books
a division of Baker Book House Company
P.O. Box 6287, Grand Rapids, MI 49516-6287

Second printing, March 2000

Printed in the United States of America

Library of Congress Cataloging-in-Publication Data

Webber, Robert.
    Ancient-future faith : rethinking evangelicalism for a postmodern world / Robert Webber.
        p.   cm.
    "A Bridgepoint book."
    Includes bibliographical references and index.
    ISBN 0-8010-6029-X (pbk.)
    1. Evangelicalism. I. Title.
BR1640.W39   1999
270.88'29—dc21

                                    99-40968

For current information about all releases from Baker Book House, visit our web site:
http://www.bakerbooks.com

ANCIENT-
FUTURE
FAITH

CONTENTS

Part 6   A Classical/Postmodern Mission

PREFACE

For the past two hundred years Western Christianity has been interpreted through the modern categories of science, philosophy, and communication theory. Today, this view, called modernity, is dying because of the current revolutions in those same fields of studies. In light of these changes, the question is being asked: "What will evangelical Christianity look like in the future?" The burden of *Ancient-Future Faith* is to say that the road to the future runs through the past.

J. Julius Scott, a colleague of mine and a fine historian and theologian, tells his classes, "If you really want to understand Christianity, you need to put it into a nine-hundred-year period. Understand the three hundred years before the first century and six hundred years after the first century, and you will grasp the origins and essence of the Christian faith." I am told that Karl Barth said to his classes, "No one dare do contemporary theology until they have mastered classical Christian thought." These two quotes capture the spirit of this book: "you can best think about the future of the faith after you have gone back to the classical tradition."

Because classical Christianity and postmodernism are areas of vast academic inquiry, the attempt to relate the two posit a third area of creativity and imagination: a dialogue between the old and the new. So this book will focus on the demise of modernity, the rise of postmodern thought, and the creative calling to re-present a classical Christianity within a postmodern world.

The fundamental concern of this book is to find points of contact between classical Christianity and postmodern thought. Classical Christianity was shaped in a pagan and relativistic society much like our own. Classical Christianity was not an accommodation to paganism but an alternative practice of life. Christians in a postmodern world will succeed, not by watering down the faith, but by being a countercultural community that invites people to be shaped by the story of Israel and Jesus.

I have written *Ancient-Future Faith* for teachers, pastors, college and seminary students, and church leaders who desire an overview of the issues and a perspective for the future. My concern is to be clear, brief, and simple. Roads into the academic discussions are found in the notes and recommended reading for those who wish to pursue the topic more extensively.

ACKNOWLEDGMENTS

The idea for this book first began when Tim Gunnett, a former employee in the Baker Books marketing department, stumbled upon a book review of my *Common Roots* (Zondervan, 1978) in an old copy of *The Wittenburg Door*. He then suggested to acquisitions editor Robert Hosack that Baker republish my book. Bob reviewed the book and agreed that many of the concerns that I had addressed there were even more relevant to the cultural context of today's church. And so a contract was given, and I set myself toward a revision. However, the more I thought about our current shift into the postmodern world, the more I sensed that more than a revision was needed to bring the book up to date. Although this book was intended as a revision of *Common Roots*, it is so thorough that it stands on its own as a new book. My thanks to Bob Hosack for encouraging me to make such extensive changes.

I also want to express my thanks to my colleague at Wheaton College, Dr. Stephen Kang, for the bibliographical help on Part 1, to the Rev. Kenneth Rick for helping me with some obscure footnotes, to Rodney Clapp for his review of the manuscript in its early stages, and to Maria E. denBoer for her careful and helpful editorial work. And thanks to Carmen Martinez, my personal assistant, who spent many hours bent over the computer typing numerous drafts and rewrites.

PART

ONE

SETTING THE STAGE

We are but of yesterday, and already
we have filled all your world: cities, islands,
fortresses, towns, market places, the camp itself,
tribes, companies, the palace, the senate, the forum.
—Tertullian, A.D. 200

My own personal history is deeply rooted in evangelicalism: I was raised in fundamentalism, educated at a fundamentalist college, and graduated from three conservative seminaries in the Episcopal, Presbyterian, and Lutheran traditions. And since 1968, I have taught at Wheaton College, a recognized institution in the evangelical tradition.[1]

Also, my family connections span the range of evangelicalism in the twentieth century. My father, who was born in 1900 and studied at Moody and Northern Baptist Seminary, was deeply involved in the issues surrounding the fundamentalist–modernist controversy. My father-in-law was a founding member of Fuller Seminary, editor of *Christianity Today,* and the author of *Battle for the Bible.* My church association since the early 1970s has been in an evangelically oriented Episcopal church.

Postmodern thought states that there is "no such thing as a completely detached observer." We always interpret reality through the eyes of our own history.[2] Therefore, when I think about the faith, I do so with the prejudices I

carry from my upbringing, my education, my family connections, my place of work, and my alignment with a historic denomination. As you read this book, I invite you to be aware of your own background and interact with me in an I-thou, not an I-it, encounter.[3] Let me begin by asking you to recognize my major prejudice: The most formidable challenge currently facing evangelicals is the shift from a modern to a postmodern worldview.

My suggestion that we re-present classical Christianity to the postmodern culture is not a call for a mere historical restitutionism, but a serious application of classical thought to a postmodern worldview. Therefore, my task in this introductory chapter is to speak to postmodernism as a movement that introduces a whole new set of questions with which we evangelicals must interact.

handwritten: 6 paradigms of time of Western church

PARADIGM THINKING

One of our first concerns is to rethink the way we interpret history. For example, when I was in seminary it was popular to regard the civilizations that preceded the Western world as inferior. This attitude has undergone significant change.[1] The new hermeneutic rejects the Enlightenment view of the steady progress of civilization, and seeks to understand and appreciate each epoch of history within its own time, taking into consideration its geographical location, culture, and philosophical presuppositions.[2]

It is now common to think in terms of six discernible paradigms of time that can be traced in the complex history of the Western church. While these divisions are somewhat artificial because history does not change abruptly, we can nevertheless speak convincingly of the following periods of Western thought: primitive Christianity (the first century); the common era, with the emergence of classical Christianity (100–600); the medieval era, with the formation of a distinct Roman Christianity (600–1500); the explosion of the Reformation and the growth of Protestantism (1500–1750); the modern era, with the growth of denominations (1750–1980): and the postmodern period now emerging (1980–) (see table A).

In each of these periods of history, Christianity wrestled with unique sets of philosophical, scientific, and cultural factors. Throughout history Christians have always struggled to incarnate the faith in each particular culture.[3] Consequently, a style of Christianity successful in one era changes as another era begins. Those who remain committed to the old style of faith subsequently freeze that style in the particular culture in which it originated.[4] This process accounts for much of the diversity

handwritten: IMP.

13

we have in the faith today and allows us to understand that the differences among Orthodox, Catholic, and Protestant groups are largely due to the cultural styles in which they have become embedded.

We now live in a transitional time in which the modern worldview of the Enlightenment is crumbling and a new worldview is beginning to take shape.[5] Some leaders will insist on preserving the Christian faith in its modern form;[6] others will run headlong into the sweeping changes that accommodate Christianity to postmodern forms;[7] and a third group will carefully and cautiously seek to interface historic Christian truths into the dawning of a new era.[8] It is this latter position that I want to espouse.[9] I will do so in the broadest strokes while recognizing the complexity of the issues.

We begin with a brief overview of the six paradigms of Christianity with the intent of viewing the landscape of two thousand years of history in a variety of cultures. This review will enable us to see that the church has gone through a number of transitions and will make us sympathetic to the current transition from a modern to a postmodern worldview.

A Summary of the Paradigms

The biblical paradigm is difficult to summarize in just a word or two for it covers many generations of people and draws from cultural settings as diverse as the liberating work of Moses, the settled reign of David, and the era of the prophets. Philosophically it may be said that the biblical era was a time for the holistic understanding of all things. In Israel reality was interpreted by the conviction that God was at work in history, most especially in the community of faith. Faith was situated in this historic religious community that passed down its teaching through oral communication from generation to generation. Like Israel, early Christians were immersed in the history of their community and found meaning and an explanation of their world through the rituals and rites of worship that handed down the faith.

During the ancient period of culture (100–600), Christianity faced the challenge of communicating the faith in an era dominated by Platonic thought. For Plato, the dominant philosopher of the period, the universal was found in the "other world." This world was a mere shadow of that true and ideal world of the other.[10] This other-worldly vision of reality caused the church to stress the biblical idea of mystery and the Pauline notion that we see through a glass darkly. God was the *mysterium tremendum*. The most often used image of God was that of light.

God dwelt in inaccessible light, a light that could not be penetrated by human sight. The church and its theology dealt with the mystery of how God who is wholly other became involved with the plight of a fallen world in the incarnation, death, and resurrection of Jesus Christ, the Son of God. While God's redemption was a great mystery, every effort was made to understand the shadow of the mystery expressed in history, embodied in the church, enacted in worship, and witnessed to in the creeds. In this period of history classical Christianity was formed.

The medieval world (600–1500) shifted its philosophy toward an Aristotelian outlook.[11] Aristotle, in contrast to Plato, insisted the universal was within the created order. This location of truth within the structures of creation led to an emphasis on the church as the institution of God on earth. It ruled the world, both the spiritual and political arms. It interpreted truth; it dispensed salvation through the sacraments; and it acted as the establishment of heaven on earth. In this period of history Christianity took on its medieval and Roman form.

The Reformation (1500–1750) was preceded by a new philosophy, nominalism. Nominalism insisted that truth is not found in an objective institution but in the mind. This philosophy weakened medieval Roman Catholic institutionalism and resulted in an emphasis on the individual and his or her mind. The Bible became the object of study that could now be interpreted by individuals who were in conflict with previous institutional understandings.[12] This Scripture-driven approach to Christianity fueled the Protestant faith. It also accounts for the rise of denominationalism, the differences of which are traced back to various interpretations of the Bible.

The modern era (1750–1980), shaped by the philosophy of Descartes, placed its emphasis on reason.[13] The rise of logic and the empirical methodology insisted that truth be based on observation and derived from the empirical method.[14] For liberals, reason led to the denial of a supernatural Christianity and to the teaching of Christianity as myth. For conservatives, the emphasis on reason led to a proof-oriented Christianity, to "evidence that demands a verdict."

Currently, Western society is in a transition from the modern world to a postmodern world. The new revolutions in science, philosophy, and communications—in all areas of life—are shifting us toward the affirmation of new values (see table C). We live, science says, in an expanding universe; we are, philosophy states, in an interrelationship with all things; and we increasingly communicate through visual and symbolic means. These shifts are resulting in a whole new culture and raise new questions about the way a biblical Christianity is to be understood and communicated (see table A).

The Value of Paradigm Thinking

This brief overview of the major Christian paradigms introduces us to a key element of postmodern thought: paradigm thinking. First, paradigm thinking asks us to understand the past contextually. Each epoch of Christian history is to be studied in its own culture. Since its beginning, the Christian faith has been filtered through a variety of cultures. In each of these cultures Christianity has been primarily communicated through one or more dominating principles. Thus, it may be said broadly that the story of Christianity moves from a focus on mystery in the classical period, to institution in the medieval era, to individualism in the Reformation era, to reason in the modern era, and now, in the postmodern era, back to mystery.

Next, paradigm thinking allows us to have a deep appreciation for the past. We Protestants usually root our understanding of the faith in one of the post-sixteenth-century renewing movements—a Reformer, pietism, revivalism, or the modernist–fundamentalist controversy.[15] We often freeze that particular moment in time, make it the standard expression of faith, and then judge all other movements or periods of time by our standard. Paradigm thinking sets us free to affirm the whole church in all its previous manifestations. Therefore, the study of other periods of history should not be looked at judgmentally, but as a dialogue and an encounter with a previous manifestation of faith that may inform and strengthen our Christian understanding in a different culture.

Third, paradigm thinking also recognizes that the major models of the past continue into the present world. For example, Christianity adapted in the Greek world remains with us in Eastern Orthodoxy; Christianity formulated in the medieval world remains with us in Roman Catholicism (note, however, that Vatican II sought to relate Catholic thought to the twentieth century). Many Reformation models are still with us—Lutheran, Anglican, Reformed, and Anabaptist. And, of course, there are those expressions of faith that have been formed by the culture of modernity—modern liberalism, for example. Through the hermeneutic of paradigm thinking we are able to understand the multiplicities of faith expressions as attempts within a particular cultural moment and geographical place to express the faith in a fresh way.

Fourth, paradigm thinking affirms the variety and diversity of the Christian faith and looks for the framework of faith that is common to the diversity. This search for a common heritage allows for the emergence of a new understanding of unity and diversity. Unity is based on what is passed down in the ecclesio-social culture of the universal church, *framework of faith stays w/ us*

whereas diversity is a particular understanding of the faith that reflects the specific cultural context in which it was expressed (e.g., medieval Roman versus sixteenth-century Reformation). So while we are all Christians, some of us are Roman Catholic Christians, Eastern Orthodox Christians, Reformation Christians, twentieth-century evangelical Christians, or some other form of modern or postmodern Christians.[16]

Finally, paradigm thinking also provides us with an intelligent way to deal with times of transition. For example, we currently acknowledge that the Christian faith incarnated in the modern culture, with its philosophical assumption of a mechanistic world understood through empirical methodology, is eroding. The cultural revolutions are in the process of ushering us into a new era. In this swirl of change, many are seeking to honestly incarnate the historic faith in the emerging culture.[17] This goal will not be accomplished by abandoning the past, but by seeking out the transcultural framework of faith (i.e., the rule of faith) that has been blessed by sociocultural particularity in every period of church history.

Therefore, the point of integration with a new culture is not to restore that cultural form of Christianity, but to recover the universally accepted framework of faith that originated with the apostles, was developed by the Fathers, and has been handed down by the church in its liturgical and theological traditions. This hermeneutic allows us to face the changing cultural situation with integrity. Our calling is not to reinvent the Christian faith, but, in keeping with the past, to carry forward what the church has affirmed from its beginning. We change, therefore, as one of my friends said, "not to be different, but to remain the same." Right now we are caught up in the throes of changing from modernity to postmodern times. So let's look at this shift more closely to figure out how we ought to change to remain the same.

17

2

FROM A MODERN
TO A POSTMODERN PARADIGM

The Modern Paradigm

I am convinced that if we want to understand the conflict taking place in churches today we need to understand the shift from the modern paradigm to the postmodern paradigm of thought. This study will help us identify the specific issues that are at stake in our cultural transition into a postmodern era. We begin with the three most central features of modern thought: (1) individualism, which asserts the ultimate autonomy of each person; (2) rationalism, which is characterized by a strong confidence in the power of the mind to investigate and understand reality; and (3) factualism, which insists that the individual, through the use of reason, can arrive at objective truth.[1]

The background to these ideas of modernity are found in the eighteenth and nineteenth centuries and in several steps that led to a thoroughgoing rationalistic Christianity. First, the cosmological revolution shifted the understanding of the world from the moral cosmology of the medieval world to the mechanistic worldview of the Newtonian world machine. Mystery was set aside in favor of an exuberant confidence in reason and science as the way of knowing objective truth. This confidence in reason led to the belief that the Christian faith could be rationally explained and defended.[2] Building Christianity around reason became the crucial task of Enlightenment Christians. Second, it was soon taught that a contradiction existed between science and the Bible, reason and the Bible, and history and the Bible. The liberal response was to claim that the structure of Christianity, with its emphasis on incarnation, atonement, and resurrection, had to be reinterpreted. According to liberals, these doctrines were myths that needed to be demythologized in order to find the core of the Christian faith.[3] For them the heart of the problem was found in the distinction between Jesus and Paul. Jesus had preached a simple gospel of love, but Paul introduced a Jesus with a heavenly status, changing Christianity into a metaphysical system. The liberal repudiated the Pauline system of thought and viewed Christian doctrine in what George Lindbeck calls the "experiential-expressive" perspective. Liberalism interpreted "doctrines as non-informative and non-discursive symbols of inner feelings, attitudes, or existential orientations."[4]

Conservatives responded to the liberal notion of "myth" with what came to be known as "evidential apologetics." Conservatives followed the Enlightenment emphasis on individualism, reason, and objective truth to build edifices of certainty drawing from the internal consistency of the Bible, the doctrine of inerrancy, the apologetic use of archaeology, critical defense of the biblical text, and other such attempts at rational proof. These attempts became inseparable from the modern notions of individualism, reason, and objective truth. In this way evangelical thought became enmeshed with modernity. Lindbeck refers to this group as "propositionalists" because they have an affinity with "analytic philosophy with its preoccupation with the cognitive or informational meaningfulness of religious utterances."[5]

René Descartes was the father of the modern emphasis on reason. His famous dictum was, "I think, therefore I am." His empirical method of scientific observation and rational deduction permeated every discipline, including biblical studies and theology. A critical methodology was developed that affirmed the ability of the mind to understand truth through science and reason. This method of rational interpretation was applied to the study of Christianity.

This Enlightenment paradigm produced three convictions shared equally by Christians and non-Christians: foundationalism, structuralism, and the notion of the metanarrative. Foundationalism is "the philosophical theological conviction that there are beliefs or experiences that are in themselves beyond doubt and upon which systems of belief and understanding can therefore be constructed with certainty."[6] Structuralism is the belief that societies construct texts to make meaning out of life and that the meaning which is in the text can be commonly agreed upon by its interpreters through the use of reason.[7] The metanarrative consists of the stories of the text. These stories make sense out of life by providing an interpretation of the world from its beginning to its end.[8]

Secular world view

For example, the modern paradigm, building on these three assumptions, has resulted in different worldviews. The dominant secular worldview insists that we can arrive at the truth of God's nonexistence through the texts of evolution and the idea of progress. Secularists have a grand metanarrative that moves from the origin of creation out of chance to the culmination of creation in some kind of golden age. And the means by which this goal will be accomplished, they argue, is through autonomous individualism, using the tool of reason to interpret the text of science to determine the meaning and the future of the world.[9]

Liberal world view

Liberal Christianity constructed a worldview in close affinity with the secular outlook. For them the foundation of thought is the use of critical reason to investigate the text of the biblical metanarrative. The liberal worldview, asserting the authority of the individual mind, insists on the mythical character of Scripture and reduces the Christian message to that of love. God is loosely construed as a nondefinable force that moves history from its uncertain origin to its equally uncertain future.[10]

Evangelical Christianity has also developed a worldview based on the modern paradigm. While reason is placed under revelation, evangelicals insist revelation can be interpreted through the use of reason, resulting in foundational truth. Following the line of structuralism, evangelicals argue that "meaning is found within the biblical text."[11] Evangelicals also insist that the single authorial meaning of each text is discoverable through the use of the grammatical-historical and theological method. This is the notion of propositional truth. For example, some time ago I was giving lectures at an evangelical seminary. After my morning lecture I was wandering around the halls and stopped outside the door of a classroom to listen when I heard the professor say in a strong and authoritative voice, "There is one single meaning to every text of Scripture and we have the tools to discover that meaning and know the intent of the author." This statement represents an evangelical application of Cartesian individualism, and a high confidence in reason to arrive at factual truth. The Bible is the foundation of truth, the tools of reason uncover that truth, and truth is emphatically, if not entirely, propositional.

The Post-Enlightenment Paradigm

In recent years the modern paradigm of rational certainty has been challenged by the revolutions that have taken place in every area of life (see table B). Because of these revolutions, evangelicals must rethink their enmeshment with modernity and construct a theology that will be consistent with historic Christianity yet relevant to our new time in culture. I have chosen to emphasize the changes that have occurred in science, philosophy, and communication theory because they illustrate the shift into postmodernism and provide good handles for an intelligent interaction with historic Christianity. Note that the shift into postmodernism is much broader; I suggest the reader reflect on the complexity of change illustrated by table C. We now examine these three revolutions to discover the kinds of changes that shift us into postmodern times (see table D).

The Scientific Revolution

The first and perhaps most fundamental challenge to modernity with its emphasis on reason and the empirical method comes from the twentieth-century revolution in science. The mechanistic worldview of the Enlightenment and the high estimate of human reason to understand the way the world works began to break down with the smashing of the atom. While it was once thought "the world stands still," it was now discovered that nothing stands still, that everything is in perpetual motion.[12] The first impact of the new science was to open the door to mystery once again. The world now appears to be complex and mysterious. While some scientists remain optimistic about the ability of the human mind to comprehend all of reality, a new scientific posture of humility before the vastness and complexity of the universe has taken shape. In the postmodern world scientists will continue to research, to explore, and to offer interpretations of creation and life, but with much more tentativeness than before.[13]

A second result of the new science with its theory of relativity and quantum mechanics is a shift from dualism to holism.[14] While our picture of the world was at one time that of a vast collection of individualized particles, externally related but essentially independent, the new revolution in physics argues for a dynamic and interrelated world. Quantum theory has demonstrated that the substance-quantity nature of the particle, a basic feature of Newtonian physics, has been replaced by a concept that is essentially dynamic, involving both space and time. Third, this shift from a world that stands still to a world that is in perpetual motion has resulted in a new approach to fact. Because matter is in perpetual movement, postmoderns argue that we cannot arrive at rational and scientific facts. So-called facts are only *interpreted* facts. Therefore, it is now recognized, even in science, that one needs to bring to "fact" a framework of thought that is based on faith. The assumption that there

21

is no God is a faith-commitment as much as the assumption that there is a God.[15]

This shift into mystery, holism, and interpreted fact, instead of necessitating a new theology, makes the historic and traditional theology of the church relevant once again. The theology of the ancient church was characterized by mystery, a holism that rejected all dualistic structures of thought and the interpretation of the Christ-fact. The understanding of God and God's relationship to the world in creation, incarnation, and re-creation, was hammered out in the framework of a commitment to a God who participates in history and works out the salvation of the entire cosmos from within the created order. This holistic understanding of God and creation as the central mystery of the Christian faith holds the greatest potential for an intelligent recovery of classical Christianity in a postmodern world.[16]

The Philosophical Revolution

It would be a mistake for us to think that the new philosophical thought arises out of a vacuum. It does not. If anything, the philosophy of postmodernism is a response to the scientific revolution. This shift from a mechanistic worldview to an open and dynamic worldview raises many new questions. However, we need to be aware that the intent of most postmodern philosophy is to dismantle not only modernity, but Christianity as well. As Bruce Benson states, "postmodernism is popularly applied to virtually everything which overturns traditional standards." The best known postmodern philosophers are "Jacques Derrida, Michel Foucault, Jean-François Lyotard, as well as the American philosopher Richard Rorty."[17] What unites all these philosophers is their negative response to the modern philosophical paradigm and to the Christianity of modernity.

We evangelicals need to listen to the philosophical interpretation of the cultural shift now taking place. These philosophers are setting the trajectories of the future by describing the dialectic, interactive view of life that prevails in our Western culture. It is in this culture that we are to communicate, embody, and live out the Christian faith. Let's look, then, at some of the major issues raised by the current philosophical analysis.

First, in postmodernism there is a shift away from the distinction between the subject and the object. Life is viewed, instead, as the dialectical interaction of all things.[18] The Enlightenment thought that the human subject could be apart from and distinct from the object examined. A person, for example, could study a historical text (the Bible, for

Symbiosis
interrelationship of all things

example) as an object and arrive at objective knowledge about it. Martin Heidegger in *Being and Time* challenged the subject/object distinction by arguing that the self cannot be fully understood apart from a relationship to others and to his or her cultural surroundings. This view has resulted in the shift from individualism to community. We are "beings in the world enmeshed in social networks," not individual autonomous selves. This postmodern concept is called "symbiosis" and emphasizes the interrelationship of all things.[19]

Second, because all things are in a symbiotic relationship with each other, the notion of absolutes has been given up by postmoderns. It is not possible, they say, to see things apart from their dependent enmeshment with all things. Consequently, we can no longer line up elements of the universe into categories of A, B, and C. Everything is relative to everything else.

Next, postmodern philosophy draws on the conclusions of science to assert there is no single unifying factor to the universe. The world is characterized by a "web of relationships," none of which is the key that unlocks the door to the universe. This view has resulted in pluralism, the notion that there are many ways, not one.

Pluralism = many ways ≠ not one!

Fourth, postmoderns have attacked the authority of language. Jacques Derrida, in *Speech and Phenomena* and *Of Grammatology*, proposes the "deconstruction" of texts.[20] The deconstruction of the text insists that language cannot present the fullness of truth, but only a "trace" of it. Therefore, truth does not reside in words but in contextual and historical situations in which words are used. Thus, language cannot give us universal truth. It is always relative to the particular context in which it was originally spoken. Since universal truth cannot be known, all so-called truth is subjective.[21] For example, Richard Rorty in *Philosophy and the Mirror of Nature*[22] dismisses foundationalism as "a vain hope" and refers to himself as "someone who holds to certain beliefs all the while knowing that they are not true in any sense other than the pragmatic sense of 'useful for the moment.'" Structuralism is also defeated by Derrida's view of language. Since language cannot bear universal truth and only reflects social constructs pertinent to particular social and historical contexts, the study of texts cannot yield universal truth, Consequently, for Rorty and other committed postmoderns the meta-narrative of a particular community only speaks for that community and has no universal truth value.[23]

imp.

The demise of the subject/object distinction, the emergence of a symbiotic understanding of all things, the failure to find a unifying factor to life, and the deconstruction of language has filled many evangelicals with fear and has resulted in new attempts to defend modernity.[24]

23

rehabilitate concepts of tradition, authority + prejudice

However, we evangelicals have a friend in the thinking of Hans-Georg Gadamer. In *Truth and Method* he points to a direction for the future by suggesting "the need for a rehabilitation of the concepts of tradition, authority and prejudice."[25] I will show how this trend, which we find in every area of life, is fertile ground for contact and dialogue with postmodern philosophical thought.

The Communications Revolution

shift from words to symbolism

The revolution in communications, birthed after 1950, has followed the same trajectory as the scientific and philosophical changes. In the modern world communication occurred primarily through conceptual knowledge. Words that dominated the ways of knowing were "reading"; "writing"; "intelligence"; "analysis"; "clarity"; "explanation"; "logic"; and "linear sequence." The new postmodern shape of communications has shifted to a more symbolic form. It is knowledge gained through personal participation in a community. The new words are "the primacy of experience"; "knowledge through immersed participation"; the "impact of the visual" such as atmosphere, environment, and space; the rediscovery of "imagination," "intuition," and a sensitivity to "spiritual realities"[26] (see figure 2).

In modernity, evangelical Christians have been committed to the use of verbal and analytical forms of communication to reach their generation. Faith has been explained as a system of thought characterized by inner coherence and logic. The Bible has been analyzed, theology systematized, and spirituality legalized.

the shift

The shift of postmodern communications to the power of symbolic communication is a call to return to the classical period when the church was an embodied experience of God expressed in life-changing rituals of immersed participation.

Here's the ?

This brief summary of the changes taking place in science, philosophy, and communication theory introduces us to the new challenge that lies before us. Where do we go to find a Christianity that speaks meaningfully to a postmodern world?

The classical tradition appears to be the most productive. It was shaped by mystery, holism, interpreted facts, community, and a combination of verbal and symbolic forms of communication. Therefore, our challenge is not to reinvent Christianity, but to restore and then adapt classical Christianity to the postmodern cultural situation.

24

THE RETURN TO
CLASSICAL CHRISTIANITY

The idea that evangelicals ought to draw from early Christian thought is by no means a new one. It began with the Reformers of the sixteenth century.

I first became aware of the relationship between the Reformation and the early church when I wrote my doctoral thesis on William Perkins, the founder of Puritanism. Perkins wrote a book entitled *The Reformed Catholic*, which created a stir and provoked a series of responses (books) in the first quarter of the seventeenth century in England. His thesis was that the Reformation was not a novelty, but a return to the early church. In presenting this thesis, Perkins reflected the position of Luther, Calvin, the Anabaptists, and the Anglican Reformers. Any fair reading of the Reformers will bear this out. Unfortunately, subsequent changes gradually led the Protestant church farther and farther away from the spirit and substance of the Reformation and thus from the early church. Today the movement to bring us back to the early church is an affirmation of the Reformers' desire to recover the spirit of the early church in its theology and practice.[1] This desire to return to the "evangelical roots" of the first six centuries is found in every branch of the church. For example, Catholic author Keith Fournier in a book entitled *Evangelical Catholics* writes, "Not only can I use evangelical to describe myself, but I must. It should be—and indeed is—a most proper description for all Christians, be they Protestant, Orthodox, or Catholic."[2] While Catholics may be rediscovering the word "evangelical," Protestants are beginning to feel much more at home with the word "catholic." This is not because they are becoming Roman Catholic, but because they are becoming catholic (lowercase) in the early church sense of the word: _universal Christian._ The leading Protestant theologian of the back-to-the-early-church movement, Thomas Oden, summarizes his willingness to use the word "catholic" and of his own journey from liberalism to the orthodoxy of the early church by quoting these words from Lancelot Andrews, the sixteenth-century Anglican Reformer: "one canon, two testaments, three creeds (the Apostles, Nicene, and Athanasian), four (ecumenical) councils, and five centuries along with the Fathers of the period."[3]

The phenomenon of the return to classical Christianity has also touched the evangelical world. In 1977 a group of forty young evangelical leaders gathered outside Chicago to hammer out _The Chicago Call._[4] This call urged evangelical churches to turn away from an ahistorical Christianity to recover new and enriching insights from the early church. The current climate of rapport between evangelicals and Catholics was heightened by the 1994 publication of _Evangelicals and Catholics Together._[5] The conflict this document has engendered is forcing us to look behind the Reformation to see our mutual commitment to classical Christianity. As Charles Colson has written: "[We] must engage the culture with the truth of God's Word and the power of the gospel. To do so, we must re-center ourselves on the key doctrines of historic Christianity."[6]

Interest in the ancient church is also visible in the Holiness tradition, rooted in the teaching and practice of John Wesley. Recently, a convocation of scholars gathered at the Nazarene Seminary in Kansas City to present papers on the influence of the Eastern Orthodox tradition, in particular on the thinking of John Wesley. These papers were published in the _Asbury Theological Journal_ and have received wide attention among people in the Holiness tradition.[7]

InterVarsity Press has shown evangelical leadership in ecumenical dialogue with its book, _Reclaiming the Great Tradition: Evangelicals, Catholics and Orthodox in Dialogue._ The goal is, as editor James Cutsinger writes, to "Test whether an ecumenical Orthodoxy, solidly based on the classical Christian faith as expressed in the scriptures and ecumenical councils, could become the foundation for a unified and transformative witness to the present age."[8]

The Holy Spirit seems to be working new convictions in the church, particularly among members of the younger evangelical generation who differ significantly from the older generation of Christians. The older generation is attracted to the details of theological systems, tends to think in exclusive either/or terms, enjoys debates over theological points, tends to be passive about social issues, and wants to maintain the status quo. They have been shaped by the science, philosophy, and communication theory of the modern worldview. Therefore, they opt for security and stability over change. But the newer generation has been shaped by the new scientific, philosophical, and communications of the postmodern world. Consequently, the new generation is geared toward change and dynamic development. Although the above characterizations of the older and newer generations are not true of everyone, they do stand as generalizations. The kind of Christianity that attracts the new generation of Christians and will speak effectively to a postmodern world is one that emphasizes primary truths and authentic embodiment. The new generation is more interested in broad strokes than detail, more attracted to an inclusive view of the faith than an exclusive view, more concerned with unity than diversity, more open to a dynamic, growing faith than to a static fixed system, and more visual than verbal with a high level of tolerance and ambiguity.

It is at these points that the link between the ancient tradition and the new generation can be made. The early tradition of the faith dealt with basic issues, and was concerned with unity, open and dynamic, mystical, relational, visual, and tangible.

Why the Early Church over That of Another Era?

Paul Lakeland, in *Postmodernity: Christian Identity in a Fragmented Age*, asks: "What kind of Christianity is needed for the future?" He writes the following:

> Theologies of redemption . . . offered only to the human race, and not something integral to the entire universe . . . are inadequate. Those that focus on the individual are positively harmful. Christologies that imagine Christ as less than cosmic are merely parochial. Theologies of the church that stop at the political, still more so those that remain ecclesiocentric, fail because they cannot conceptualize Christian discipleship in the service of a sick planet. Eschatologies that imagine that the spiritual can have a reality aside from the material are simply naïve.[9]

Lakeland is right, and I will show how classical Christianity speaks to a holistic and integrated view of life.

The Fathers of the early church era hammered out their theology in the context of the mystery religions, polytheism, gnosticism, cults such as Manichaeism, and the philosophies of Plato, Aristotle, Stoicism, and Neo-Platonism. Their theology, being in such close historical, geographical, linguistic, and conceptual proximity to the New Testament era and to its parent religion, Judaism, is characterized by a sustained

27

attempt to remain faithful to the apostolic tradition. Consider, for example, the following six ways in which this may be demonstrated.

First, the early church was responsible for summarizing the general doctrines of the faith in creedal form, such as the rule of faith, the later Old Roman Symbol, and the Apostles' Creed. To this day the whole church frequently confesses its faith in God within the liturgy by reciting the Apostles' Creed or the Nicene Creed. Second, we recognize the early church's role in the development of the canon of Scripture. This was a process occurring after the apostolic age and one which took several centuries. Yet, in more than fifteen hundred years since the affirmation of this canon, it has not been repudiated, even though it has been the subject of controversy and continual scrutiny. Third, the early church ecumenical creeds have given definition to a trinitarian concept of God (Nicene Creed) and to an affirmation of the human and divine natures in the person of Christ (Chalcedonian definition). While these creeds are written in the Greek language and use Hellenistic concepts, they preserve and even expound on the biblical kernel of truth they seek to defend. In spite of our contemporary questions, they remain models of theological thought and methodological inquiry.

Fourth, the ancient church has provided foundational thought on ecclesiology, ministry, and sacraments. While less binding on the thinking of all Christians than the Nicene Creed and the Chalcedonian definition, this thought has nevertheless become the basis for all future thinking on these subjects. Fifth, the ethical approach of the first three centuries to war, abortion, infanticide, marriage, and numerous other subjects and its thinking about the church's relationship to society in general and to the state in particular have shown how penetrating early Christian thought is in the social, political, economic, and psychological areas of human existence. Finally, during the same era, the church was wrestling with its worship. The form of worship, together with the approach to baptism, eucharistic prayers, the Christian year, architecture, the lectionary, and ceremony was being developed at the same time as were the creeds, canon, and ethics.[10]

It is clear that the early church has defined the theological issues and established the framework or the "rules" in which the church does its theological reflection. Anyone who defends the canon, subscribes to the Apostles' Creed, advocates the Trinity, or adheres to the full humanity and divinity of Jesus is already affirming essential aspects of classical Christianity. Evangelicals already have a commitment to historic Christianity and only need to be reminded of what that means. The work of the early church fathers represents foundational Christian thought, which has been the subject of interpretation, reinterpretation, and debate throughout the history of the Christian church. The importance of the Fathers is crucial to every epoch of the faith. Therefore, no Christian dare wrestle with postmodern thought until she or he has studied classical Christian thought. To give special attention to the period of classical Christian thought is to be orthodox, evangelical, and ecumenical. Novel ideas of the faith will come and go, but the classical Christian tradition will endure.

Thus the primary reason to return to the Christian tradition is because it is truth that has the power to speak to a postmodern world. Early Christian teaching is simple and uncluttered, it cuts through the complexities of culturized Christianity and allows what is primary and essential to surface.

Furthermore, the classical tradition is sorely needed because so many people have come to the end of their patience with the modern version of evangelical faith and with current innovations that have no connection with the past. Rationalism and every new trick in the book need to be replaced by resurrected old treasures that still have meaning and can offer direction into the future.

Retelling the Christian tradition also accents what is common in the faith. It refuses to condone divisiveness between churches based on differences in secondary theological issues. What is truly important are those truths the universal church holds in common. My own search for the unity that exists among believing Catholic, Orthodox, and Protestant Christians has taken me back to the common era, and to those convictions that *precede* a time when the church became *Eastern* Orthodox, *Roman* Catholic, or *Protestant*.[11] This "telling the Christian tradition" again links the past with the future. The old adage that those who would shape the future must know the past still stands. If we would shape the future of the church in continuity with its past, we need to know its tradition and why it has endured for so long.

Communicating Classical Thought to the Postmodern World

The question of whether it is actually possible to apply classical thought to the postmodern world must be addressed. First, philosopher Hans-Georg Gadamer speaks of the possibility of communication from one paradigm of history to another through the "fusion of horizons." This line of thought supports the idea that we are able to re-present an original presentation in a different paradigm in such a way that the re-presented content remains faithful to the spirit of the original, even

29

though the cultural setting and the language forms of the new paradigm are somewhat different.[12]

A second helpful insight comes from George Lindbeck, who posits the "cultural-linguistic" concept of conceptualizing the significance of classical theology for the postmodern world. This approach to theology is an alternative to the modern conservative insistence on propositional truth and the liberal view of doctrines as expressive symbols. Lindbeck regards both conservative and liberal constructs of truth as "extratextual" because they search for the "religious meaning outside the text or semiotic system either in the objective realities to which it refers or in the experience it symbolizes."[13] The propositionalists insist that the language of doctrine corresponds with an exact objective truth while the expressionists locate the value or the "truth" of the doctrine in the subjective experience of the believers without any need to correspond to an external objective truth. Rejecting both of these concepts, Lindbeck describes the "cultural-linguistic" view of doctrine as "intratextual." That is, the "meaning is constituted by the uses of a specific language rather than being distinguishable from it."[14] In other words, its truth value is determined by how it "fits into systems of communication or purposeful action, not by reference to outside factors."[15]

For example, the truth value of the Nicene Creed is not to be found in words that correspond with an exact reality, but in words that truthfully signify the religious reality of the Trinity in the system of thought (in this case, Hellenistic) in which it is articulated. This means that it is truth within the system of language and thought that conveys the Christian message in that particular culture.

The "fusion of horizons" and the "cultural linguistic" hermeneutic allow us to speak meaningfully of the application of classical Christian thought to a postmodern setting. We are able to communicate classical Christianity within a postmodern view of reality in such a way that its truth value remains consistent with the original. In this way it may be said that the original presentation of classical Christian thought has been faithfully re-presented in a different paradigm—the postmodern culture in which we live. These two hermeneutical assumptions will drive our search for connections between classical Christian thought and a viable Christianity in the postmodern world.

The Structure of *Ancient-Future Faith*

I have structured *Ancient-Future Faith* around the phenomenon of the origin of the Christian faith. I have not started where evangelicals usually start—with the Scriptures. Rather, I begin with the work of Jesus Christ, the primordial event of the living, dying, rising, and coming again. I have then attempted to unfold the Christian faith in a phenomeno-logical manner—as it happened in those first several centuries. First, Christ; then, the church, its worship, its spirituality, its mission to the world; and finally an appendix on the authority by which the church speaks and acts within the world. This method, as I will show, repre-sents the shift from rationalism to the mystery of the interpreted faith grounded in the Christ event.

Not starting with the Bible does not represent a lower view of Scrip-ture than that which is generally held among evangelicals. Instead, the Christocentric method acknowledges the place of the Scriptures in the early Christian tradition. In the early centuries Scripture was not sepa-rated from the church or from the development of classical Christian thought, but was inextricably linked with the whole phenomenon of the rise of Christianity. In modern times the act of lifting the Bible out of its phenomenological context of the work of the Holy Spirit in the church has resulted in making the Bible the object of rational criticism. In post-modern Christianity the authority of the Bible will be restored, not by more rational arguments, but by returning it to its rightful place in the development of the entire spectrum of Christian thought in the first six centuries of the church and by learning to read it canonically once again.

I begin, therefore, in part 2 with the work of Jesus Christ, the pri-mordial event of the Christian faith. I show that God of very God became incarnate with the specific purpose of entering history to recover God's creation through the victorious defeat of the powers of evil. As we will see, the ancient *Christus Victor* theme of the work of Christ is central to the classical Christian vision of reality. It does not stand alone, but is connected to all other aspects of the Christian faith as the central thread to the entire tapestry. In subsequent sections I develop the relationship of *Christus Victor* to the main concerns of the Christian faith, such as the church, worship, spirituality, evangelism, education, social action, the Scriptures, creeds, and theology.

In part 3 the relationship between Christ and the church is discussed. Early believers presented the church as the new community made up of the people who constitute the beginning again of the created order. The church is the new society, the people of the future living in the pres-ent, the people of the *Christus Victor,* the people who are defined by the living, dying, rising, and coming again of Christ. All Christian truth that flows from Christ converges in the church. Worship, Scripture, theol-ogy, spirituality, education, evangelism, social action, and creeds all belong to the church and are all defined by the work of Christ. Thus, the church is the community in which the vision of a renewed world is anticipated and experienced.

Part 4 presents the relationship between Christ and worship. The early church presents worship as the church's celebration of *Christus Victor*. Worship proclaims and acts out the Christian metanarrative. In its daily prayer, weekly service, and yearly cycle of sacred time, the church tells and dramatically reenacts the living, dying, rising, and coming again of Jesus. In both the preached Word and the celebrated Table the underlying reality is the salvation of the entire universe in Christ's action on behalf of the world. Worship renewal, then, is not a matter of gimmicks, but the recovery of the Christian vision of reality enacted by the community of God.

Part 5 presents the relationship between Christ and spirituality. The early church taught that true spirituality draws its life from the power of *Christus Victor*. This kind of spirituality arises out of our baptism into his death and resurrection so that by the power of the Spirit we are called to put off the "old man" and put on the "new man." In this way spirituality is a participation in Christ's victory over sin that results in a commitment to witness against the powers of evil. Christ, the church, and its worship are the source of spirituality while evangelism, teaching, and social action are spirituality's fruits. Therefore, the hope of the spiritual life is the restoration of all things through Christ.

Part 6 presents the relationship between Christ and the mission of the church. In traditional Christian thought the mission of the church is threefold: evangelism, education, and social action. The early church teaches how each of these aspects of mission is rooted in Christ's victory over sin and death. Evangelism defies the claim of Satan, confounds the power of evil, and brings the new creation into existence. It is an evangelism into the ongoing life of Christ in the church, its ministries, and its mission. Education forms the convert by the Christian vision of reality. This formation takes place in the context of community through the celebration of worship and the guidance of the Scriptures, and results in participation in the mission of the church to the world. Social action, rooted in *Christus Victor,* applies the victory of Christ over the powers of evil to nature, to society, and to society's institutions. Social action is the politics of Jesus anticipating the hope of a restored world.

Part 7 looks at the matter of authority. The final authority over all things is Jesus Christ. He gained his authority by virtue of his victory over the powers of evil. The apostles are the authoritative source for the interpretation of Christ. Therefore, the rule of faith, a summary of apostolic Christianity, plays an authoritative role in the interpretation of the Scriptures, the authoritative substance of the Christian faith. Creeds and theology are witnesses to the redemptive story that sweeps from creation to consummation. The true function of theology is to witness to Christ and to bring us to the worship and service of God.

Conclusion

At the beginning of this section I described the background that I bring to the study of the role of classical Christianity in a postmodern world. You will bring *your* own history to the reading of this book. Therefore, I want to conclude by suggesting some ways in which you might read this book for the greatest personal benefit.

First, *Ancient-Future Faith* may be read as *a primer on the Christian faith*. I intend to spell out in a clear fashion the most essential truths of traditional Christianity and suggest ways these truths function in a postmodern world. Unfortunately, we often deal with specific aspects of the Christian faith in isolation from the whole. We get caught up in the details of the tapestry, dwelling on this or that thread or color. Consequently, we fail to see the interwovenness of the absolute essentials, those main threads that bind the tapestry together and create the pattern. As a primer, this book looks at the basic threads, the threads that we deal with in our everyday experience of the Christian life. And since these are the basic threads of the faith, they are the common threads, the ones that unite all Christians. Therefore, the book has value for our personal quest to understand the Christian faith in its most basic elements woven into a single tapestry.

Second, you may read the book as an *explanation of what is happening in the church today*. There are many people involved in churches today who have not been given an interpretation of their personal and corporate experience. This, of course, is not unusual. Frequently, when we are in the midst of change, we may know things are changing, but we may not understand where the change is taking us. Hopefully, by reading this book people who are involved in a church that addresses postmodernism will understand what is happening not only in their local church, but in the church throughout the world.

Finally, this book may be read as *a self-portrait*. I didn't grasp this dimension of the work until a young friend of mine read the manuscript. As he was reading, he exclaimed, "Why, this is like a self-portrait. . . . I see myself and my experience everywhere!" This person felt the book identified what he had experienced, but was not yet able to articulate.

33

Throughout history a revived interest in the insights of the early church has usually been accompanied by significant renewal in the church. For example, both Luther and Calvin drew heavily on the early church fathers. Then, in the seventeenth century, when the fires of the Reformation were burning low, Philipp Jacob Spener, the leader of the pietist movement in Germany, called upon the people to recover the kind of Christianity taught and practiced by the early Christians. After citing Tertullian, Ignatius, Eusebius, Justin, and others, Spener wrote: "It [the early church] demonstrates that what we are seeking is not impossible . . . it is the same Holy Sprit who is bestowed on us by God, who once effected all things in the early Christian, and he is neither less able nor less active today to accomplish the work of sanctification in us."[16]

If Luther, Calvin, and Spener could speak to us today, they would assure us that the faith of the early Christian tradition is simple and compelling. They would call on us to restore the early traditions, to let what is central to Christianity shine forth in bold relief.

Finally, I hope you will read this book with the expectation that classical Christianity can do something for you. You may sense that you are on a spiritual journey; you know that you cannot remain where you are; you know something is happening inside you. You may not be able to put your finger on it, but you know that some very profound changes are occurring in your spiritual outlook. Classical Christian thought will help you understand yourself and will point you in the direction of a more fulfilled Christian experience.

Allow classical Christianity to interpret you and your world by putting yourself under the communal authority it holds in the life of the church. By allowing classical Christianity to act as interpreter with yourself as the interpreted, you will avoid the deadend street of modernity, which proudly thinks the human is autonomous and the individual mind is the final arbiter of truth.

Table A: Paradigms of Church History

Ancient	Medieval	Reformation	Modern	Postmodern
Mystery	Institutional	Word	Reason	Mystery
Community			Systematic	Community
Symbol			& Analytical	Symbol
			Verbal	
			Individualistic	

Each paradigm of history is characterized by one or more central ideas through which the Christian faith is interpreted. Transitions from one paradigm to another are complex and include the breakdown of the old and the development of new ideas that eventually culminate in a new paradigm. Western history is now in a time of transition from the modern to an uncertain postmodern period. Indications of a postmodern worldview suggest that mystery, with its emphasis on complexity and ambiguity, community, with its emphasis on the interrelationship of all things, and symbolic forms of communication, with an emphasis on the visual, are all central to the new way of thinking.

Table B: The Seven Stages of Postmodernity

- 1870—Prehistory
  Arnold Toynbee in 1875 saw Western history as the final phase of a
      proletariat civilization
- 1950—Modernity in decline
  The questioning of modern assumptions in science and philosophy
- 1960—Deconstruction
  The countercultural shift
  The desire to break away from traditional norms
- 1975—The rise of eclecticism
  New respect for minorities, variety, and different lifestyles
  Pluralism
- 1979—A new interest in historical memory
  A postmodern classicism emerged in art and architecture
- 1980—Critical reactions to contemporary culture
  The consumer culture and the manipulations of the information
      age are brought under attack
- 1990—The emergence of the postmodern paradigm
  Revisionary postmodernism begins to construct a worldview
      through "a revision of modern premises and traditional concepts"

Adaptation from Charles Jencks, ed., *A Post-Modern Agenda* (New York: St. Martin's, 1992), 10–39.

Table C: Modern Hybridized to Postmodern

Modern Hybridized	Postmodern
in politics	
1. nation-states	regions/supranational bodies
2. totalitarian	democratic
3. consensus	contested consensus
4. class friction	new agenda issues, green
in economics	
5. Fordism	post-Fordism (networking)
6. monopoly capital	regulated socialized capitalism
7. centralized	decentralized world economy
in society (First World)	
8. high growth	steady state
9. industrial	postindustrial
10. class-structured	many-clustered
11. proletariat	cognitariat

(continued)

Table C: Modern Hybridized to Postmodern *(continued)*

Modern Hybridized	Postmodern
in culture	
12. purism	double-coding
13. elitism	elite/mass dialogue
14. objectivism	values in nature
in esthetics	
15. simple harmonies	disharmonious harmony
16. Newtonian represented	Big Bang represented
17. top-down integrated	conflicted semiosis
18. ahistorical	time-binding
in philosophy	
19. monism	pluralism
20. materialism	semiotic view
21. utopian	heterotopian
in media	
22. world of print	electronic/reproductive
23. fast-changing	instant/world-changing
in science	
24. mechanistic	self-organizing
25. linear	nonlinear
26. deterministic	creative, open
27. Newton mechanics	Quantum/Chaos
in religion	
28. atheism	panentheism
29. "God is dead"	creation-centered spirituality
30. patriarchical	postpatriarchal
31. disenchantment	reenchantment
in worldview	
32. mechanical	ecological
33. reductive	holistic/holinic/interconnected
34. separated	interrelated semiautonomous
35. hierarchical	heterarchical
36. accidental universe	anthropic principle
37. anthropocentric	cosmological orientation
38. absurdity of "man"	tragic optimism

From Charles Jencks, ed., *A Post-Modern Reader* (New York: St. Martin's Press, 1992), 34–35. Used with permission.

Table D: A Comparison of the Modern, Postmodern, and Classical/Evangelical Worldviews

The Modern Worldview	The Postmodern Worldview	A Classical/Evangelical Response
The Scientific Revolution		
• mechanistic world	• mysterious world	• recovery of the mystery of Christ and a Christocentric worldview
• knowable is attainable	• knowledge not attainable	• knowledge in community
• facts are objective	• only interpreted facts	• apostolic interpretation
• universal truth based on the scientific method	• no universal worldview —all is relative	• Christianity rightly understood and embodied is the universal faith for all
The Philosophical Revolution		
• distinction between subject/object	• symbiosis—all things are interrelated	• Christocentric worldview—Christ interrelated to all things
• idea of progress	• the new hermeneutic of history views each epoch within its own culture	• appreciation of early church as well as other paradigms of faith
• optimistic view of humanity	• recognition of dualism —the conflict between good and evil	• spiritual warfare
• individualism	• the importance of community	• primacy of the church
• by reason we can find one overarching metanarrative that speaks the truth about the world	• the world is full of competing narratives, none of which are universal truth	• restoration of the Christian metanarrative in worship
The Communication Revolution		
• conceptual knowledge	• symbolic knowledge	• preanalytic and preexperiental knowing
• propositional knowledge (facts)	• the return to myth, image, metaphor, story, analogy (knowing in community)	• communal knowledge and authority
• knowledge as information	• knowledge as wisdom construct with no universal	• education and nurture as character formation
• language corresponds to truth	• language is a social meaning or authority	• universality, antiquity, and consensus "establish rule of faith" within the Christian community

Table E: The Relationship of the Work of Christ to Christian Thought

CHRIST	Church	*The primary extension of Christ in the world* The community of God's people through whom the work of Christ is extended to the world is the church, the sign of redemption.
	Worship	*The primary celebration of the church* In worship the church proclaims and acts out Christ and his redeeming work, making it present in all its power among God's people.
	Spirituality	*The primary life of the church* Spirituality is a participation in Christ, a personal sharing in the victory of Christ over the power of evil.
	Mission	*The mission of the church* The mission of the church is to witness to the binding, dethroning, and destruction of the powers of evil through evangelism, nurture, and its life in the world.
	Authority	*The primary document of the church* The authority of the church is the apostolic authority of Scripture summarized in the rule of faith and proclaimed in the ecumenical creeds and interpreted by the antiquity, universality, and consensus of the church.

A CLASSICAL/POST-MODERN CHRIST

So the Lord now manifestly came to his
own, and, born by his own created
order which he himself bears, he
by his obedience on the tree renewed
and reversed what was done by disobedience in
connection with a tree.

—Irenaeus, A.D. 180

As a child, I loved to put puzzles together. Whenever
I became sick with a cold or the flu, my mother would
ask, "What do you want to entertain yourself with until
you are well enough to go back to school?" I always
said, "Get me a puzzle—the bigger the better."

My mother would spread the puzzle out on a large
card table by my bed, and I would enthusiastically analyze it before making any attempt to put it together.
My first concern was always to find the key, the central image around which all other parts of the puzzle
fit. Once I found the key, the rest of the puzzle seemed
to fall quickly into place.

In the Christian faith the key to the puzzle is the
work of Jesus Christ. Once we have a solid grasp of
the meaning of his work, the rest of the faith falls
together around it.

As far back as I can remember I was told that Christ
was central to the Christian faith. However, when I

began to reflect on the teaching I had received, I realized that the importance of Christ was always explained in terms of my personal salvation, little more.

I have come to see through the study of the early Christian tradition that my view of Christ was severely limited. It wasn't that I didn't believe rightly. I simply didn't understand how far-reaching and all-inclusive Christ really was. When I discovered the universal and cosmic nature of Christ, I was given the key to a Christian way of viewing the whole world, a key that unlocked the door to a rich storehouse of spiritual treasures.

This classical understanding of Christ speaks to two problems posed by postmodernists. First, there is the search for a unifying principle. Although postmodernism rejects the notion of a unifying principle to the world, this rejection has not kept scientists from a search for a possible unity. As David Ray Griffin writes, "A number of factors today are moving toward a postmodern organism in which science and the world are reenchanted. Besides providing a basis for overcoming the distinctive problems of modernity that are due primarily to disenchantment, this postmodern organicism gives science a better basis than it has heretofore had for understanding its own unity."[1] While Christians do not deny the validity of scientific inquiry, they affirm the unity and coherence of all things in Christ (Col. 1:16–20). Second, postmodernists in contrast to the modern doctrine of the goodness of humanity recognize the presence of evil but have an inadequate answer. For example, Charles Jencks refers to the postmodern anthropic principle as the recognition that "we inhabit a universe full of violence and unpredictability."[2] But this principle asks us to think of our world not only in terms of "original sin," but also in terms of "original blessing." The blessing is that within "suffering, real evil and constant warfare we can clarify . . . the question . . . is the universe a fundamentally good place, should we be optimistic? The answer, of course, hangs in the balance and depends on how we treat the earth and ourselves, as well as other endangered species."[3] Christians also recognize the descriptive presence of evil, but do not place the overcoming of evil in the hands of an ecologically sensitive humanity, but in Jesus Christ who defeats evil by his death and resurrection.

In this part I explore the classical understanding of the cosmic Christ, the Christ who stands at the very center of the universe, the Christ who gives meaning to all of life.[4] And I will also explore the problem of evil as it is related to the work of Christ. Classical Christianity affirms the centrality of Christ to all creation and offers a distinct way to deal with the problem of evil. It sees the presence and power of evil in society as the impact of original sin, which permeates all the structures of existence. But it rejects the "original blessing" of postmodernism which teaches that millions of years of evolution will bring the creation and humanity to its perfection. For classical Christianity the original blessing is the second Adam who by his redeeming event has entered into history to reverse the effects of original sin. He alone has bound, dethroned, and will ultimately destroy all the powers of evil and will restore the created order. This is the gospel that frees and liberates us to be ecologically active. We now turn to an exploration of how the classical perception of Christ speaks effectively and creatively to the culture of postmodernity.

CHRIST WITHIN
THE PARADIGMS OF HISTORY

There are three main interpretations of the work of Christ in Scripture and in history: His work is (1) a sacrifice which (2) won a victory over the powers of evil and (3) left us an example to follow. These views should all be held together. However, the church in this or that paradigm of history has emphasized one aspect of the work of Christ, but has seldom presented all three views as a whole (see table F).

The dominant interpretation of the work of Christ for the first thousand years of history is the proclamation that his death and resurrection constitute *a victory over the powers of evil*.[1] This interpretation obviously presupposes a strong awareness of the principalities and powers, a sensitivity that we find in the New Testament writings and in the liturgies and teaching of the ancient church. The creeds of the early church deal specifically with the defeat of the powers of evil and teach that it was God who became incarnate and was united to humanity in Jesus, the second Adam, who defeated the powers "for us and our salvation" (this statement is found in all the ancient creeds).[2]

During the medieval era, the interpretation of the work of Christ as a sacrifice overshadowed and then replaced the *Christus Victor* interpretation. The medieval era was not nearly as sensitive to the powers of evil. The work of Christ was best understood through the economics of the feudal system of society. For example, society was made up of numerous manors that were complete societies within themselves. The lord of the manor was responsible for ruling the manor in all respects, including matters of justice. In the event that one of the persons in the manor offended the lord of the manor through breaking one or more of the rules of the manor (theft, for example) the honor of the lord of the manor was offended. The offense against the honor of the manor required a satisfaction in order for the person to be forgiven and to continue living in the manor. These satisfactions ranged from a beating to death. Once the satisfactions had been accomplished, the honor of the lord of the manner was restored. It was out of this cultural practice of feudalism that Anselm wrote his famous *Cur Deus homo* (Why the God-man?).[3] His argument was that sin has offended God's honor and therefore requires a satisfaction. Jesus offered that satisfaction in his sacrificial death. The interpretation of the death of Jesus as a victory over the powers was replaced by the satisfaction theory.

The Reformers continued to emphasize the sacrificial nature of the death of Christ but taught it was a satisfaction offered to God against God's offended holiness. Because the satisfaction met God's demand for righteousness, Jesus' work was representational for all who had faith in him. His righteousness, imputed to us through faith, makes us acceptable to God, grants us forgiveness of our sin, and saves us.[4] Except for Luther, the *Christus Victor* interpretation remained largely ignored.

The third interpretation of the death of Christ, which emerged with Abelard[5] in the medieval era, became the watchword of liberals in the modern era. The focus was on the example Jesus set by his willingness to go to the cross in weakness and humility. The liberals took the example theory away from its association with *Christus Victor* and the satisfaction theory and let it stand on its own. For them it was a perfect nonsupernatural way to interpret the death of Jesus. Jesus was a prophet whose mission was misunderstood. He was unjustly condemned and crucified. His death was neither a victory over the powers nor a satisfaction to the Father. Instead, his death as an example exerts a positive influence on society and makes us turn away from selfishness to a life in service of others. This theory fit the idea of social progress as the controlling idea of the relevance of Christ to the future. It was a theology for the social gospel. Modern liberals were convinced the world was progressing toward a utopia in which all peoples would live out of the ethic of the church, rooted in the self-giving love of Jesus. Ultimately, God's reign would be established over the whole world.

Today, postmodernists reject the notion of the idea of progress. The industrial, scientific, and technological revolutions have not advanced civilization to a new threshold of evolution. Instead of facing a steady, upward movement of history that will end in utopia, we appear to be standing on the brink of self-destruction. Our current precarious world situation is in great need of a decisive word from the church—namely, that Christ by his sacrificial death has won a victory over the powers of evil.

The Problem Regarding Christ Inherited from the Enlightenment

The primary problem we evangelicals have inherited from the Enlightenment is its emphasis on the foundational nature of Scripture. The church has from its very beginning confessed that Jesus Christ is the foundation of faith: "No one can lay any foundation other than the one already laid, which is Jesus Christ" (1 Cor. 3:11). This foundation of Christianity is the incarnation of God into our humanity to do for us what we cannot do for ourselves: Defeat the powers of evil and restore the creation in the new heavens and the new earth.[6]

It was during the Enlightenment that the foundation of the Christian faith shifted from the centrality of the person and work of Jesus Christ to the centrality of the Bible. Theology shifted from the God who acts to the God who spoke. In the worst scenario faith shifted from trust in Christ to trust in the Book. Therefore, the first question we must address as evangelicals in a postmodern world is this: Do we believe in a book or a person?[7]

The Starting Point: Book or Person?

The Book-oriented approach to the Christian faith, which dominated during the Enlightenment, makes several presuppositions: (1) the Bible is the mind of God written; (2) the mind is the highest faculty of our creation in the image of God; (3) truth is known as the human mind meets the mind of God in the study of Scripture. The Bible as observable data is an exact science that leads to rational answers. These answers are objective propositional truths.[8]

Both conservatives and liberals have approached the Bible through empirical methodology in search of truth. Liberals used reason to demythologize the Bible and reduced the essence of the faith to love. On the other hand, conservatives argued for the exact correctness of everything in the Bible, based on the doctrine of inerrancy. In this vicious circle the liberals tore the Bible to shreds with biblical criticism while the conservatives continually followed the liberals in trying to put the pieces back together with rational arguments.[9] In the meantime for many the message was lost. For example, in seminary I enrolled in a course on the Pentateuch. I was eagerly anticipating more insights on the exodus event and on the meaning of Israel as well as thoughtful analysis of Israel's communal life. The message of the Pentateuch was never addressed. The entire course dealt with a defense of Mosaic authorship and the denial of the liberal source analysis of JEDP.

In the postmodern world, this old modern battle for the Bible is no longer the primary issue. The empirical method based on modern science and reason is under question. Postmodern philosophy has shifted away from the subject/object distinction that stands behind the modern search for propositions of truth. The issue in a postmodern world is not to prove the Bible, but to restore the message of the Bible, a message which, when proclaimed by the power of the Spirit, takes up residence within those who know how to hear.

This message is an event-oriented perception of the world.[10] The framework of that message is that God created the world; that the world fell away from God in the disobedience of the first Adam; that God rescued the world through Jesus Christ, the second Adam; and that at the end of history God will complete the rescue operation in the establishment of the new heavens and the new earth. The center of the message is the person and work of Jesus Christ. The Bible is the authoritative interpretation of this event. Therefore, the Bible takes us to the person and work of Jesus Christ in whom we have faith. In this classical/postmodern view we have shifted from an understanding of the Bible that results in faith to a faith that results in understanding the Bible. Christianity is not an I-It relationship but an I-thou personal relationship with the center of the universe, a relationship established by divine initiative when God became united to humanity in the incarnation and destroyed the power of death by his death and resurrection. The mystery of the person and work of Christ proclaimed is the starting point of faith, not rational argumentation that seeks to prove the Bible to be correct.

The Conflict with Evil

The second problem inherited from the Enlightenment is its failure to focus adequately on the cosmic power of evil. The New Testament is highly conscious of the powers of evil and their debilitating effect on human life and on political, economic, social, institutional, and family structures. It is impossible to read the Gospel accounts without continually encountering a story that deals with the powers of evil.[11] The entire ministry of Jesus revolves around binding the powers, dethroning the powers, and assuring his disciples and followers that the powers will be utterly destroyed and routed out of the world at the end of history.[12] In the Gospel of John alone there are more than seventy references to the conflict between Jesus and the powers. Throughout his text John focuses on this conflict culminating in the destruction of evil. He reminds his readers that Christ has come to be the light of the world (John 1:9); that the powers have "no hold" on Jesus (14:30); that the "prince of this world now stands condemned" (16:11); and that "now is the time for judgment on this world; now the prince of this world will be driven out" (12:31). Therefore, "Take heart! I have overcome the world" (16:33). The Epistles are equally full of admonitions regarding evil. Paul summarizes the issue when he states that "our struggle is not against flesh and blood, but against the rulers, against the authorities, against the powers of this dark world and against the spiritual forces of evil in the heavenly realms" (Eph. 6:12). This same sensitivity to the powers of evil permeates the works of the early church fathers, particularly in the baptismal instruction, which is a call to put off evil and put on Christ.[13]

Whatever happened to the prominence given to the powers of evil and to the overcoming power of Christ? After the conversion of Constantine in the fourth century, the church set about to create a Christian society in which evil was contained and tamed (or so they thought). Even the Reformers continued the medieval idea of Christian society. During the Enlightenment, the idea of progress resulted in an optimistic view of history. Church leaders were characterized by an enormous confidence in the future. The twentieth century was to be the Christian century: The church was going to permeate the world with its message of love; society was to become one family under the reign of God; nations would cease their warring against each other; disease and poverty would be practically unknown!

However, the twentieth century has been anything but utopia. It has not been a century of progress, but of regression. Two World Wars shattered optimism. Millions of people have been slaughtered: six million people under Hitler; untold millions of Russians put to death by Stalin; the massacre of millions of Armenians; the wholesale slaughter of millions of Chinese. And the world is now faced with the omen of nuclear war, massive deaths from new and seemingly uncontrollable diseases, the disintegration of Christian values, and little hope for tomorrow.

Postmodernism takes the contemporary situation in hand and says we must abandon the idea of progress and return instead to the sense of a dualism in life, to the recognition that in this life there is a continual struggle with the powers of evil. But postmodern philosophy has no answer to the problem of personal and corporate evil other than to say we are dealing with a "tragic optimism" (see table C, no. 38).

The Christian story speaks to the realism of the postmodern world. It says, "We agree with you. There is a fundamental conflict between good and evil that expresses itself in every aspect of the human personality and in all the institutions of society. As Christians, we can address that problem in the person who is the centerpiece of human history—Jesus Christ, who is the victor over the powers of evil." We turn now to an examination of *Christus Victor* in the early Christian tradition; first in the New Testament, then in the Fathers of the church. For here lies a new starting point for an evangelical witness in a postmodern world: the centrality of Christ and his victory over the powers of evil.

5

CHRISTUS VICTOR
IN THE APOSTOLIC WRITINGS

The New Testament material concerning the victory of Christ over the powers of evil is extensive. However, we can organize this vast amount of material under several themes that will help us grasp more firmly the earliest Christian creed, the shout of victory expressed in the words, *Jesus is Lord!* (Acts 2:36). These themes are that Christ has bound Satan, has dethroned the powers of evil, and will utterly destroy the powers of evil at the consummation. The consequence of Christ's work is that the powers are now limited and that we are called to live in the expectation of a restored creation. These themes lie at the heart of the Christian understanding of reality[1] and are relevant to the postmodern search for a unity to all of life and to a way of dealing with the problem of evil.

Christ Has Bound Satan and All Demonic Powers

In a confrontation with the Pharisees, Jesus makes the claim to have bound Satan (Matt. 12:22–29). The occasion for the confrontation was the healing of a blind and mute man who was possessed by demons (v. 22). According to the Pharisees' interpretation, "it is only by Beelzebub, the prince of demons, that this fellow drives out demons" (v. 24). Rather than seeing Jesus as one who had power over the demonic, they saw him as subject to and even as an agent of the demonic. But Jesus, showing them the absurdity of this conclusion, argued that "if Satan drives out Satan, he is divided against himself" (v. 26). More important, Jesus categorically stated, "How can anyone enter a strong man's house and carry off his possessions unless he first ties up the strong man?" (v. 29).

The point made by Jesus is that he has power over the demonic because he has already entered into the domain of evil and found its source. The event in the life of Christ where this "binding" most likely occurred is the temptation (Matt. 4:1–11). Generally, exegetes are united in their recognition that the temptation of Jesus by Satan was not a test of his moral character but of his messianic calling. This messianic interpretation asserts that in the temptation Satan attempted to divert Jesus from the work his Father had called him to do, offering him the kingdom of the world if he would bow down and worship him. Jesus' final answer was, "Away from me, Satan! For it is written: 'Worship the Lord your God, and serve him only'" (v. 10). Jesus' refusal to bow to Satan signaled an important moment in the work of overcoming the power of Satan. Jesus' rejection of Satan's power and affirmation of his service to God alone reversed the trend initiated by Adam when he chose Satan over God in the garden. Just as Adam was seduced by the word of Satan and brought the whole human race under his influence, so Jesus broke the power of that seduction and set in motion the chain of earthly events that would ultimately and conclusively destroy the power of Satan. Thus Paul writing to the Romans was able to say, "For just as through the disobedience of the one man the many were made sinners, so also through the obedience of the one man the many will be made righteous" (Rom. 5:19).

The Gospel writers pointedly accented the power of Jesus over Satan to their readers. Matthew saw that the power of Jesus over evil was in fulfillment of the Old Testament prophecies (Matt. 8:16–17) and came as a result of the "Spirit of God" (12:28). Mark and Luke also acknowledged that Jesus had power, even authority, over evil (Mark 1:21–28; Luke 9:37–43). The exercising of Christ's power over Satan had the effect of restoring to wholeness God's creation that had become demented, twisted, distorted, and corrupted by Satan. When Jesus cast out demons, healed the blind, made the lame walk, restored health, and raised the dead, he demonstrated that his purpose was to restore, renew, and re-create his universe. In order to re-create the creation, it was first necessary for Christ to dethrone that power which was distorting the creation. Evil was perverting the purposes of the structures of existence that had been created to provide order and meaning to the world so these structures—the powers—had to be dethroned in order to set the creation free from "its bondage to decay" (Rom. 8:21).

Through the Death and Resurrection of Jesus Christ, the Power of Satan Has Been Dethroned

Paul expands the idea of God's victory over Satan in his letter to the Colossians. He writes that Christ's death and resurrection had "disarmed" the powers and authorities and "made a public spectacle of them, triumphing over them by the cross" (Col. 2:15).

According to Paul, the death and resurrection of Christ has "disarmed" the powers and authorities. The force of the word "disarm" is that of taking away, like stripping a soldier of his guns, thereby putting him in a position of vulnerability. So Christ's death has had the effect of exposing the deception that Satan exercises through the structures of existence. Christ is seen as Lord, not only over death, but over all other evil influences that seek to distort our lives. The illusion that life or death, humanly devised religious observances, or human social regulations are ultimate is now exposed for the lie it is. Likewise, all other aspects of the created order that people elevate to positions of ultimate authority are stripped of the power to deceive. Now people can be free from these illusions. It is no longer necessary to be bound by the power of a false understanding and the distorted functioning of the created order. Faith in Jesus Christ, who is the ultimate ruler over all of life, can break the twisting of political, economic, social, and moral structures into secular salvation. Because those structures that promise secular salvation are disarmed, they can no longer exercise ultimate power in our lives. The powers have been dethroned by the power of the cross.

In the Consummation, Satan's Influence over the Powers Will Be Utterly Destroyed

Although the influence of Satan, which he exercises through the powers, has been overcome through the life, death, and resurrection of Christ, the final blow to Satan will not occur until the consummation of Christ's work in his second coming. Even though Jesus spoke of an "eternal fire prepared for the devil and his angels" (Matt. 25:41), a more elaborate development of the idea of Satan's ultimate destruction occurs in the thought of the early church. In Paul's classic statement on the power of the resurrection over death (and the disintegration of the created order implied in the symbol of death), he reminds his readers that the end will come "after he has destroyed all dominion, authority and power. For he must reign until he has put all his enemies under his feet" (1 Cor. 15:24–25). The apostle John, in his apocalyptic vision of the end times, declares that "the devil, who deceived them, was thrown into the lake of burning sulfur, where the beast and the false prophet had been thrown" (Rev. 20:10). This chorus of voices affirms the total destruction of satanic forces and assures us that the work of Christ which we have seen linked to the temptation (the binding of Satan) and the cross (the overcoming of Satan) is concluded by the consummation (the final defeat of Satan).

Between the Resurrection and the Consummation the Power of Satan Is Limited

It would be naive to conclude that Satan no longer has power in the world. He is still the master of deception. He still blinds the eyes of people to the truth. He still masterminds faith in false gods and creates messianic illusions that people follow to their own destruction. Yet his influence is limited, for Jesus has overcome him. "In this world you will have trouble," said Jesus. "But take heart! I have overcome the world" (John 16:33). In his first letter, John interprets this saying of Jesus to describe those who believe in him as overcomers. "For everyone born of God overcomes the world. This is the victory that has overcome the world, even our faith. Who is it that overcomes the world? Only he who believes that Jesus is the Son of God" (1 John 5:4–5).

Yet the overcoming is still not an established reality, as Paul indicates when he uses two words that mean "coming to nothing" and "expectation." The first word is used in his First Letter to the Corinthians: "We do, however, speak a message of wisdom among the mature, but not the wisdom of this age or of the rulers of this age, who are coming to nothing" (1 Cor. 2:6). The force of the word translated "coming to nothing" is "being put out of action." In the military sense, it means the war is over; now the cleaning up of the final matters must occur. Guerrilla pockets may still exist, confrontation may still occur here and there; but the tide has been turned, the oppressor has been definitely routed, and it is only a matter of time until the end.

The second word, "expectation," describes the state of those who are to be released from the ravages of war. Paul uses this word in the Letter to the Romans: "The creation waits in eager expectation for the sons of God to be revealed" (Rom. 8:19). This passage suggests a cosmic victory over a cosmic bondage. Satan has brought the entire creation under his dominion and influence, but that pervasive power has been so thoroughly broken that the entire creation—all the structures of existence— now experiences an expectation of their release.

These passages point to the importance of preaching as the means by which Satan continues to be exposed to his defeat. For it is through faith in Jesus Christ (as the one who has defeated Satan and all his attempts to distort the creation) that the extent of Satan's activity is limited. Satan may continue to deceive some, perhaps many, but not all.

Preaching Christ continually unmasks the power of Satan; faith in Christ opens a person's eyes to the reality of Satan's deception, so that whenever anyone believes in Christ, the limitation of Satan's power is exposed.

Creation Ultimately Will Be Reconciled to God

The contest between Satan and Christ will have an end even as it had a beginning. Furthermore, as Paul states, the course of its cosmic conflict is under "the mystery of his will" and "according to his good pleasure." The will and pleasure of God are being fulfilled in Christ, whose purpose it is "to bring all things in heaven and on earth together under one head, even Christ" (Eph. 1:9–10). Paul mentions this same theme in his First Letter to the Corinthians, telling his readers that God has put "everything under him [Jesus Christ], so that God may be all in all" (1 Cor. 15:28). For Paul, this means nothing less than the re-creation of the entire universe, including the structures of existence. Restoration of these structures is made more clear in his Letter to the Colossians, when he tells his readers that it is God's purpose through Christ "to reconcile to himself all things, whether things on earth or things in heaven, by making peace through his blood, shed on the cross" (Col. 1:20).

In these passages, Paul does not imply that Satan and the fallen hosts which represent the demonic in this world will be reconciled to God. They are defeated and cast into the lake of fire (Rev. 20:10). What is redeemed, restored, and re-created is God's work of creation. In this sense, the new heavens and the new earth will be a restored Paradise—the world as it was before the Fall and more.[2]

The Kingdom of God Is among You

The result of the cosmic work of Christ is that the kingdom of God, God's rule over all things, is now manifest.

When Jesus began to preach, his message was the kingdom of God. Although John the Baptist preceded Jesus and had already preached the coming of the kingdom, Jesus' proclamation was something new. The Baptist was speaking as a prophet of the one who was to come. But Jesus was the event John proclaimed; the kingdom had arrived in him. To understand the meaning of the work of Christ, then, we must understand the meaning of the kingdom.

The basic meaning of the Greek word *basileia* (kingdom) is twofold. It refers to the *realm* of a king and to the *rule* of the king. These two meanings may be applied in three ways: Some passages refer to the king-dom as God's *reign;* others refer to God's kingdom as the *realm* of his kingship; and still others refer to a *future realm* after the return of the Lord Jesus Christ when all creation will be under his reign. These dis-tinctions force the serious Bible student to examine every reference to the kingdom in its context in order to know which of the aspects of the kingdom is being mentioned.

Despite different usages of the word *kingdom,* however, three under-lying themes permeate the *kingdom* uses.[3] First, the underlying theme is the rule of God in Christ over all areas of life. It is this rule that Jesus proclaimed. In effect he was saying, "The ruler of the universe has come to rule in your life. Turn away from all other demands for ownership of your life. Enter into my reign. Let me rule in the life of the world through my rule in you." Jesus called people away from following their false gods to follow the one true God manifested in himself.

To grasp the meaning of the rule of Christ we must take into account the New Testament contrast between the kingdom of Christ and the kingdom of Satan. We see Christ's kingdom as a "rule" more clearly when we view his kingdom over against the anti-kingdom of Satan. It is of primary importance to recognize that the contrast is between two rules in the world order.

Satan's rule in this world is not some kind of ownership of creation. (This is a gnostic doctrine which has crept into the thinking of many people, i.e., the world belongs to Satan and therefore everything in it is evil.) On the contrary, the ownership of the world belongs to God by virtue of creation. It is God's world and it is good! Due to the Fall, how-ever, a new force or power has been unleashed—the power of the evil one who rules in the hearts of people and in the life of the world through them. So the conflict between Jesus and Satan has to do with reigning and ruling: By whom will creation be ruled? By the king of evil or by God's king, Christ, the victor over evil?

The next underlying theme of the kingdom is that it is a gift. Jesus pointedly emphasized that people must be born into the kingdom. The kingdom comes to a person without a person's help or actions (John 3:5–6, 8; Mark 9:1; Luke 17:20–21). Although entrance into the kingdom is viewed as a gift, there are also correlatives that look at entrance into the kingdom from a person's point of view. The way a person is to receive the rule of God is as a child (Mark 10:15). The self-righteous Pharisees and others like them won't get into the kingdom because of their refusal to repent (Matt. 21:31–32).

The third underlying motif is that Jesus himself is the embodiment of the kingdom (Matt. 19:29; 21:9; Mark 10:29; 11:9–10; Luke 18:29–30).

It was the king-god who "became flesh and made his dwelling among us" (John 1:14). It is this king who was made flesh, who died and was buried, who was raised from the dead, who is present in the church, who is returning for those he rules. He is the one who is announced and is present in the proclamation.

To preach Jesus Christ, then, is to preach the kingdom. In Jesus both the publication and the actualization of the Good News are brought together. He not only proclaims the Good News but he *is* and *does* the Good News. He is the content of his message.

We should note, then, that it is this theme (Jesus—the kingdom) that the apostles preached. Jesus sent the disciples "to tell everyone about the coming of the Kingdom of God" (Luke 9:2 LB). The ministry of the apostles began after Pentecost and as a result of the persecution "the believers who had fled Jerusalem went everywhere preaching the Good News about Jesus!" (Acts 8:4 LB). The apostles were not preaching mere facts, but an interpretation of an event. The message was that Jesus lived, died, and rose again for their sin! Salvation is no mere assent to the facts about the king, but an actualization of repentance, faith, and obedience. This is the Good News that saves (1 Cor. 15:2).

The special feature of this new era is that God himself has entered into human history (John 1:15). It is the age in which the king of glory has appeared in human flesh and lived out before the eyes of people the rule of the king. Because he is that king, he calls people to follow him, to live under his rule, and to establish him as the Lord of their lives. The presence of his kingdom is within them (Luke 17:20–21) and someday will extend over the whole world (Rev. 11:15).

The full-blown development of this kingdom concept as it relates both to the presence of the kingdom in the here and now and to the ultimate fulfillment and establishment of the eternal kingdom means that there can be no area of life that escapes the rule of the king. His rulership extends over *all* of life. What we do, say, and think must be executed under his rule. Our eating, sleeping, drinking, judging, and loving must all take place under the rule of the king. He is the lord of life—all of life. Thus the inauguration of the new age is not merely some intrusion into the secular world, or a spiritual component that runs alongside of life. It is the center through which all of life is interpreted. In the ancient world the Fathers of the church called this the theology of recapitulation and it is this theology which is pertinent to our postmodern world.

THE THEOLOGY
OF RECAPITULATION

I have shown in the preceding chapter that the classical understanding of Jesus is that he came into the world to rescue the world from the powers of evil and restore all things to the Father's glory. To use a postmodern term, the work of Christ is the "original blessing" that reverses the "original condition of sin." To demonstrate this interpretation of Jesus, we turn to the early church—to its worship and to the writings of the Fathers.

Christus Victor in the Worship of the Early Church

The experience of Christ as the victor over the powers by the primitive Christian community was first expressed in its worship. The proclamation of Christ as victor over the powers of evil is found in worship acts such as hymnology, baptism, preaching, prayers, the Eucharist, and the practice of Christian year. Because these matters will be dealt with later, three liturgical examples will suffice at this point.

First, the oldest prayer of thanksgiving said over bread and wine and preserved for us by Hippolytus in *The Apostolic Tradition*, written about A.D. 215, points to the *Christus Victor* theme. The climactic point of the prayer brings the sacrifice and the resulting victory of Christ over the powers of evil together in these words:

Fulfilling your will and gaining for you a holy people, he stretched out his hands when he should suffer, that he might release from suffering those who have believed in you. And when he was betrayed to voluntary suffering *that he might destroy death and break the bonds of the devil, and tread down hell* (italics mine).[1]

These words were prayed every Sunday and shaped the thanksgiving of the Christian community around the central image of a conquering Christ.

Christus Victor was also a frequent subject of the Christian sermon. One of the earliest extant sermons of the church comes from the pen of Melito of Sardis (A.D. 195). Here are his concluding words to an Easter sermon:

> But he rose from the dead
> and mounted up to the heights of heaven.
> When the Lord had clothed himself with humanity,
> and had suffered for the sake of the sufferer,
> and had been bound for the sake of the imprisoned,
> and had been judged for the sake of the condemned,
> and buried for the sake of the one who was buried,
> he rose up from the dead,
> and cried with a loud voice:
> Who is he that contends with me?
> Let him stand in opposition to me.
> I set the condemned man free;
> I gave the dead man life;
> I raised up one who had been entombed.
> Who is my opponent?
> I, he says, am the Christ.
> *I am the one who destroyed death,*
> *and triumphed over the enemy,*
> *and trampled Hades underfoot,*
> *and bound the strong one,*
> and carried off man
> to the heights of heaven,
> I, he says, am the Christ.[2]

The theme of *Christus Victor* is also found in numerous prayers of the early church. The date of the following prayer used in the Orthodox Church is unknown, but it reflects the themes of early Christian worship:

> Unceasingly do we adore thy life-giving Cross, O Christ our God,
>   and glorify thy Resurrection on the third day; for thereby, O Almighty One,
> thou didst renew the nature of man, which had become corrupt, and didst restore to us the way to heaven: For thou only art good and lovest mankind.
> Thou hast done away with the penalty of the tree of disobedience,

O Saviour, in that thou, of thine own good will, wast nailed to the tree of the
Cross; and when thou hadst descended into Hell, O Mighty One, thou didst
break the bonds of death, in that thou wert God: For which cause we
worship
thy Resurrection from the dead, joyfully crying unto thee: O Lord Almighty,
glory to thee.
Thou hast destroyed the gates of Hell, O Lord, and by thy death hast
annihilated the kingdom of Death, and hast freed the human race
from corruption, giving life and incorruption and great mercy unto
the world.
Glory to the Father, and to the Son, and to the Holy Spirit,
now and ever, and unto ages of ages. Amen.[3]

The central theme of liturgical theology in the early church clearly
points to *Christus Victor*. The whole human race has been subjected to
death and is under the penalty of disobedience. But God has by the incarnation, death, and resurrection of Christ trampled down death, destroyed
the gates of hell, and overcome the powers of evil. In Christ the nature
of humanity has been renewed and the way to heaven has been opened.
These rich images of the liturgy are found in the writings of the early
Fathers, and in their theology of recapitulation.

Christus Victor in the Writings of the Fathers

The theme of *Christus Victor* permeated the writings of the early
Fathers, especially the anti-gnostic works of Tertullian and Irenaeus in
the latter part of the second century.[4] The gnostics taught that the material world is evil. But the Fathers stood in the New Testament tradition
of the incarnation of God as a real enfleshment in material reality. Therefore they wrote in defense of the victory of Christ over the powers of evil
in creation and argued for the redemption of the entire creation. Irenaeus proclaimed the purposes of Christ in these words: "that He might
destroy sin, overcome death, and give life to men."[5] This analogical way
of presenting the faith is called the theology of recapitulation.

When Paul wrote to the Ephesians, he spoke of the recapitulation of
all things in Christ. The word *recapitulation* appears in the middle of a
long sentence in Ephesians 1:

And he made known to us the mystery of his will according to his good
pleasure, which he purposed in Christ, to be put into effect when the times
will have reached their fulfillment—to *bring* [recapitulate] all things in
heaven and on earth under one head, even Christ (Eph. 1:9–12, italics
mine).

For Irenaeus the theme of the recapitulation of all things was seen as the fundamental result of Christ's death. It was the thread into which everything else was gathered, for it reached out into every piece of the tapestry and put the entire Christian vision of reality in focus. Irenaeus summarized the Pauline theme of the recapitulation this way:

> So the Lord now manifestly came to his own, and born by his own created order which he himself bears, he by his obedience on the tree renewed and reversed what was done by disobedience in connection with a tree. . . . He therefore completely renewed all things.[6]

Irenaeus showed how the work of Christ was understood in terms of the salvation of the entire creation. God not only saved persons, but through the work of Christ, the restoration, renewal, and re-creation of the entire universe was foreshadowed. This overarching view of history is built on the vision of Isaiah (65:17–25) and Paul (Rom. 8:20–24).[7]

The theme of recapitulation is developed through three motifs set forth by Irenaeus: He teaches how the entire universe and all of history, from the creation of the world to the new heavens and earth, are gathered into Christ. We now turn to these three themes to develop the theology of recapitulation which lies at the heart of *Christus Victor*.

First, for Irenaeus and the early church fathers redemption begins with the incarnation. In the incarnation God is "born by his own created order which he himself bears." In these words, Irenaeus brings together the biblical theme of a fallen creation with the incarnation. In the incarnation humanity was grasped by God; the human condition of sin and the resulting death was borne by God, who took into himself the reality of death. This concept of incarnation can be explained better by putting it into story form.

When God created the universe, God looked at the created order and declared that it was good. God was pleased with what had been brought into existence out of nothing, for it was the product of God's own creativity. God had created time, space, sound, color, shape, life, animals, humankind—all things. The sight of it gave God great pleasure. As a result of the power of the evil one, however, the harmony and beauty of God's work of creation had been spoiled. Now hate, greed, chaos, and disharmony raged in the creation. And although creation itself remained good, the power of evil working through people and the institutions of society such as government and the economic order brought the pain and misery of dehumanization into the creation. God could have destroyed the creation and started over. Instead, God chose to *become* the creation. God united with humanity and took a body "under death" in order to defeat the consequence of sin, which was death. This is the meaning of the phrase "born by his own created order which he himself bears."

The second aspect of *Christus Victor* is expressed in the words "he by his obedience on the tree renewed and reversed what was done by disobedience in connection with a tree." By death God in Jesus Christ has defeated all that is sin and death in the world.

Irenaeus and the Fathers taught that when Adam and Eve fell, the demonic powers of evil were unleashed against the created order. Paul related that these powers "in which you used to live when you followed the ways of this world" are the powers of evil which are at work in the creation (Eph. 2:2). Like the wave that washes over the sand castle, the powers of evil distort and pervert God's good creation. They make social institutions become evil things, terrorizing people, plundering the environment, aborting babies, threatening nuclear holocaust. The powers of evil rob the earth of its joy and turn history into madness. But Christ, the second Adam, broke the power of sin by his obedience to the Father and through his death reversed the effects of the Fall. Because of the death of Christ, sin is conquered and the creation is set free. What the Fathers developed was the Pauline theme that "the creation itself will be liberated from its bondage to decay and brought into the glorious freedom of the children of God" (Rom. 8:21). In this way the Christian teaching about creation and the Fall are intrinsically linked with the work of Christ. Creation and the Fall are not intellectual objects of inquiry. Rather, they are parts of the story of existence, parts of the story that can only be truly understood in the light of *Christus Victor*. Through Christ the powers of evil have suffered an irreversible defeat!

Third, the resurrection motif of *Christus Victor* speaks to us about the future: "He therefore completely renewed all things." *Christus Victor* shifts attention away from a focus on the events surrounding the end times to the meaning of the coming of Christ for the world: We are to live in the eschatological hope of the full recapitulation of all things. Christ, the early church proclaims, will rule over a restored and renewed universe. This is no mere creedal statement, but a living hope that we are to celebrate in worship and experience in our lives.

This hope, this expectation of the renewal of all things in Christ, is also the vision in which the whole church lives. No matter how effectively the powers of evil now rage, they are doomed. Evil is not ultimate. Evil is not the final word in human existence. The final word is Jesus Christ. The vision of new heavens and a new earth is no fantasy. It is the reality, the truth. Therefore, it is the hope that lies behind everything we do as Christians.

In sum, the *Christus Victor* message provides the Christian with an interpretation of all reality. It speaks to the origins of all things; it deals with the problem of evil; it affirms a God who is involved in the created order; it answers the human quest for meaning; it provides a hope for the future. This message is the mystery of "God . . . reconciling the world to himself in Christ, not counting men's sins against them" (2 Cor. 5:19). This mystery is the message, the good news for a postmodern society. God has become involved in the creation and God will restore the creation God's way.

CHRIST, THE CENTER

One of the major conclusions of postmodern science is that there is no center to the universe, no single link that ties together the forces of nature. The philosophers, drawing from current scientific theories, therefore conclude that all things are relative. In theology this concept has resulted in "pluralism," the belief that no religious view may be regarded as better than the others. As evangelicals, we have always affirmed the apostolic interpretation of the centrality of the living Word to the entire creation. This message is the "framework of faith" through which we interpret the world. The Fathers of the church wrestled with this framework of thought in the great creeds of the church. How they perceived the centrality of Christ is highly pertinent to the postmodern search for a center to the universe and for a God who becomes involved with the creation.

The Centrality of Christ

The centrality of Christ to the entire created order is never merely a reasoned argument, but always a matter of faith expressed in the worship of the church. The hymn of praise in John's Gospel proclaims that through him all things were made (1:10). This same cry of praise characterizes the great hymn of Paul in Colossians: "by him all things were created: things in heaven and on earth, visible and invisible, whether thrones or powers, or rulers or authorities; all things were created by him and for him" (1:16). In this hymn the church proclaims another astonishing mystery: "in him all things hold together" (1:17) and through him there will be a "reconciliation" of "all things, whether things on earth or things in heaven" (1:20). This is the same theme in the Johannine hymn in which the one who is the center of the universe comes among us as "the Word [that] was made flesh and made his dwelling among us" (John 1:14). And again, this theme of God descending to us in Jesus Christ is the object of praise in the great hymn of Philippians: for the one who is in the "very nature of God" was "made in human likeness" and "became obedient to death" is that one to whom "every knee should bow, in heaven on earth and under the earth, and every tongue confess that Jesus Christ is Lord" (Phil. 2:6–11). This is the faith of the church, its story, its basic paradigm through which it views all reality. It is affirmed and received not by reason, although it has been the subject of intelligent discussion for centuries. Rather, it is received by faith, a faith that leads to understanding.[1]

Creation—Incarnation—Re-creation

Any attempt to understand the centerpiece of the puzzle needs to begin with the relationship of the center to the whole.[2] As we saw in the previous chapter, the Fathers of the church thought out of the interrelationship of creation, incarnation, and re-creation. The God who created becomes incarnate in order to re-create. This story of faith contains several crucial issues. The first one is *who became incarnate?* Was it God, or was it a Son whom God created out of nothing and appointed to rescue the world?

During the first three centuries of the church, the incarnation of God in Jesus Christ was affirmed in the liturgy of the church, in the apostolic writings, and by the Fathers, but without elaborate explanation. However, in the fourth century Arius challenged the tradition that the Son is God and proclaimed that the Son was not God but a son of God. Arius insisted that the Son was a created being who was not the same essence of God. The Son of God, he taught, was the first act of God's creation and thus a different essence than God. There was, he said, "a time when he was not." Therefore the Word was divine by appointment but not by essence.

The threat Arius posed for the church and its doctrine of incarnation was this: Someone other than God was the redeemer. God did not become incarnate. Instead, the Son of God who is not God became incarnate for our salvation and won a victory over the powers of evil.

Athanasius,[3] the major opponent of Arius, retorted that if the Son of God who is not God saves us, then God has not saved us. The Nicene Creed was written to deal with this issue in A.D. 325. The consensus of the church was that it was God of very God who saves us. The language of the creed repeatedly expresses the relation of the Word to the Father in the language of sameness, thus teaching that in Jesus there is an incarnation of God:

> We believe in one Lord Jesus Christ,
> the only son of God,
> eternally begotten of the Father,
> God from God, light from light
> true God from true God,
> begotten, not made,
> of one Being with the Father.
> Through him all things were made.
> For us and our salvation
> He came down from heaven
> by the power of the Holy Spirit
> He became incarnate from the Virgin Mary
> and was made man.[4]

There is a crucial philosophical issue that stands behind the creed. Greek philosophy of the day insisted on the separation of the spiritual from the material. It saw spirit and matter as two distinct spheres of reality that could not coinhere. Consequently, systems of salvation at that time such as gnosticism, Neo-Platonism, or Manichaeism always posited some kind of eternal material creation that mediated between the eternal spirit and temporal reality. Arius was committed to this philosophical school and thus presented the Son as *made*, not *eternally begotten*. For Arius, the Son of God was a created go-between, mediating between spirit and matter. In the thought of Arius it wasn't God of very God who saved the world, but his Son whom he made and appointed as a God. Athanasius and his followers insisted "only God can save." For Athanasius, God who is immaterial actually took on materiality in the incarnation. The Nicene Creed affirmed that *immateriality is communicated to us through materiality*. Divine encounter does not occur apart from the material as in some fuzzy and nondefinable esoteric spirit, but through the physical and material reality of a man named Jesus. Through him, the enfleshed God, God encounters humanity, takes the human burden of sin and death into himself, cancels the debt of sin, destroys death by death, and rises from death, bringing creation to a newness of life now experienced in the church.[5]

The church's consensus that it was God, not an appointed being, who became enfleshed in Jesus raised the second question about the incarnation. *How do the immaterial and the material unite?*[6]

While the relationship between the human and divine in Jesus was a question discussed for several centuries, it was the heresy of Apollinarius that stimulated the church to work toward an answer. In the middle of the fourth century Apollinarius asserted that the Logos simply "took up residence in the human shell" of Jesus. In other words, he asserted that Jesus did not have a human interior. On the outside he was flesh. But on the inside he was divinity. It was this heresy that prompted the Synod of Alexandria in 360, and through the influence of the Cappadocian Fathers, to insist on the axiom "only that which God becomes is healed."[7] So the church affirmed that the incarnation was not God hidden within flesh, but that God had become one of us, taking our full and complete humanity.

In the course of time two axioms had been affirmed: The first, from above, taught that "only God can save"; and the second, from below, taught "only that which God becomes is healed." These axioms affirmed that it was God who was in Christ "reconciling the world to himself" (2 Cor. 5:19). Jesus Christ, the center of the universe, is fully divine and fully human. But how does the immaterial divinity of Jesus and the material humanity of Jesus coinhere?

There were various constructs. The Alexandrian school of thought shaped by Platonic idealism put the emphasis on the divine side. For them the human nature was absorbed into the divine (monophysite). Because this denied the axiom that "only that which God became is healed," however, it was not an adequate doctrine of incarnation. It fell short of affirming the full humanity. On the other hand, the Antiochean school of thought tended to overemphasize the human side of Jesus. They argued that the Spirit of God came upon Jesus like the Spirit came upon David or Gideon for the special work to which they were called (Spirit Christology). This overemphasis on the human denied the axiom that "only God can save." It was an inadequate incarnation because it did not have a Christ who was fully divine.

The issue was settled in the Chalcedon Creed of 451, when the coinherence of the two opposites was affirmed. It emphasized that Jesus Christ is fully divine, for only God can save. It affirmed that Jesus was fully human for he was the second Adam, the representation of the human race. That is, God became one of us so that by participating in our humanity and our condemnation to death God might as the God-man die to destroy death and open the way to heaven.

The Chalcedon Creed has become the received tradition of the church. It describes the faith of the church that enjoys universality, antiquity, and consensus. Therefore, it establishes a normative pattern for Christian understanding of Jesus Christ. The creeds are, as George Lindbeck has pointed out, "communally authoritative teachings" of the church.[8] The Nicene Creed and the Chalcedon Creed tell us that, to quote Scripture, "surely it is God who saves us." This is a 'rule of faith' that must be worked out in each period of history in relation to the culture of the time. Today the scientific concept of quantum physics with its dynamic concept of materiality and the philosophical concept of symbiosis which affirms the interrelationship of the subject and object seems especially open to the ancient affirmation of a cosmic salvation through the identification of God with the plight of the world in Jesus Christ. God is not an absent observer of the world, but in Jesus Christ God has participated in history and taken into himself our fallen condition. God himself has participated in our suffering and by his suffering on the cross has rendered suffering and death ineffective. His victory over the power of evil is now extended to the church by the power of the Holy Spirit, whose special ministry is to "proceed" into our lives in the church and through the church to proceed into the world.

Conclusion

In the introduction to this section, I described how, as a child, I always looked for the central piece of the puzzle. There is also a centerpiece in the Christian faith. And that center, that focal point around which everything else is gathered, is Christ.

I have shared with you how the apostles and Fathers take us back to the biblical idea that the victory of Christ over evil results in the *recapitulation*. His victory over evil is the key not only to the early Christian tradition but to the renewal of our personal faith and to the renewal of the life of the church. I want to show how every aspect of the Christian life relates to Christ's victory over the power of evil and to the ultimate renewal of all things.

The early church saw how faith centers in Christ. For them faith did not begin with the church, with worship, with Scripture, with theology, with spirituality, with education, with evangelism or social action. All these aspects of Christianity, important as they were, were servants of this central theme of faith: Christ became one of us in order to destroy the power of evil and restore us and the world to God.

From this center there is a true understanding of history itself. God is at work in history to accomplish his purposes. This biblical and historical view of Christ speaks to the desire of postmodern thinkers like Paul Lakeland, who wrote "Theologies of redemption . . . offered only to the human race and not . . . integral to the entire universe . . . are inadequate."[9] The classical view that God in Christ is the cosmic redeemer is the message that will be most readily heard in the postmodern world. In the disparaging relativism of postmodernity the Christian faith speaks directly to the desire for a unified center to the world and to the search for an "original blessing" that will bring an end to all evil and establish the Shalom of God over the entire creation. The future of the world does not rest in the hands of an ecologically sensitive humanity, but in God who in Christ has rescued the world. In anticipation of the new creation we witness to its reality by being ecologically sensitive.

Table F: Christ in the Paradigms of History

Ancient	Medieval	Reformation	Modern	Postmodern
Christus Victor	Anselmic Sacrifice Theory Moral Theory of Abelard	Luther combines sacrifice and *Christus Victor*	Liberal: Example Theory	By his sacrifice he won a victory over the powers of evil and left us an example to follow
Rule of faith, 180 Nicene Creed, 325 Chalcedon Creed, 451		Calvin: Sacrifice	Conservative: Proposition-alism Liberal: Expressive-Experiential	*Regula Fidei* View of Christ regulated by the creeds

The first goal of an evangelical theology in a postmodern world is to recognize that the sacrificial view of Christ's death is incomplete. The second goal is to become reconnected with the biblical and historical witness to Jesus Christ as the unique incarnation of God in history who by his sacrificial death and glorious resurrection has defeated the powers of evil, reconciled the world to God, and established a new community of people, the church: See especially Gustav Aulen, *Christus Victor* (New York: Macmillan, 1986).

THE CLASSICAL/POST-MODERN CHURCH

He who hath not the church for
his mother hath not God for
his father.
—Cyprian, A.D. 250

Some time ago, I had the opportunity to speak in a church in rural Michigan. As I was traveling there, I wondered what I would encounter.

Some churches are cold, fixed, and rigid in their views and judgmental of those who disagree with them. Some churches pride themselves on being the only church in town that has the truth. This negative spirit usually spills over into the personality of the whole church and stifles a spirit of joy. So I always wonder what kind of attitude I'll encounter in the churches I visit.

Happily, this church was an extended family that received me as one of their own and drew me into their fellowship immediately. The congregation was only seven years old and had grown from a nucleus of thirty-five people to more than seven hundred.

I asked someone, "Why has this church grown so much in a short period of time? How do you account for this

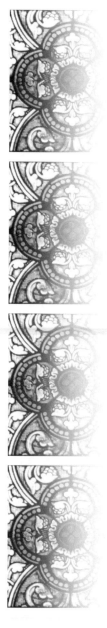

phenomenon?" "Well," the person said, "I think it's all very simple. We love each other so much that we simply talk about how wonderful it is to be a part of this community." This person didn't have to explain further because the very atmosphere of this church was the experience of Christ making all things new. Many of the people were new converts; others had come from churches that were lifeless or characterized by a stifling spirit. So there was an obvious sense of joy among the people.

In theological terms, you could describe this community as an *extension of Jesus*. They were, in a very real way, the new creation, the recapitulation coming into being, experiencing an extension of the victory of Christ over evil in a local body of believers. This is the same kind of experience that the Fathers of the church described.[1]

During my seminary education, I never felt we really addressed the question: "What does it mean to be a member of the church?" Later, when I turned to the early Christian tradition and began, for the first time, to understand what it meant to be a member of the body of Christ, it was like removing blinders that had covered my eyes.

I learned from the early Fathers that the church is intrinsically connected with Christ and his victory over the power of evil. The church is therefore to be regarded as a kind of continuation of the presence of Jesus in the world. Jesus is not only seated at the right hand of the Father, but is visibly and tangibly present in and to the world through the church. This is an incarnational understanding of the church. It is a unique community of people in the world, a community like no other community because it is the presence of the divine in and to the world. This concept of the church has specific relevance to the world of postmodernism.

Postmodern thought has shifted our attention from an atomistic and individualistic view of reality to the interconnection of all things. This scientific and philosophical concept of interrelationship has led to the affirmation of community. As Daniel Bell states, "The post modern industrial society . . . is a 'communal' society in which the social unit is the community rather than the individual."[2]

We already see the move toward community in the globalization of the world and in the communication revolution through which we have instant contact with other people in all parts of the world. Furthermore, the trend, according to political and economic scientists, is that the world, which was once organized around geographical civilizations, is now being reorganized around cultures. Future clashes, skirmishes, and even wars are likely to be cultural wars rather than civilization wars. This has already been seen in the Middle East (Jews and Arabs), and in Bosnia and Kosovo (Christians and Muslims). The rise of Muslims around the world and here in America is another case in point. Muslims will always be Muslims before they will be Americans or members of any other culture or civilization.

What this means for the church is that Christians must recover the primacy of being a Christian community. It means that the primary question we must ask is, "What does it mean to be a citizen of the local and global church?" This question must precede the question, "What does it mean to be a good citizen of the United States?" All Christians are members of the church before they are members of an American, African, Asian, Spanish, or any other culture. For the church transcends all the cultures of the world and defines all believers as the culture of the presence of Jesus Christ in and to the world.[3]

In this section we will review the classic understanding of the church as God's presence in the world through the biblical images and the historic marks of the church. These signs map out a route for us to follow in the postmodern world. The argument of this chapter is that the church is the primary presence of God's activity in the world. As we pay attention to what it means to be the church we create an alternative community to the society of the world. This new community, the embodied experience of God's kingdom, will draw people into itself and nurture them in the faith. In this sense the church and its life in the world will become the new apologetic. People come to faith not because they see the logic of the argument, but because they have experienced a welcoming God in a hospitable and loving community.

CHURCH WITHIN
THE PARADIGMS OF HISTORY[1]

There was a time in my life when I sought the continuity of truth in "the trail of blood," the communities who defined themselves against the established church. As I began to study the history of the church, I became particularly concerned when I discovered that "the trail of blood" generally included the gnostics of the early church who denied the incarnation and the Catharists of the medieval era who denied the Trinity and practiced communal marriage.[2]

When I turned away from a sectarian view of the church to embrace the whole church with all of its triumphs and failures, I sensed a belongingness to this vast community of people. I also experienced a connectedness to history that broke the arrogance of my sectarian attitude and created a humility that allowed me to be defined by the church as the worldwide community of people to which I belonged. This means that I am able to affirm the whole church in all the various paradigms of history. As Origen said, "I want to be a man of the church; I do not want to be called by the name of some founder."[3]

In the classical period the chief understanding of the church was that it was a visible continuation of the presence of Jesus in the world. As Henri de Lubac writes, "If Christ is the sacrament of God, the church is for us the sacrament of Christ."[4] This incarnational view of the church saw Jesus present in the assembled people, in the ministry of bishop, presbyter, and deacon, in word and song, and at the Table. In this way Christ continues to minister to his church and to dwell among his people. This divine nature of the church was organized around the three-fold order of ministry (bishop, presbyter, deacon) whose responsibility it was to receive and pass down orthodox teaching, to shepherd the flock, and to appoint others to be faithful ministers of Word and sacrament. As the church expanded, bishops over the church took on increasing responsibility. By the end of the sixth century the unity of the church was based on the unity of the bishops, with the bishop of Rome as the first among equals.[5] Truth, it was argued, originated in the church with the apostles, and was handed down in Scripture, summarized by the creeds, and guarded and interpreted by the church.

Roman Catholicism as we know it did not emerge until the thirteenth century. By then, the central characteristic of the church was that God's presence had become institutionalized in the papacy, the hierarchical concept of authority.[6] The church was no longer a community of equals, but of unequals. The clergy was the source of all power. Their decisions filtered down to the lay person, who passively obeyed. The church had adopted the juridical model of the state. Canon law defined all of its actions and prescribed in detail the laws of the church and the penalties for infraction. Salvation came through the church as grace was made available through the sacraments.[7] During the last two centuries of the medieval era the institutional church became morally and politically corrupt and was in great need of reform.

The Reformation burst on the scene with a new understanding of the nature and organization of the church. Protestants turned away from the church as the presence of God in history, and looked for the purpose of the church in its calling to proclaim the gospel.[8] Avery Dulles calls this the "herald model" of the church. The Reformers identified the presence of the church as "wherever the word of God is rightly preached and the sacraments rightly administered."[9] The classic threefold order of ministry was replaced in most Protestant churches with a presbyterial model (government by an appointed group) or congregational (government by the local church) model. The true church, it proclaimed, was not found in this or that body of people, but in the invisible church which existed in the mind of God—what Luther called "a spiritual, inner christendom."[10]

The shift from the visible church to the "invisible" church dominated modern Protestant thought. Consequently, the modern church is characterized by numerous denominations, the rise of the independent church movement, and the emergence of the parachurch movement. In this invisible church model, the church on earth is not a divine presence, although it does have a divine calling. Its calling is to witness to the world and serve the needs of the world. This servant model of the church is accomplished not by the corporate church, but by individuals within the church who hear the call to full-time ministry.[11] In this way the church has reflected the individualism of the modern era.[12]

In the postmodern period we can expect a new interest to emerge in the visible church, both local and universal. The local church will increasingly work toward an experienced community of faith, a community that has historical continuity with two thousand years of history, a community that is related to the global church. Once again, the church in society will seek to be the incarnate presence of God in tangible form[13] (see table G).

Problems Inherited from the Enlightenment

In order to be effective in a postmodern world, it is necessary for evangelicals to deal with two specific problems inherited from the Enlightenment: (1) the emphasis on pragmatism, which has resulted in an a-theological understanding of the church; and (2) the emphasis on individualism, which has resulted in an a-historical view of the church.

Pragmatism Results in an A-Theological View of the Church

In the pragmatic view of the church, the church as the body of Christ has been replaced by an efficient corporation. The pastor is the CEO and everyone else functions under the pastor's strong leadership.[14] A meaningful and effective ministry is developed using marketing techniques and corporate organizational structures instead of attempting to recover the theological reality of the church.

A second theological view of the church is the model of the church as a political power base. For example, the religious right and its national organizations apply political pressure on the church to elect Christians to office and legislate morality. The desire of these groups is to become a strong political presence and to control behavior through legislation. They mobilize the church as one more competing subculture, demanding its right to be heard. This model of the church fits into the modern paradigm of competing subcultures, each attempting to assert its will over that of others, thus misunderstanding the theological nature of the church and its function in the world.[15]

Individualism Results in an A-Historical View of the Church

The second problem we have inherited from the Enlightenment is an a-historical attitude. Not all denominations and fellowships are equally a-historical. But for many, history is of little value. There is also a strong bias against the history preceding the Reformation.

Unfortunately, many independent church movements, small denominations and fellowships, and parachurch movements are about reinventing the wheel. The attempt to "start over again" arises from a negative view of history. The argument is that all one needs is an intelligent view of the Bible and a grasp of the current culture. Because of this attitude toward history, the church has been unknowingly shaped by social, political, and philosophical forces: democracy and capitalism have given rise to the rugged individualism expressed in the fierce concern for independence among many of our autonomous churches; denominationalism has reflected the social divisions of society; the industrial movement has produced wealth and, with it, the church has become a landed institution, a corporation wielding economic power through heavy investments; and Enlightenment rationalism has robbed the church of its mystical self-concept, so that it is now regarded as little more than a human organization made up of individuals.

Individualism often exhibits itself in a failure to realize the importance of involvement with other Christians in a local church, in a failure to recognize that being a Christian is not something a person does alone, and in an emphasis on personal experience. It devalues the corporate life of the church. This neglect of the whole body of Christ for what has been called "freelance" Christianity is a dangerous rejection of the body in which Christ dwells. As Rodney Clapp points out, "It misconstrues human personhood as fundamentally atomistic (rather than social) and the church as the collection of individuals—rather than as a corporate body whose members have identity and purpose by being a part of the church."[16]

The origin of this kind of individualism lies, to some extent at least, in the failure of a misguided revivalism: a revivalism geared toward the personal experience of the individual with Christ to the neglect of the individual's corporate experience in the body. Because revivalism has crossed denominational boundaries, there is a tendency to tell converts to "attend the church of your choice," often without a sufficient definition and explanation of what it means to be part of the church. Thus, certain kinds of evangelism tend to make the church less important than experience and unwittingly support the "Christ is in" but the "church is out" syndrome.

What are we to do about the failure of evangelicalism to have a strong theology of the church as God's earthly community? What are we to do about our failure to affirm our visible connection with God's earthly community throughout history and around the world? These questions are addressed in the two chapters that follow.

RESTORING THE THEOLOGY
OF THE CHURCH

Several years ago as I was walking down the corridor of The Billy Graham Center where the Wheaton Graduate School of Theology is housed, I was greeted by one my colleagues. "Hey, Webber!" he cried. "You're going to love the new college statement of faith that is being announced today." "Why?" I was curious. "Because for the first time in Wheaton's history we have included a confessional statement on the church." I quickly got a copy, and here is what I read:

> We believe that the one, holy, universal Church is the body of Christ and is composed of the communities of Christ's people. The task of Christ's people in this world is to be God's redeemed community, embodying His love by worshipping God with confession, prayer, and praise; by proclaiming the gospel of God's redemptive love through our Lord Jesus Christ to the ends of the earth by word and deed; by caring for all of God's creation and actively seeking the good of everyone, especially the poor and needy.[1]

I was elated with this statement because it spoke directly to a theology of the church and to the need to be connected with the whole church. The early Christians did not think that Christ had defeated the powers of evil in his living, dying, and rising without leaving a means by which this redeeming action would continue in the world. The church is seen as the sign of *Christus Victor*, the community of people where the victory of Christ over evil becomes present in and to this world. For this reason Paul spoke of the church as the community through which "the manifold wisdom of God should be made known to the rulers and authorities in the heavenly realms" (Eph. 3:10).[2]

Because it is impossible to give a succinct definition of the church, the biblical writers and the early church fathers always referred to the church through picture images. Paul Minear states there are more than eighty images of the church in the New Testament.[3] Most Christians are familiar with some of these images like salt and light, ark, or sojourner. But Minear's study led him to conclude that the four most dominant images of the church are the people of God, the new creation, the fellowship in faith, and the body of Christ. These images speak to us of the theology of the church as the presence of Christ in the world. This theological insight, that the church is the "community of God's presence" will have a far-reaching effect in the postmodern world, both for those who are within the church and for the unchurched.

The People of God

The most basic definition of the *ecclesia* in the New Testament is found in the image of the church as "all the saints in Christ Jesus" (Phil. 1:1). These people are the people *of God;* God creates, calls, sustains, and saves the church.[4] The origin of the church lies, then, in the work of the redemption through Jesus Christ. Just as the origin of Israel is rooted in the exodus event so the church is grounded in the Christ event, the primordial event of the Christian faith. For this reason, the church is designated by words that compare it with Israel. The church is "a chosen race," "a holy nation," "the true circumcision," "Abraham's sons," "heirs of David's throne," "a remnant," and "the elect." Even the life of the church is often compared to the life of Israel. Christians are making their "exodus" to the "promised land." They are "aliens" in a strange land, and Christ is the "bread" from heaven.

The church, like Israel, is also viewed in terms of the future. The idea of the church as a historical community moving toward a destination is common in the Bible (see Heb. 12:2; Phil. 14:1): The church is a pilgrim people that has not yet entered into Sabbath rest (Hebrews); an exiled people (Peter); a people who are at enmity with the world (James); a people who wrestle with diabolic powers (Eph. 6); and a bride (Rev. 19:8). The future toward which the church travels is the new heavens and the new earth.

This image of the people of God is highly pertinent to us in a postmodern world because it says the church is the continuation of the presence of Jesus Christ in the world and a sign of God's presence in history. There is a people of God in the world today chosen to be a unique manifestation of God. This historical people is a community, "brought together from the ends of the earth in your kingdom."[5] And, as Ignatius wrote, it is to be "a standard for the ages."[6] The goal of the church is to be a divine standard, a sign of God's incarnational presence and activity in history. In a postmodern world the most effective witness to a world of disconnected people is the church that forms community and embodies the reality of the new society. People in a postmodern world are not persuaded to faith by reason as much as they are moved to faith by participation in God's earthly community.

The New Creation

The second image, "the new creation," speaks to the nature of God's earthly community. It is the community in which a new start in life has begun. As Paul said in 2 Corinthians 5:17: "Therefore, if anyone is in Christ, he [or, more accurately, the community] is a new creation; the old has gone, the new has come." This new creation is to be taken in both an individual and a corporate sense—a new person, a new community of people. This soteriological concept of the church is clearly enunciated by Cyprian in his treatise *On the Unity of the Church* (A.D. 250). He states, "You can not have God for your Father if you have not the church for your mother!"[7]

At first glance an evangelical may think of Cyprian's view of the mothering role of the church as a Roman Catholic view. However, this view has been clearly affirmed throughout history. Calvin states,

> But as our present design is to treat the visible church, we may learn even from the title mother how useful and even necessary it is for us to know her; since there is no other way of entrance into life, unless we are conceived by her, born of her, nourished at her breast, and continually preserved under her care and government till we are divested of this mortal flesh, and "become like angels." For our infirmity will not admit of our dismission from her school; we must continue under her instruction and discipline to the end of our lives. It is also to be remarked, that out of her bosom there can be no hope of remission of sins, or any salvation.[8]

This "new creation" is the context in which our journey of faith is taking place. The fellowship of the community itself nurtures and forms our pilgrimage.

The Fellowship in Faith

This is why the church as a fellowship in faith emphasizes the divine presence taking form in a new fabric of human relationships—a fellowship of people. This fellowship shares a corporate life. For example, Luke describes the early Christians as being of "one heart and one soul" (Acts 4:32). They even sold their possessions and lived in common, although, as the rebellion of Ananais and Sapphira illustrates, this original common community was difficult to administrate. Living together was not easy, and the principles of being the church together had to be learned as each member of the community submitted to the rule of Christ. But faith in the end was to overcome the boundaries that separated people, transcending racial, economic, and sexual differences. "There is neither Jew nor Greek, there is neither slave nor free, there is neither male nor female" (Gal. 3:28). The character of the "fellowship in faith" is to be far different from the character of other communities.

The difference is rooted in a common slavery to Jesus Christ. The image of a slave, so often overlooked, is an image that Paul often used of himself in relation to other believers, "For we do not preach ourselves, but Jesus Christ as Lord, and ourselves as your servants for Jesus' sake" (2 Cor. 4:5). A slavery to God immediately transforms relations on the horizontal level. No longer can one person "lord it" over another. All God's people are equal before God and each other. For this reason the church is called the "family of God" (1 Peter 4:17). We all serve in God's house under God's authority. Thus, the church is a fellowship in faith, a corporate existence under God, a mutual slavery to each other.

The church as the realized experience of the "fellowship of faith" will break down our extreme individualism. Modern individualism is something different from a personal relationship with God in Christ. It is a form of Christianity that fails to understand the integral relationship that exists between the members of Christ's body. We need to reflect on the teaching of Ignatius, bishop of Antioch (A.D. 110), who wrote to the Ephesian church: "your accord and harmonious love is a hymn to Jesus Christ."[9] When the "fellowship in faith" is actualized, the church as a true fellowship makes Christianity real to the individual, as Ignatius indicated when he described the church "as a choir able to sing in unison and [with] one voice."[10] The mandate to break through the façade of individualism and create dynamic Christian relationships is demonstrated in this new fabric of human relations.

Consequently, the challenge of the church in the postmodern world is to recover community within the local church and the community of the entire church throughout history. We must learn that we are members of the *whole* church, the living and the dead, who constitute the fellowship in faith. Our calling is to deconstruct our sectarianism and to enter into dialogue with the whole church with the intent of recovering our relationship to the whole family of God—Catholic, Orthodox, and

Protestant. The more we experience the "fellowship in faith," the more deeply we will experience the church as the body of Christ, a body that will attract and hold the postmodern seeker.

The Body of Christ

The image of the body proclaims that the people of God are a physical body of people who truly are the continuation of the presence of Christ in the world. In Paul "the body of Christ" is understood as antithetical to the "body of death." This contrast is expressed in Romans 5:12–21, a recapitulation passage. Here, there are two humanities: those who stand in solidarity with Adam and constitute the body of death, and those who stand in solidarity with Christ and constitute the body of life.

Paul's reference to the church as the body of Christ is therefore not a mere metaphor containing social and psychological value, but a statement about the relationship that exists between Christ and his body. It says that Christ is one with the church, that the existence of the church is an essential continuation of the life of Jesus in the world; the church is a divine creation which, in a mystical yet real way, coinheres with the Son who is made present through it.

This incarnational motif regulated the early Christian perception of the church. For them, the body image of the church is that of a revolutionary society of people. The church is a new order, a new humanity, which has the power to be an explosive force in society and in history. It is called not to contain its message but to live its message, calling all people to repentance from the old body into the new body.

These four images—the people of God, the new creation, the fellowship of faith, and the body—describe the connection that exists between the Christ victorious over sin and the Christ immediately present in the church. It is a new society that acts as the sign of redemption to the world. The power of this recovered tradition results in a new commitment to the church as the people of God, a love both for Christ and for the church, a recognition that Christ and the church cannot be separated from each other, for they are intrinsically linked. The emphasis is not so much on the church as an institution or a denomination, but on the church as the people, that community of people created by God in whom and through whom Christ is present in the world. In the postmodern world the most effective churches will be led by those who turn their backs on the corporate market-driven view of the church and return to the theological understanding and practice of the church as the community of God's presence in the world. It is this kind of church that will grow not only in numbers, but in depth and openness to others. The most significant witness in the world will emanate from the church as the embodied presence of God on earth. For example, one of my students, Barry Spencer, related the following story to me, a story that illustrates my point. I'll tell it in Barry's words:

This is a story of a conversation that I had with a customer when I worked at a department store. I'll call him Mark.

He approached the counter in the common dress of college students today: baggy jeans with extra wide bottoms, oversized shirt, the latest in Doc Martens, and a hoop earring. The conversation began as a normal one. He wanted to check out the latest Tommy Jean bib overall. After trying on the largest size, he asked if there was a larger size. After taking his name and phone number for the contact list, he stayed at the counter and did not seem in much of a hurry. Since it wasn't busy, I asked him some questions about himself, like where he lived, where he went to school, and what he planned to do. The more we talked the more comfortable I felt with him so I decided to ask him more probing questions about his life and his future and Christianity. At this point and for the next forty-five minutes he told me all the things that he, as a second-year college student, was dealing with. He told me about the heartache his friends were experiencing: one has an infant child at the age of 19. The father feels obligated to marry the girl since she decided to keep the child. Another friend has HIV. Another has had multiple sexual partners. Most of his friends are dealing with situations that they are completely unprepared to face: early parenting, life-threatening diseases, and marriage.

Mark does not have a child, or a threatening disease. But he does relate to his friends in many ways. Like his friends, he has had little direction and instruction from his parents on how to live a fulfilling life. His parents have had addiction problems ranging from alcohol addiction, to sexual addiction, to work addiction. A genuine love from loving parents is a nonexistent reality. Emptiness of heart reigns in their lives, and their futures look bleak from where they are standing. Why do he and his friends have sex with who they want and not take school or the future seriously? Because from where they are standing there seems to be no other way to live. They feel stuck in a way of life that has little hope and no fulfillment, which leads to an emptiness in the heart.

At this point we were standing next to his car in the parking lot on a bitter cold day. But as the sun glistened off the snow, I told him about another way to live. I told him about the hope and meaning that comes through Jesus Christ. I told him that life can be lived with an unspeakable fullness. I told him that the church is designed for people who want to support one another and who together want to experience community, genuine love, the fullness of hope, and fulfillment in life. When I asked him if he would like to be a part of a people like this, he said that he certainly would. In fact, his face lit up as I talked about the church. But he concluded by saying that such a people does not exist. And I responded by saying that I am proof that it does and I can introduce him to my community where he can experience it.[11]

The challenge in a postmodern world is to be the presence of a transcendent reality here on earth, the embodied community that draws others to Christ through participation in his incarnate presence, the church.

RECOVERING OUR
HISTORICAL CONNECTION

Another ecclesial mandate for evangelicals in a postmodern world is to pay greater attention to breaking with our a-historical attitude and recover our connection to the entire visible church. The Nicene Creed states: "We believe in one Holy, Catholic, and Apostolic Church." This confession is not a belief *about* the church, but an experienced reality of Christ's presence in the church. We therefore need to reconsider our emphasis on the "invisible" and "spiritual" church, and restore the ancient concern for the visible church, where Christ's presence is experienced in the unity we have with the whole church.

The Church Is One

We find a desire for the oneness of the church in the words of Jesus that "all of them may be one . . . that the world may believe that you have sent me" (John 17:21). In the early church Jesus' statement meant "visible" unity.[1] For the Fathers, any break with the church was taken as a serious breach against Christ's body. For example, in a letter to the Corinthian church on the occasion of a revolt by some of the younger members of the church against the elders, Clement, the bishop of Rome (A.D. 96), pointed to the seriousness with which he took the unity of the body: "Why do we divide and tear to pieces the members of Christ, and raise up such strife against our own body and have reached such a height of madness as to forget that we are members of one another?[2] Likewise, in the *Didache* (c. 100), a prayer over bread at the Eucharist, points to the esteem in which unity was held: "Even as this broken bread was scattered over the hills and was gathered together and became one, so let thy church be gathered together from the ends of the earth into thy kingdom."[3] It was this kind of spirit that stood behind the more elaborate portrayal of unity in *On the Unity of the Church,* written by Cyprian, bishop of Carthage (A.D. 250): "As there are many rays of sun, but one light; and many branches of a tree, but one strength based in its tenacious root; yet the unity is still preserved in the source."[4]

The church throughout history has unfolded in many cultures and therefore no one expression of the church stands alone as the true visible body of Christ. This means that we must affirm the church in its different paradigms. This is difficult to do consistently, even for those of us who wish to be interpreted by the oneness of the church. For example, I was speaking on evangelism and referred to a specific type of evangelism in a way that was negative. A layman in this church came up to me afterward and said, "I like everything you said except your illustration about such-and-such type of evangelism. You see," he said, "I believe that God works in every one of our churches in different ways. And I don't like it when any Christian group is put down."

A goal for evangelicals in the postmodern world is to accept diversity as a historical reality, but to seek unity in the midst of it. This perspective will allow us to see Catholic, Orthodox, and Protestant churches as various forms of the one true church—all based on apostolic teaching and authority, finding common ground in the faith expressed by classical Christianity. One way of experiencing the unity of the church is to affirm that it is a "community of communities"[5] (see table G, figure 1). In this view there is only one church, but it is expressed in many cultural ways.

The Church Is Holy

One major block for many evangelicals against accepting the unity of the church is the issue of the church's holiness. Shouldn't the church, it will be asked, be pure and holy? The Christological dimension of the church speaks to this issue: The church is fully divine, yet fully human.

The holiness of the church is expressed in the admonition "Be holy, because I am holy" (1 Peter 1:16). This statement may be understood as standing for the whole body of Christ, for Peter defined the church as "a chosen people, a royal priesthood, a holy nation, a people belonging to God" (1 Peter 2:9). While all Christians agree that the church is holy, not all concur on the specific content and meaning of holiness. The majority of Christians admit that it does not refer to a state of holiness achieved by individual members of the church. Holiness belongs to Jesus Christ; the church that is baptized into him is holy because of his holiness. Nevertheless, Christ through the Holy Spirit summons the church to holiness (Rom. 1:7; 1 Cor. 1:2).

The early church in general agreed with Callistus of Rome that the visible church is like Noah's ark, containing both the clean and the unclean. Pointing to the parable of the tares, Callistus insisted that the wheat and the chaff grow side by side; thus, the church contains both sinners and saints. The early church taught that holiness, as a quality of perfection, belongs to Jesus Christ by virtue of who he is and to his church by virtue of what he has done for it. Therefore, the holiness of Christ's church is not a realized holiness but an anticipated holiness. The church that is "holy and blameless," without "spot and wrinkle," is the one the Son will present to the Father. Thus, the church on earth may be regarded as both holy and unholy.

We evangelicals need to turn our backs on the old separatist model of "if you don't agree, start your own denomination." We will also need to be more tolerant of the human weaknesses of the church. For example, at one time I was convinced that my particular brand of Christianity was the right one and that my church alone was correct in all the views it held. Therefore, I was hesitant to associate with other churches—the wrong ones, or at least the ones that I believed had a lot of wrong views. It was a freeing experience for me to discover that the church was not yet holy, that its perfection (both doctrinal and ethical) was essentially an eschatological expectation. Now I am able to embrace the whole church and to affirm that my faith is catholic.

The Church Is Catholic

The word *catholic* was first used by Ignatius when he wrote, "Wherever Jesus Christ is, there is the catholic church."[6] By this designation he pointed to the fullness of truth: the church that is catholic has all the truth—Jesus Christ.

The early church also used the word *catholic* to mean universal. Saint Cyril of Jerusalem in his *Cathechetical Lectures* said the church is called catholic because it

> extends all over the world from one end of the earth to the other; and because it teaches universally and completely one and all the doctrines

which ought to come to men's knowledge, concerning things both visible and invisible, heavenly and earthly.[7]

Today evangelicals and Catholics are enjoying spiritual camaraderie that was nonexistent a few years ago. For many years evangelicals were taught that Catholics were not fully Christian. At Wheaton College, where I teach, as in other evangelical schools and institutions, there are a small but growing number of Catholic students. I have had several deeply committed Catholic Christians in my course on Christian thought. One of them, a young man who was the youth director at the local Catholic church in Wheaton, had the following inscription painted on his briefcase: *God Loves Protestants Too.* He always set it up in class so everyone could see it. And, of course, the point was well taken in good spirit. We recognize that we belong to each other because there is only one church that results from Christ's victory over the power of evil.

The full meaning of the word *catholic* may be defined by such words as "universal," "identical," "orthodox," "continuous," and "wholeness or fullness." The church is universal not only in the sense that it is worldwide, but also in the sense that it is grounded in the universality of the atonement. The church is identical in that it always remains true to itself in history; the church is always to remain orthodox. To identify with catholicity, then, is to believe in the continuity of Christ's work in history and to affirm the whole faith.[8]

This affirmation that the church is all over the world is another reason to reject a sectarian spirit and to affirm an ecumenical view of the church. Evangelicals in a postmodern world will increasingly feel at home with Catholics, Orthodox, and other Protestant bodies as we recover the faith of the common era of the church, a faith based on solid content, the apostolic tradition.

The Church Is Apostolic

The concept of apostolicity indicates that the church is intimately linked to and built on the past. It points to the church built "on the foundation of the apostles and prophets," and in this way affirms a view of continuity from one generation to the next (Eph. 2:20). This concept of continuousness reaches back into the way God was made known in Israel's history. For a Jew, Israel's past is always present. Abraham, Moses, David, and the prophets, as well as the fortunes and misfortunes of Israel as a people, have always been looked on as a present reality— guiding, informing, and directing Hebrew life. This sense of the presence of the past is so strong that, at the Passover Seder, the one presiding says, "When I was a slave in Egypt . . . " In the same way the evangelical church needs to be guided by the witness and authority of the apostles.

One of the major problems we evangelicals have with our Catholic and Orthodox brothers and sisters is the matter of apostolic succession. Most evangelicals do not have the ancient threefold order of ministry— bishop, presbyter, and deacon—nor do we have an emphasis on the historical succession passed down through the episcopate. Naturally this is a huge barrier to union with the historic churches.

The postmodern world with its emphasis on variety and pluralism may be a creative setting in which we can deal with the problem. Evangelicals can stand with Catholics and Orthodox in the affirmation of the apostolic tradition as summarized in the rule of faith, the Apostles' Creed, the Nicene Creed, and the Chalcedon Creed. We can also affirm that the work of the church is to "hand down" this apostolic tradition. We evangelicals believe in the succession of truth, not through a specific body of people as in the episcopate, but in the handing over of the whole church from generation to generation. For example, Catholic theologian Hans Küng suggests that "the whole church and every individual member shares in this apostolic succession."[9] The argument is that the "church as a whole is the successor to the apostles." The church is a community of faithful Christians, all of whom stand in apostolic succession in the broadest sense of the term. The church, in other words, hands down the church.

We evangelicals also agree that within this apostolic succession there is a special succession of the apostolic pastoral services. Thus, the church, to be apostolic, ought to have within it all the charismatic gifts that were present in the primitive church and these gifts should be practiced within the body. This includes the specific succession of particular functions of the charismatic offices of *presbyter* (pastor), *episkopos* (bishop), and *diakonos* (deacon). These stood out with increasing prominence in the early church as it was recognized that the church must have overseers, teachers, and servants. In most of our evangelical churches we have these three apostolic functions, but we have dropped biblical language and adopted a secular language ("executive minister," for example). We need to restore the language of bishop, presbyter (pastor), and deacon and be brought one step closer to our common roots in the classical church. The recovery of apostolic language will be a uniting rather than a dividing matter. We will be able to affirm that the whole body of Christ shares in the apostolic faith, handed down in the life of the church through the centuries. For example, I once believed that the church became apostate at the close of the first century and hadn't emerged again until the Reformation. I jokingly say to my students, "We Protestants act as though Pentecost occurred on October 31, 1517, when Martin Luther tacked his 95 Theses on the door of the Wittenburg church." This attitude results in a negative view of the early church fathers and Christianity prior to the Reformation. The fact is that God's church has existed from *the Pentecost described in Acts.* We belong to the whole church and need, for our own spiritual health, to affirm every part of it.

Because evangelicals fear that a respect for the early church fathers will turn them into Roman Catholics, a distinction needs to be made between *catholic* and *Roman Catholic.* The early Fathers are catholic in the sense that they defined the classical Christian tradition for the whole church. This is a tradition, as I have been presenting, common *to every branch of the church. Roman* Catholicism, as such, is a tradition that has added to the common tradition. I believe in the common tradition and share that tradition with my Catholic brothers and sisters. But, I do not believe in some of the added traditions of the Romanization of the church in the medieval era. The late medieval church is accused of salvation by works, valuing tradition over Scripture, indulgences, and the like. When we understand Catholicism as a particular paradigm that developed in the medieval period, we can understand the added traditions as the cultural accretions of medievalism. We evangelicals also have our cultural baggage drawn from the Enlightenment. What we have in common with each other is a Christianity rooted in the apostolic tradition.

The early Fathers can bring us back to what is common and help us get behind our various traditions, not in the sense that we deny our own tradition, but that we give a priority to the common teaching of the church. Here is where our unity lies.

To summarize, the words *One, Holy, Catholic,* and *Apostolic* point to the oneness of the church, as a matter of faith. Christians do not believe something *about* the oneness of the church; they believe *in* the oneness of the church. Consequently, evangelicals need to go beyond talk about the unity of the church to experience it through an attitude of acceptance of the whole church and an entrance into dialogue with the Orthodox, Catholic, and other Protestant bodies. This is already happening in the "Evangelicals and Catholics Together" consultation, in an evangelical-Orthodox dialogue, in scholarly societies such as the Society of Biblical Literature, and in local ecumenical settings in which evangelicals are involved.

The importance of recovering our historical and global connection to the church as the community of God's presence in the world was brought home to me in a recent encounter with an atheist.

I had been invited to debate a University of Wisconsin professor of philosophy who was an atheist on a radio show aired over WGN in Chicago. I didn't want to do the debate because I knew he would concentrate on undermining the so-called rational proofs for the existence of God. Since I didn't place any confidence in these arguments, I feared there would be little to talk about.

In the first few minutes of the program, I excused myself from the use of rational arguments for the existence of God, pulling the rug out from under the philosopher and preventing a discussion on rational counterargumentation.

The host, immediately taken aback, said "Bob, what are we going to talk about?" "Let's talk," I said, "about the phenomena of Israel and the church in the world. How does the exodus event and the people of Israel and the Christ event and the people called church interpret us and our world?" We ended up having an engaging conversation on the metaphysics of presence, the significance of interpreting God and ourselves, out of the existence of these two communities that represent the presence of God in the world.

When the discussion was over the philosopher professor took me aside and said, "I'm an atheist, but I'm also a practicing Jew. We keep a kosher home and celebrate all the Jewish feasts and fasts. I'm fascinated at how the community presents God and interprets me. This discussion has given me much to think about."

In a postmodern world the rational arguments for the existence of God are cold and lifeless. But a community of people who allow themselves to be interpreted by God's saving event in Jesus Christ and become formed as a true and living example of a local and universal oneness will speak volumes to the world about the saving Christ who dwells within them.

Conclusion

In the introduction to this section I referred to the evangelical church in the postmodern world as one that will recognize itself as an extension of Jesus in the world. The distinguishing characteristic of allowing ourselves to be interpreted this way is the recovery of a supernatural experience of the church and a new sense of connection with the whole church, visible and invisible. During the modern era we evangelicals have not been serious enough about the connection of the church with Christ and we have been indifferent about our relationships with the church throughout history and around the world. These attitudes need to change.

My argument is that the postmodern world is a rich cultural context for the recovery of a classical view of the church. The scientific emphasis on the interrelationship of all things allows us to speak intelligently of the interdependence of the church historically and globally. The philosophical shift from reason to mystery provides an opening to the discussion of a supernatural view of the church connected with the work of Christ. The shift from individualism to community is a cultural change that permits us to speak once again of the significance of the church as a reflection of the eternal community of God expressed in the Trinity; the emphasis in communication theory and a language of images and metaphors allows us to recover the biblical images and historic marks of the church, which can be mined for their rich variety of meanings; and the notion that communication best occurs through participation invites us to experience the church and to be interpreted by its meaning not as an abstract idea, but as a present reality. This approach to the church as a "metaphysical presence" is the strongest kind of apologetic to the reality of God in a postmodern world.

Table G: The Church Throughout History

Ancient	Medieval	Reformation	Modern	Postmodern
The continuation of the incarnation: the body of Christ	Institutional Visible Sacramental	The herald model; the true church is an invisible inner Christendom	Rise of denominations	Return to incarnational model
The unity of the church	Juridical		Invisible	Visible
Mystery				Church is the mystical presence of the body of Christ on earth

The postmodern emphasis on the interconnection of all things drives us back to the biblical recovery of the church as the body of Christ, the continued presence of Christ in and to the world. This emphasis will create a new apologetic that focuses on the church as a "metaphysical presence," the door into Christ. Consequently we will need to stress the unity of the church and seek fellowship in the family of faith based on a mutual affirmation of the classical Christian heritage.

Figure 1: The Church as a Community of Communities

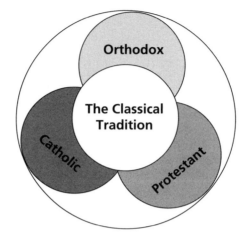

What Orthodox, Catholics, and Protestants have in common is the classical Christian tradition of the first five centuries. While our unity is not now an actual oneness, we can start by embracing the common ground we all share in the classical tradition. It at least allows for a sense of spiritual unity that accents the common identity in classical thought and recognizes that differences are the result of cultural formation.

FOUR

A CLASSICAL/POST-MODERN WORSHIP

As this piece of bread was scattered
Over the hills and then was brought
Together and made one, so let your
Church be brought together from the
Ends of the earth into your Kingdom.
For yours is the glory and the power
Through Jesus Christ forever.
  —A Prayer from *The Didache,* A.D. 100

Several years ago, I was invited to give lectures on worship to a group of evangelical theologians. I was more than pleasantly surprised by the strong interest these theologians had in the thinking of the early church. A number of them indicated they were rediscovering the Fathers of the church and were interested in how the classical Christian tradition of worship could be applied to the church today. The central point I made—and the one that piqued the interest of my audience—is that worship is a rehearsal of the saving deeds of God in history. God's saving actions culminate in the work of Christ, the overthrow of the powers of evil, and the ultimate establishment of the kingdom in the new heavens and the new earth. This is the story of the meaning of history; it shapes the church, forms spirituality, and motivates the mission of the church. It is what we call the Christian metanarrative.

This metanarrative of Israel and the church is no invention of human ingenuity. It is instead the revelation of God's presence in history working out the salvation of the world. In worship we proclaim and enact God's mighty deeds in history and offer our prayer of praise and thanksgiving to the Creator and Redeemer of the world.

The postmodern world is fertile ground for this classical understanding of worship for two reasons. First, postmodern people are turning away from their faith in reason to recognize the mysterious nature of the world in which we live. Catherine Pickstock writes that the Enlightenment hope for a "universal rational humanism" is now exhausted and defeated. Unfortunately, various postmodern approaches are "needlessly nihilistic." We are left with a "radical [Christian] orthodoxy" that concedes along with postmodernism "the indeterminacy of all our knowledge and experience of selfhood," but "construes this shifting flux as a sign of our dependency on a transcendent source which 'gives' all reality as a mystery."[1] Historic worship is an experience of the mystery of salvation and thus the doorway through which a person may approach the complexities of life to rest satisfied in the mystery of God's transcendent presence experienced in worship.

Second, the postmodern shift in communications from the verbal to the symbolic allows evangelicals to recover the classical Christian approach to communication and to creatively apply it to worship renewal. Pierre Babin, a leader in Christian communication, points out that in an audiovisual world understanding occurs through participation in "the way of beauty" and "the symbolic way." People of the new communication era are "more attracted to beauty than in the proofs for the existence of God."[2] In worship we engage in the mystery of God at work in the world. How we do so needs to take into account the changes that are occurring in the shift from a print-oriented to an audiovisual society. Once again, it is the classical view of worship adapted for the twenty-first century that holds the greatest promise for evangelical faith and practice. But there are two problems with which we must deal.

First is the problem of the postmodern commitment to the relativity of all metanarratives. According to postmodern philosophy, every culture in the world has its own metanarrative rooted in its own religion. So in the cultures of the world we have Hindu, Confucian, Buddhist, Jewish, Muslim, or Christian narratives. Each narrative has its own story to tell, its own history to remember, and its own religious teachings and precepts to live by. According to postmoderns all these narratives are of equal value and no one narrative can claim universality. While Christians recognize the existence of the many narratives, and their importance to the communication of the religious view of each culture, the evangelical problem with postmodern thought is with the relative nature assigned to all narratives. Classical Christianity makes a universal claim for the Christian narrative, and evangelicals stand in continuity with this conviction. Therefore, the idea that the Christian metanarrative is one of many equally valid metanarratives (pluralism) is not acceptable to evangelicals. Evangelicals take the universal character of the Christian metanarrative as an essential aspect of the framework of Christian faith. In this matter evangelicals will need to stand against postmodern relativism.

The second problem has to do with the communication of our metanarratives. Modern communications stress con-

ceptual communication that centers on reading, reason, logic, linear sequence, and understanding that derives particularly via the mind. Evangelical worship has followed the modern theory of communication with its emphasis primarily placed on verbal communication. Postmodern theories of communication have shifted to the centrality of symbolic communication through an immersed participation in the event. This emphasis represents the shift from a print-oriented society to an audiovisual society.

In sum, evangelicals will remain steadfast in affirming the universal nature of the Christian metanarrative, but will need to draw from the well of symbolic forms of communication.

WORSHIP WITHIN
THE PARADIGMS OF HISTORY[1]

In biblical and ancient times worship was the primary way of experiencing God's saving work in history. Early Christian sermons (as in Acts) and liturgies (both Eastern and Western) are oriented around the proclamation and enactment of God's saving work from creation to the consummation. This historical and symbolic recitation expressed the identity of the church, gave shape to its communal self-understanding, and signified its place in the world. During the first three centuries of the church, worship took place in homes or the catacombs. Its content was primarily the proclamation of God's salvation and the anticipation of Christ's return. The culminating praise of worship celebrated the work of Jesus Christ in the Eucharist. Because believers did not meet in churches, worship was informal and intimate.[2]

After the conversion of Constantine, worship became more public. Constantine donated numerous large basilicas to the church and these were turned into places of worship. Because congregations were huge, it was necessary to shift worship from the intimacy of the first three centuries to theater. Drawing from the picture of worship in Revelation 4 and 5, earthly worship was patterned after heavenly worship. Consequently, considerable pomp and ceremony was introduced into worship: processions, great choirs, a more dramatic sermon style, fixed liturgies, vestments, sign of the cross, genuflection, and music forms such as the Gregorian chant. Worship space was modeled after heaven. In worship one joined heavenly worship with the angels, the archangels, and the whole company of saints. In this way worship reinforced the heavenly standing of God's people on earth. Worship was a mysterious participation in God's saving action and a joining in heavenly worship where God and God's saving work were continually praised.[3]

In the medieval era the liturgy underwent significant change. The familiar pattern of ancient worship, with "singers, readers, congregation and celebrant with their respective parts," was changed into a clericalized worship with the congregants watching. Rich ceremony was marked by "multiplication of signs, gestures, genuflexions, striking of the breast, kissing of the altar, kissing of the missal, and so on, and these were invested with sacred allegorical significance." Most of all, worship became the Eucharistic Mass, an unbloody resacrifice of Christ that could be purchased for the dead. Worship was in great need of reform.[4]

The Reformation shifted worship from the visual form[5] to worship that centered around the Word, with a primary emphasis on preaching. This emphasis fit well with the invention of the Gutenburg printing press, the rise of literacy, and the emergence of the Renaissance. In the shift from the visual to the spoken word, truth was not seen so much as it was heard. Truth was in the Bible and the Bible alone. Truth was no longer mysteriously acted out in the liturgy. Instead, truth was available in the words of Scripture, words that could be explained and understood. The consequence of this move to a Word-oriented worship can be seen in the structure of Protestant worship, which focuses on the reading and preaching of the Word; in the architecture, which is plain; and in the hymns, which reinforce and teach the message of the Bible.[6]

This Word-oriented approach to worship dominated the modern era of Christianity. In the seventeenth and eighteenth centuries worship was the means of educating the people. Sermons were often two hours long; time would be set aside after the sermon for discussion of its relevance to the moral, social, and political issues of the day. This heady approach to worship was challenged by the rise of romanticism in the nineteenth century, with its emphasis on feeling and intuition. Revivalism, following the more subjective line of thought, introduced an evangelistic model of worship. In this approach worship was directed toward the sinner and the goal of conversion. Intellectual sermons were replaced by emotional evangelistic sermons and the Eucharist was replaced by the invitation.[7]

These two modern views of worship (pedagogical and revivalistic) have been in continual conflict within evangelicalism. Some churches have maintained the strong Word-centered approach to worship that intends to edify the saints. Others continue to have an evangelistic thrust in worship directed toward sinners. The seeker service has tried to deal with the problem by separating worship from evangelism. Saturday night and Sunday are given to the seeker outreach, whereas a midweek service is directed toward educating God's people in the Word.[8]

In the twentieth century the rise of Pentecostal, charismatic, and praise and worship has stressed style over substance and in some instances has fallen into a kind of entertainment worship.

In the postmodern world evangelical worship is faced with the challenge and opportunity to bring the traditions of worship together in a creative way.[9] From the ancient church, we derive the emphasis on the content and the fourfold order; from the Reformation, we obtain the emphasis on the Word; from free church history, we receive the Christocentric emphasis; and from the younger contemporary churches of our time, we inherit the sense of the Spirit and of intimacy. Worship renewal in the twenty-first century that draws from the Scriptures, and from the rich treasuries of history, will be concerned for contemporary relevance (see table H).

Problems Inherited from the Enlightenment

Three significant problems in evangelical worship have resulted from the Enlightenment. First, there is a loss of the theology of worship. Evangelical issues involving worship seem to be rooted in the conflict between the Enlightenment emphasis on reason and the nineteenth-century romantic stress on emotion. The emphasis on reason during the Enlightenment resulted in a heady form of worship. Worship assumed the nature of a lecture hall, where the primary emphasis was given to the sermon. This intellectual worship was challenged by revivalism, which began in England under the influence of John and Charles Wesley and George Whitefield and in America through the ministry of Charles Finney. Finney introduced the "New Means," which directed worship toward the sinner. Revivalism worship, following the more intuitive and emotional approach, clashed with the older worship, which was directed more toward the mind. One evangelical group located the meaning of worship in the shaping of the Christian mind; the other evangelical stream pointed to the meaning of worship in the experience of the heart. This conflict of style has continued in the twentieth-century debate about traditional versus contemporary worship. Traditional worship seems to be hanging on to modernity while contemporary worship has capitulated to pop culture. In either case the debate continues to rage about style with little concern for a biblical theology of worship. This emphasis is curious, considering the evangelical emphasis on the Bible. In worship many evangelicals are driven more by the market than they are by the Scriptures. No wonder there is no theology of worship among us.

Second, there seems to be little understanding of the order of worship. Evangelicals generally reject order in the name of freedom and spontaneity. But traditional evangelical worship has become as dead and as ritualistic as the worship rejected. Even contemporary worship, which adopted the order of music-driven worship followed by the sermon, has fallen on hard times. The instruments play and the leaders sing, but loudness stifles the human voice (the best instrument of praise) and worship degenerates into a program or production for the entertainment of the people. This form of worship initially draws large crowds but has no staying power.

The third problem of evangelical worship is the rejection of symbolic speech. The dominant word-oriented culture inherited from the Enlightenment is based on conceptual language: reading, notions, abstractions, precision, intelligence, clarity, analysis, idea, explanation, linear sequence, and logic are all the forms through which communication occurs in the modern era and in most evangelical churches. We are accustomed to simple and straightforward language. The use of imagery, symbols, and even subtle language is relatively unknown among many of us. We have locked ourselves into discursive speech as the preferable, if not the only form of communication. One reason why we evangelicals prefer verbal communication over symbolic speech has to do with our view of the Bible. We see the Bible as a book of words. It is God's *written* revelation. This emphasis on the written words of Scripture coupled with neglect of the symbolic forms of communication (which constitute a large portion of Scripture) cause a loss of understanding. Another reason we focus on words as the major means of communication is found in our sense of persons as *reasonable* creatures. A strong emphasis is placed on the mind. Because the mind is rational, it is able to investigate the words of Scripture and derive from them the correct meaning of things. Therefore, the emphasis falls on *words* and *cognitive understanding* in communication. So we must ask, How do we communicate in worship? How can we integrate symbolism in a verbal community?

This modern rejection of visual forms of communication resulted in the loss of the sacraments as "visual words."[10] In evangelicalism the notion of a sacred presence through divine action is largely denied. In the desire to make Christianity as rational as possible and to steer clear of the rituals of the Catholic Church, we have denied the power of symbol to create and form the Christian community. For us truth resides in words, not in images, symbols, and actions. Consequently, we have shifted baptism and Eucharist from God's action to human action. Baptism has become the means by which the converting person declares his or her faith; the Lord's Supper has been reduced to an intellectual recall of Jesus hanging on the tree. We have reduced the ritual of water and of bread and wine to understandable actions. The mystery is gone.

It was this same spirit of rationalism that relegated the Christian concept of time to the list of nonessentials. In the meantime we have baptized the secular calendar. We celebrate national holidays and Mother's Day while neglecting the story of God's saving action in Advent, Epiphany, Lent, and Pentecost. (Christmas and Easter have always been celebrated, but not with the pomp and ceremony they deserve.)

We now live in a new communication era. Communication is shifting from conceptual language to symbolic language. Information is no longer something that can be objectively known and verified through evidence and logic. Knowledge is more subjective and experiential. Knowledge comes through participation in a community and in an immersion with the symbols and the meaning of the community. This emphasis on experience stresses the importance of worship as the celebration of God's saving deeds. We turn now to the classical Christian tradition to find a deeper sense of the Christian metanarrative and to recover ways to communicate this story in worship.

RECOVERING THE THEOLOGY
AND ORDER OF WORSHIP

I teach a course on worship at Wheaton College. In the early part of the semester we do a Jewish liturgy. I want my students to be aware that Christian worship is rooted in Jewish worship and that the metanarrative of Christian worship is always that of "Israel and Jesus."

Jewish worship is characterized by its own metanarrative, which it celebrates through recitation and dramatization. The synagogue with its emphasis on the Word brought the Jewish worshiper into an encounter with God through the recitation of the Word—reading and preaching. Jewish family worship—weekly worship, the festivals, and especially the yearly reenactment of the exodus in the Passover—rehearses the relationship God established with Israel when they were brought out of Egypt. Consequently, Jewish worship celebrates those events in history through which God acted decisively to redeem Israel, to enter into relationship with them as God's special people, and to lead them into the promised land. The celebration of the exodus experience through recitation (synagogue) and dramatization (Passover) is the key to understanding the meaning of Christian worship.[1] In worship we tell the story of Israel and Jesus in the service of the Word and we enact the story at the Table. Like Israel, we rehearse God's mighty deeds of salvation and offer thankful praise and worship to God who saves us.

Recovering a Theology of Worship

I have already made the point that the centerpiece of our worship is Jesus Christ, his incarnation, death, resurrection, overthrow of evil, and return to establish his kingdom. This metanarrative is the key to the content and meaning of worship. Jews who became Christian saw the coming of Jesus as the fulfillment of their worship. Their theology of creation, sin, the redemption of Israel out of Egypt, and the covenantal relationship they had with God found new meaning in Jesus Christ. Christ did not abolish the Old, but fulfilled it by actualizing it in himself. Salvation was an accomplished fact. History had come to its unique turning point. Therefore, the worship of the church became the fundamental expression of the content of both the Old and the New Covenants. The Old, which anticipates the New, was preserved in the liturgy of the Word. And the New, which fulfills the Old, was expressed in the liturgy of the Eucharist, the remembrance of Christ's death and resurrection that inaugurated the New. Consequently, both Word and sacrament celebrate Jesus Christ and his work of creation, incarnation, and re-creation.

This Christian metanarrative sweeps from creation to consummation with Christ at its center. It is through Christ that Christians interpret creation. For through the work of Jesus fallen creation has been redeemed and will be completely renewed and restored at the end of history. Therefore, the place of creation in worship affirms that the meaning of the world is more than what we see, feel, touch, taste, and smell. There is an interiority to the universe that provokes a worshipful position toward the Creator. (For this reason, God set aside one day to be a sign of his Lordship over all our time and our activity. Through it we recognize God's rightful claim to every moment of our lives.) Even the creation itself is set free to worship because the work of Jesus Christ is a victory over the powers of evil that rage in the creation and a promise that creation will be delivered from its "bondage to decay." Therefore, worship uses tangible signs and symbols, chiefly bread and wine, to testify to the meaning of Christ's work in the re-creation of the whole universe. Even the material world is able to signify the redemption and point to the future kingdom.

The content of worship is a rehearsal of the covenantal relationship God has established with Israel and the church. For example, at Mount Sinai God entered into a covenantal relationship with Israel, sealed with blood. They became "a people holy to the LORD . . . chosen . . . to be his people" (Deut. 7:6). The Lord became Israel's God, and Israel became God's special people. And in this relationship there emerged tangible signs of that union—the sanctuary, the priesthood, the offerings, and the appointed feasts and seasons. In this way Israel's worship looked back to the exodus event and forward to the promised land. In the New Testament there is another covenant, sealed with the blood of Christ, through which the church becomes Christ's peculiar possession, "a chosen people, a royal priesthood, a holy nation, a people belonging to God" (1 Peter 2:9). This new relationship is the body—the body of Christ, an extension of the incarnation, the continued presence of Christ on earth, a divine organism inhabited by the presence and power of the Holy Spirit. In the church, his body, there are tangible signs of the presence of Christ in worship—the assembled people, the Word, the sacraments, ministry, fellowship, discipleship, prayer, and love. All these expressions of worship look back to the Christ event and forward to the new heavens and the new earth.

In sum, the content and meaning of classical worship tells and acts out the story of God's saving work in history, culminating in the work of Christ to overthrow the powers of evil and to ultimately establish his kingdom over creation. This story is in our hymns and songs, in our prayers and testimonies, and, supremely, in the reading of Scripture, preaching, and the Eucharist.[2]

One word of caution is needed: This commitment to the Christian metanarrative will not be received well by postmoderns, who believe in the relativity of all narratives. Therefore, the idea that the Christian metanarrative is one of many equally valid metanarratives (pluralism) is not acceptable to evangelicals. Evangelicals take the universal character of the Christian metanarrative as an essential aspect of the framework of Christian faith. And the thoughtful recovery of this narrative is the first step evangelicals need to take to recover the theology of worship. This is the mystery of God at work in the world bringing healing and salvation, the mystery that will, as Catherine Pickstok indicated, give all reality as a mystery.[3]

Recovering the Order of Worship

The earliest description of New Testament worship is found in Acts 2:42. According to Luke, the early Christians "devoted themselves to the apostles' teaching and to the fellowship, to the breaking of bread and to prayer." There is general recognition of the twofold form of worship described in this verse: the gathering around the apostolic teaching and the breaking of bread. In brief, the primitive form of worship centered around Word and Table.[4]

One of the most immediate consequences of recapturing worship as a telling and acting out of the Christian vision is the impact it makes on the order of worship. The rule of thumb is that this order, rooted in the living, dying, and rising of Christ, which it re-presents, is *the vehicle through which the story of the work of Christ is proclaimed and enacted.*

Figure 2
A Comparison of Enlightenment
and Post-Enlightenment Communication

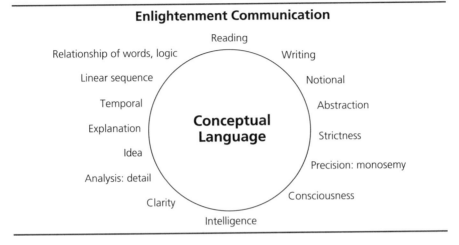

Enlightenment Communication

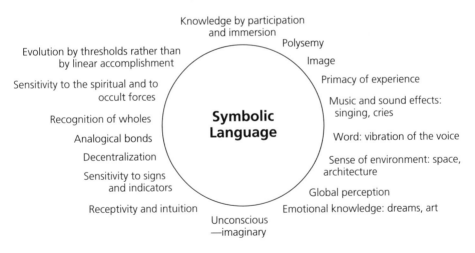

Post-Enlightenment Communication

The form of communications that dominated the Enlightenment and affected the worship of the church was that of conceptual language. The new form of communication of the post-Enlightenment world is that of symbolic language. Used with permission of Pierre Babin, *The New Era in Religious Communication* (Minneapolis: Fortress, 1991), 150–51.

The order of worship itself is active, not passive. Fortunately, for our study, we have manuscripts of actual liturgies from the third and fourth centuries that show us the theological structure of worship.[5]

In this pattern, we gather to tell and enact the story and to go forth to live by the Christian metanarrative. In this way worship is *the rehearsal of the Christ event through which one's experience with God is established, maintained, and repaired.*

This broad and general order of worship sets the pattern for Sunday worship, but does not do so in a rigid and formal way. One can choose in this pattern to be liturgical, or to be spontaneous and free, or to find a place somewhere on the spectrum between liturgical repetition and the creativity of doing worship differently from week to week.[6]

Throughout history this structure of worship has been seen as a prescription for order and not a mere description. Evangelicals who recover this order will find a form that will more perfectly communicate the mystery of the Christian metanarrative in the postmodern world.

RECOVERING SYMBOLIC COMMUNICATION

Communication specialists point out that we communicate in three ways. First, the language of everyday speech uses words to communicate; second, the language of science uses concepts to communicate ideas; and third, the language of religion uses symbols to communicate.[1] In worship we use everyday words, we speak the language of faith, and we communicate symbolically. We evangelicals are strong on concepts, but weak in symbolism.

Peter Roche de Coppens points out that "symbols are the 'language' and the vehicles . . . of the supernatural. They deal with the intuition, with imagination, and with emotion rather than with thinking, sensations, or the will." Symbols function "as 'a mine' which must be mined, a seed which must be planted and allowed to grow to reveal its flowers and fruits." In short, symbols are the "psychospiritual means by which we invoke a certain presence, induce a certain state of consciousness, and focus our awareness, by which we recreate, in ourselves, an image, facsimile, or presentation of that which is without or above us."[2]

The role of symbolism in a postmodern world is not to re-create the ceremonial symbolism of the medieval era, but to understand and apply the symbolism of atmosphere such as the sense of awe and reverence, to recover the beauty of space and the symbolic actions of worship, and to restore the sounds of music and the sights of the arts. For in these symbolic ways God's presence and truth are mediated to us. In these symbolic actions we take the known and lift it into the unknown so that it is returned to us as the mystery of the transcendent.[3] We will briefly look at this principle in seven examples: space, the order of worship, music, baptism, the Eucharist, the Christian year, and the arts.

Space

We are all familiar with Marshall McLuhan's adage that "the medium is the message." This theme is concretized in the use of worship space. Some worship spaces feel ordinary and are similar to an office, a theater, a school gymnasium, or a bank lobby. Other spaces such as cathedrals create a sense of "The Holy" and deliver the feeling of "otherness."[4]

In the 1980s evangelicals sought to neutralize space to make the seeker more comfortable. This worked in the 1980s but is not the way to go in the postmodern world. The inquirer needs to be immersed within a space that bespeaks the Christian faith. The very narrative of faith which we seek to know and to live is symbolically expressed in our space. We take the ordinary aspects of life—stone, wood, windows, tables, and chairs—and form them into voices of the Christian mystery. Space becomes the visual image of the connection between the known and unknown. God's presence on earth is symbolized by the body assembled in chairs or pews surrounded by the images of heaven. God's active presence in history is clearly symbolized by the image of the body assembled, by the central image of the table that speaks to his death and resurrection, the pulpit that symbolizes the proclamation of the event, and the baptismal pool or font that speaks of entrance into the church through baptism. In a postmodern world that has become increasingly interested in communication through space, it will be necessary to feature the relational seating of God's people around the symbols of water, the pulpit, and the Table. These are the primary visual images of God's work in the history of salvation.

The Order of Worship

Worship orders our relationship to God. We can see an analogy of worship as relational by comparing the fourfold pattern with the simple act of entertaining guests in our home. When guests arrive we greet, assemble in the foyer, move into the living room for the purpose of communicating with each other, gather around the table to eat and enjoy each other's company, and return to the foyer, where we bid our guests farewell. These four acts are never announced or singled out for attention. They are just done—with great formality, with informality, or somewhere in between. And we all know instinctively, without any need to comment, analyze, or dissect, that in these four acts relationships have been established, deepened, and transformed.

The analogy to the fourfold pattern of worship is obvious. These four acts symbolically represent our entrance into the presence of God, our listening and responding to the spoken Word of God, our fellowship with God at the Table, and our going forth to love and serve the Lord. These four concrete acts are lifted up into the mystery of a relationship with God and returned to us in such a way that the ordinary symbols of relationship become transformed and order and organize our divine relationship with God in worship.[5]

Music

In postmodern thought there is a new appreciation for the role of sound in communication. Music is an auditory stimulant that is capable of evoking an experience with the transcendent. In music we take ordinary sound and through its arrangement we are able to lift the hearer into the ineffable. This generally happens when the pattern of ordinary sound is interrupted by the sound of otherness. For example, I am writing this the day after a workshop in Columbus, Ohio, where I spoke on the principle of connecting known sounds with interrupted sounds that broke the beat of the known and created the experience of transcendence. Two musicians who knew what I was talking about volunteered to lead the group in an example of music that accomplished the experience of transcendence. We sang "Seek Ye First" and "Alleluia" at the same time. The sound and beat of "Seek Ye First" provided the ordinary while the sound of the "Alleluia" broke through the ordinary into the unknown and created an experience of transcendent otherness. This kind of music, which has been used very effectively in worship and in the communication of the other, is found in Taizé's music, which has spread around the world in renewal worship over the past several decades.[6]

Baptism

Postmodern evangelicals need to restore the rich symbolism of baptism. For the most part we evangelicals have regarded baptism as an important symbol. Yet, our emphasis has been on baptism as an act done by the convert. We have failed to understand the divine symbolism of baptism. A consequence of our overemphasis on the human side of baptism has resulted in the replacement of baptism by the conversion experience. For example, some time ago I addressed a group of evangelicals on the importance of understanding the divine side of baptism. One person became extremely upset and began to argue that baptism is totally unnecessary. In this person's church, at least one-third of the people had never been baptized and baptism was optional for all new Christians.

This attitude misses the point of the symbol. A symbol participates in the reality which it represents. Water is an ordinary element of creation that participates in the extraordinary. In creation God separated the ground from the waters; in our first birth we are formed in water; Noah and his family passed to safety on the waters; the Jews passed through the waters of the Red Sea to safety; Israel crossed the waters of the Jordan into the promised land. All these instances of water point to God's actions and creative activity in respect to water.

When we enter into the waters of baptism, we enter into a divine connection with the suffering of Jesus and with his resurrection. We are brought into a pattern of life that is an actual identification with Jesus. Baptism is therefore not only an identification with Christ but a calling to live the baptized life.[7] The calling which baptism symbolizes gives concrete form to our spirituality—a matter we will look at in the next chapter.

Eucharist

A Presbyterian minister friend of mine who is a professor at a major evangelical seminary said to me, "Bob, if we don't restore the Eucharist to its rightful place in our churches, we are going to lose many of our children to the liturgical churches." Many people *are* moving into evangelically alive liturgical churches and are doing so, at least in part, because of the weekly celebration of the Eucharist. In the early church, the central meaning of the Eucharist was to give thanks for the living, dying, and rising again of Jesus, looking forward to the coming again of Christ to establish his kingdom. Many evangelicals are being drawn back to the classical experience of Table worship, an experience both Calvin and Luther desired to recover.[8]

Some evangelicals are also reconsidering the memoralist view of the Lord's Supper in favor of a view that emphasizes the active saving and healing presence of Christ at the Table. The earliest description of Christ's presence at the Table, written by Justin Martyr in A.D. 150, is becoming increasingly acceptable.

For not as common bread and common drink do we receive these; but in like manner as Jesus Christ our Savior, having been made flesh by the

Word of God, was made both flesh and blood for our salvation, so likewise have we been taught that the food which is blessed by the prayer of His word, and from which our blood and flesh by transformation are nourished, is the flesh and blood of that Jesus who was made flesh.[9]

The emphasis of the early church, as seen in Justin, is that the saving action of God rooted in the incarnation and the atonement is made present to the worshiping community through the power of the prayer that sets the bread and wine apart as special agents of divine action. When the elements of bread and wine are taken in faith, the transforming and nourishing power of Christ for the salvation and the healing of the person is made available.

Those who have allowed this historical interpretation of Table worship to shape their experience of bread and wine have discovered the healing power of Christ through the Eucharist.[10] For them, worship has broken through the lifeless nature of what, for some, may be an empty form and has opened them to the joy and healing that come from the gracious and active presence of Christ in the sacrament.

Sometimes students or other persons struggling with a painful experience in their lives will come to me for counsel. I always say to them, "I'm not a counselor and I don't have the tools necessary to help you with this problem. But I can suggest one thing—flee to the Eucharist. Get to the Table of the Lord just as fast as you can, because it is there that God can and does touch his people in a healing way." In all the years that I have been giving this advice, not a single person has come back and told me it is not true. On the contrary, many have affirmed that God through the Eucharist reached into their pain and touched them with his healing presence.

The Christian Year

The secularization that worship has undergone is perhaps most obvious in the typical evangelical calendar. Generally, the evangelical calendars are full of special events revolving around Mother's Day, Father's Day, Children's Day, Memorial Day, Independence Day, and Labor Day. In some churches special attention is even given to Boy Scout and Girl Scout Day, as well as other national or even local days. This strange mixture of the patriotic, sentimental, and promotional shows how far removed we are from a Christian concept of time.

Some may object to the above analysis, pointing out that most Protestants do have a Christian year because Christmas and Easter are observed. While this is true, the celebration of these events too often lacks meaning because they are frequently entered into with haste, and sometimes even take commercial or promotional shape in the church.

The place from which we stand to develop a Christian view of time is not only Christmas or Easter but also the weekly Eucharist. Here we have, as Gregory Dix observed, "the enactment before God of the historical process of redemption, of the historical events of the crucifixion and resurrection of Jesus by which redemption has been achieved."[11]

From a Christian point of view, the life, death, and resurrection of Jesus Christ are at the center of time, for from Christ we look backward toward creation, the Fall, the Covenants, and God's working in history to bring redemption. But from the time of the incarnation of Christ we also look forward to the fulfillment of history in his second coming. For this reason time is understood, from the Christian point of view, in and through the redemptive presence of Jesus Christ symbolized in the bread and wine.

Oscar Cullmann has dealt with the biblical concept of time in his well-known book *Christ and Time.* He describes another way of rendering time meaningfully through the Christian concept of eschatology, for the Christian believes that history is moving toward a fulfillment, not an ending. In this sense, the Christian view of time is similar to the Hebraic understanding. The Old Testament believer looked toward the fulfillment of time in the coming of the Messiah. Jesus' coming did not render the events of the Old Testament meaningless, and especially here we may think of the Hebrew sacred year, but by fulfilling them he established their meaning. In the same way the Christian believes that the end of time will fulfill and complete the life, death, and resurrection of Jesus Christ.

For this reason the Christian year is based on the events in the life of Christ that shape the Christian's understanding of time.[12] By observing the church year, time is aligned with the living, dying, rising, and coming of Christ. The Christian, in his or her view of time, makes a dramatic break with a secular view of time and begins to consciously meditate on the aspect of Christ's life currently being celebrated by the church. Time is actually experienced as *Christus Victor* time, a time that lives in the expectation of the recapitulation (see figure 3).

The Arts

A professor once said to his class, "There is only one God-ordained communication, and that is the use of words." Some time later this professor drew a circle on the board and said, "This circle represents God." An astute student, seeing the contradiction, said, "But, professor, you told us that the only God-ordained form of communication is words, and here you are using a symbol." The professor immediately cleared his throat and said, "You're right. I did say that." Then he walked to the blackboard, erased the circle, and said, "I'm sorry, I'll never do that again."

While not all evangelicals are hostile to the symbolic communication through the arts, there does seem to be some question about the value of the arts. The fear of the arts goes all the way back to the Reformation. Abraham Kuyper in his *Lectures on Calvinism* argues that the "alliance" of religion and art represents a *lower* stage of religious development. Because verbal communication is the highest form, "Calvinism has . . . abandoned the symbolic form of worship, and refused, at the demand of art, to embody its religious spirit in monuments of splendor."[13]

Thankfully, evangelicals are rediscovering the arts in worship and using them effectively.[14] The arts, whether drama, storytelling, liturgical dance, banners, environmental hangings, or artistically designed bulletins, are always servants of the text. That is, an art form speaks to us and acts upon us as it serves the text of worship. For example, a dance should never be a performance; it accompanies an act like a procession, a reading of scripture, or a song. In this way a dance speaks the Word and communicates God's presence. The new emphasis on the arts by evangelicals is a positive move toward the communication skills that will impact postmoderns.

Conclusion

In the introduction to this section I referred to a group of evangelical theologians and their interest in worship. There is wide interest among evangelicals in worship today. However, the greater part of evangelical clergy, worship leaders, and congregations are fascinated with a market-driven pop culture worship.

For this reason there is a great need among us to restore a biblical and historical theology of worship which is an epiphany of God's saving work in history. We also need to recover the fourfold pattern of worship and recognize the power of symbolic language in communication.

Worship is first upward and then outward. If we concentrate on the outward, it will not go upward. But if we focus on the upward, offering our worship in content, structure, and style to God, the theology will inform our heart, the order will deepen our relationship, and the symbolic will function as the praise of the whole person. This kind of worship will draw the seeker and nourish the faithful in a postmodern world.

Table H: Worship Throughout History

Ancient	Medieval	Reformation	Modern	Postmodern
God-oriented	Worship became clericalized	Worship was returned to the people through a translation into the language of the people	Conflict: should worship be directed toward the education of the believer's mind or should it be directed toward the sinner?	Return to God-centered worship
Mystery	Worship was turned into the Mass, an unbloody sacrifice of Jesus	Reformation developed Word-oriented worship		Emphasis on the mystery of God at work in the history of salvation
Historical recitation	Ritual			Restoration of classical understanding of content
Eschatological anticipation	Latin	Rejection of symbolism	Rejection of symbolism	Restoration of symbolism
Word and Eucharist Symbolic Participatory Worship is upward				

The shift into mystery and symbol is fertile ground for the adaptation of classical worship to postmodern times.

Figure 3

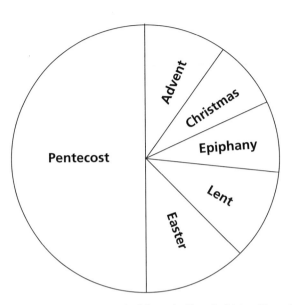

From Advent to Pentecost the Christian calendar follows the life and ministry of Jesus. The season after Pentecost follows the growth and development of the early church. The feasts and fasts of the Christian year symbolically mark the mystery of God's saving events. Those who worship with intention will find their lives defined and shaped by the content of God's saving deeds.

A CLASSICAL/ POSTMODERN SPIRITUALITY

Christians belong to another world,
They are the sons of the heavenly Adam,
A new people, children of the heavenly
Spirit, radiant brothers of Christ, like
Unto their Father: the spiritual and
radiant Adam.

Marcarius, A.D. 350

I frequently have students ask questions about subjects that range from career guidance to specific matters of theology and, of course, spirituality.

After four decades of teaching, I can say without reservation that the most difficult matter for people to grasp is spirituality. I can speak for myself and for my students as well as for other people to whom I've spoken. Most Christians deeply desire to achieve an authentic spirituality, yet it remains elusive.

For example, I recall an incident from my days in seminary. A pastor from the West Coast was scheduled to speak in chapel on the subject of reality in the spiritual life. When the topic was first announced, my heart leaped within me as I hoped to get some solid direction. I longed

to have a spirituality that was genuine. I no longer remember what he said, but I do know that it did not satisfy my quest.

For most of us brought up in the evangelical branch of Christianity, spirituality has been defined almost exclusively in terms of a handy list of do's and don'ts. On the negative side, spirituality means abstinence from worldly habits such as drinking, smoking, dancing, and card playing; on the positive side, spirituality is defined in terms of church attendance, prayer, regular Bible reading, and witnessing. This formula is usually set forth as a sure way to grow spiritually. But for me it led to a spiritual legalism lacking authenticity and life.

When I became a student of church history, I began to look at the struggles of various leaders of the church and at the insights on spirituality from different movements in the church. While spirituality will always remain an open-ended subject for me, I do feel that the classical tradition has provided me with a grasp of what it means to be spiritual and that its insights are particularly relevant to the postmodern era.

The cultural context of the postmodern society is actually a fertile ground for the recovery of classical spirituality. We have shifted from the secular humanism of the 1970s to New Age spirituality that has permeated every area of life.

New Age spirituality is based on the pagan concept of an impersonal God whose being is extended into creation. Consequently, New Age spirituality is an integration with creation and an awareness of a spiritual connection to all things in the created order. This connection breaks down the dualisms between material and spiritual, divine and human, goodness and evil. Through the awareness that the oneness of all things is in the One, a person can transcend all the dualities of human existence and enter into a spiritual relationship with the One. The view has expressed itself in meditation, various views of prayer, and earth issues of ecology. Interestingly, New Age spirituality is quite relativistic in ethical matters, particularly regarding the question of moral standards.[1]

While evangelicals soundly reject the presuppositions of the New Age movement, the shift from atheistic secularism to a mystical but amorphous spiritual view of the universe sets a good stage for the adaptation of classical spirituality.

We evangelicals can look for points of contact with people who are seeking to be spiritual. For example, I recently conversed with a woman who was converted from paganism to a New Age philosophy. This conversion led her to the church, and it was in the church where she was nurtured into a Christian spirituality. Her experience may become increasingly common in a postmodern world. We can come alongside of people, affirm their spiritual longing, and bring them into the church, where they can be nurtured into the Christian faith.

14

SPIRITUALITY WITHIN
THE PARADIGMS OF HISTORY

The spirituality of the ancient church is related to the conflict between God and the powers of evil. Ancient Christians were intensely aware of demonic power and influence. For them, spirituality was located in Christ, the God-man, who by his death and resurrection defeated the powers of evil and established his kingdom. New Christians were baptized into the death of Christ, which meant death to all sin and evil in one's life and being united with Christ in his resurrection. They were to put on a new life patterned after the life of Christ, empowered to live by the fruits of the Holy Spirit. Therefore, classical spirituality means living in the pattern of death and resurrection.[1]

In the latter centuries of the ancient church and throughout the medieval era a number of approaches to spirituality were birthed. After the canonization of Scripture, a spiritual form of reading the Word, the *lectio divina*, emerged.[2] The reader personally savored every word of the text and meditated upon it in a desire to discover a personal meaning. In addition, various monastic groups were founded in the medieval era illustrating, perhaps, the institutional nature of spirituality.[3] Because monastics were concerned about the worldliness of the established church, they established communities where the imitation of Christ was made possible through solitude, prayer, chastity, poverty, and obedience. For the monastics, spirituality was a full-time vocation. On the other hand, the spirituality of the masses of lay people was oriented around acts of devotion, such as prayers to the saints, pilgrimages to holy places, involvement in the festivities for holy days, and devotion to the Eucharistic Host. Lay spirituality was primarily penitential.[4]

The Reformers reacted to the monastic movement and the superstitions of lay spirituality and turned toward a spirituality of understanding objective truth. It was enough to grasp the notion of justification by faith. But the Reformers did not neglect the inner experience of spirituality. They spoke of the heart finding great joy and gladness in God's truth. Calvinists, for example, emphasized the objective nature of truth and developed a spirituality based on an affirmation of a biblical framework of thought and strict adherence to its teaching. Because the Reformed framework demonstrated how God was active in history, in national affairs, and in the life of the family, spirituality was returned to the people. Every person's vocation was a calling from God, a calling that, when followed, was a "lived out" spirituality.[5] The Anabaptists stressed the spirituality of discipleship[6] within the community, and the Anglicans emphasized the spirituality of the liturgy,[7] with its focus on Scripture, creed, Eucharist, and episcopacy.

In the seventeenth century modern evangelical spirituality made a decisive shift toward the subjective. The rise of pietism, revivalism, fundamentalism, and evangelical Christianity moved from the objective spirituality of the Reformers to the inner experience of being born again. (Exception to this shift into subjectivism is found in those groups today who distinguish themselves as Reformed, i.e., the Presbyterian Church of America.) The new birth, it was taught, results in a new life characterized by the love of Scripture, obedience to the Great Commission, and a walk with God shaped by a dying to the world.[8] The more liberal side of Christianity saw spirituality expressed in the care of the poor and needy and in the support of justice.[9] However, in the past several decades, with the demise of liberal Christianity, evangelicals have taken on the concern for justice and the needy as part of their spirituality.[10] There is also a strong current among evangelicals to recover the spirituality of the inner disciplines that flowered during the medieval era.[11]

Postmodern spirituality will be characterized by an affirmation of all the spiritualities throughout history. Because of the shift toward subjectivity, however, there will be increasing attention to the inner spiritual disciplines. There will also be a recovery of the image of baptism into a death to all that is sin and death and a resurrection into all that is life-giving in the spirit. Personal spirituality will be worked out not only in the inner chamber of the heart, but in the common ethic of the Christian community—an ethic that will increasingly be in conflict with the loss of ethics in society (see table I).

Problems Inherited from the Enlightenment

The two most significant problems of evangelical spirituality of the modern era are found in what we negate and what we affirm. Instead of standing in the historical stream of negation and affirmation, we tend to distort the classical tradition.

The Spiritual Failure of Our Negations

First, we fail spiritually when we ignore the resources the Holy Spirit has given us throughout the history of the church.[12] For fifteen centuries prior to the Reformation a vast reservoir of spirituality had developed within the church: hours of prayer, exercises of devotion, personal and corporate discipline, communal values, and harmony with nature had been introduced, to say nothing of schools of spirituality such as the monastic movements, the spiritual writings of the early church fathers such as Ignatius (A.D. 110), Irenaeus (A.D. 180), Tertullian (A.D. 200), Athanasius (A.D. 325), the Cappadocian Fathers (A.D. 320), and the desert spirituality like that of Evagrius of Pontus (A.D. 399) and John of St. Catherine (A.D. 600). Unfortunately, when the Reformers attempted to rid the church of its bad devotional habits, such as the excessive emphasis on Mary, a preoccupation with the saints, the worship of relics, and devotion to the Host, they failed to retain other positive approaches to spirituality that had emerged in the early church.[13]

Second, we fail spiritually when we act as though Christ's work does not relate to history and to culture.[14] The gradual secularization of culture, along with the retreat of Christianity from culture, has resulted in a spirituality of the closet. God is "up there" and "out there." God's relationship to the world is seen almost exclusively in terms of the "spiritual" as over against the "secular." God is to be found in church, in the Bible, or in prayer, but not in the field, in the lab, in the computer industry, or on Wall Street. Consequently, spirituality is gradually reduced to something that runs alongside of life and is no longer the central dynamic force of life itself. For some, the spiritual life has lost its connection to daily activities, to the values by which decisions are made in business and politics, and has become instead the "hour with God," a matter of the closet, shut away from life.

A third failing is that we have acted as though Christ did not save the mind.[15] In the past several hundred years Christianity has gradually retreated from the intellect into the heart. In the modern world, science and reason, philosophy and psychology, sociology and anthropology, based on a humanistic and not on a theistic worldview, have taken over the minds of even Christians. This has resulted in a cadre of Christians who live "with two caps." The one cap is worn in church or in the doing of "religious" things; the other is worn when thinking or living in the world. Spirituality no longer connected to thinking has become, for some, an indefinable and contentless matter of the heart, merely experiential and emotional, and all too often just a romantic feeling.

The Spiritual Failure of Our Affirmations

The second set of problems in contemporary evangelical spirituality is expressed in what is often unthinkingly affirmed. For example, there is the insistence on conformity to subcultural standards. Spirituality, instead of being free to affirm what the Bible teaches and what the church has always affirmed, is reduced to legalism. Spirituality is measured by a separation from definable "worldly" practices. While these rules may produce a well-trained "spiritual army," they often fail to bring a person into a deeper spiritual life.[16]

Next, a focus on external rules fails to help a person grow into a more holistic relationship with all of life. If anything, legalistic spirituality tends to make a person fearful of those who are not part of the subculture; it produces negative attitudes toward the world and a lack of confidence in what one believes. Spiritual responsibility is reduced to readily defined limits, both in terms of what a person may do and in terms of with whom a person may associate. And, tragically, it divides the body of Christ by claiming a privileged position for itself and denying that those in other Christian traditions are true Christians. Yet an individualistic, personalistic spirituality cannot come to grips with the expanded spiritual responsibilities of the Christian to culture and to thought.

Then, there is a spirituality that emphasizes an *overfamiliarity* with God. The recent emphasis on sensitivity, community, and getting to know one another, which certainly has its good qualities if developed within the total framework of the nature of the church and of the Christian's relationship to God, often leads to "warm fuzzies." Suddenly, God is no longer "the Holy One of Israel"; God is no longer the God of judgment, whose holiness inspires fear and awe, but just our buddy, our pal, our friend. When you need "somebody to love you"—God is there. When you are lonely and down—God is there.

These notions do contain some truth. God is there. But when God is oversentimentalized in contemporary music, poetry, and books, the view of God borders on blasphemy. It becomes idolatry because it substitutes part of the truth about God for the whole truth. It panders to me-ism—

God's chief value is in making me feel good. In this view, there is neither majesty nor dignity left in our relationship to God. God is no longer the King before whom we bow. The end of this kind of familiarity is not reverence, but a loss of the awe and respect due God.[17]

In another variation of this view, beautiful buildings, large crowds, three-hundred-dollar suits, Cadillacs, and a beautiful home in the suburbs measure spirituality. "God does not want you to be poor or weak or sad; God wants you to be rich, strong, and happy." The danger is that of measuring spirituality in terms of wealth, power, beauty, popularity, and acceptance. When Christianity is made attractive, the result may be an exchange of the true quality of spirituality as a life of humble service that affirms true Christian values for Western values dressed up to look Christian.

In summary, the root of the problem of our confusion over spirituality may be found in the failure to understand the implications of the incarnation. When the humanity of Christ is overemphasized, spirituality concentrates almost exclusively on personal experience. When Christ's divinity is overemphasized, spirituality concentrates on the otherworldly. The hope for the future lies in the recovery of an incarnational spirituality that affirms both our experience of the other world and our experience of this world.[18]

CLASSICAL SPIRITUALITY

When we reflect on spirituality in Scripture and history, two strands or broad emphases of spirituality emerge. One like the divine side of Christ emphasizes detachment from the world and the pursuit of the inner life; the other like the human side of Christ stresses involvement in the world. These are not contradictory, however, for no writer stresses one to the exclusion of the other. Nevertheless, the emphasis as a distinctive is clearly there. Two examples will suffice: Paul and Matthew.

The Spirituality of Paul

Paul's central emphasis is on the death and resurrection of Christ.[1] In the Christ event, something new happened. Paul describes this "new" reality in words that convey a contrast between the old and the new. He uses opposites such as flesh and spirit; law and grace; the present age and the age to come; Adam and Christ. We were "in Adam," and we participated in the old "man," in the old humanity, in the old order. But now, because of faith in Christ, we are "in Christ"; we participate in a new humanity, in a new order. The Christian has been "clothed with Christ," "walks in the Spirit," has Christ living "in" him or her, lives in the "body" of Christ, and is "adopted" into the family of God, to use only a few of the famous Pauline metaphors. Consequently, this new person "puts off the old" and "puts on the new."

These motifs lie at the heart of Pauline spirituality. They indicate the transfer of loyalty from one master to the other—complete and full identity that can be described in terms of death to the one and life and resurrection to the other. "You died, and your life is now hidden with Christ in God. . . . Put to death, therefore, whatever belongs to your earthly nature . . . put on the new self" (Col. 3:3, 5, 10).

In Paul's writings there is a strong emphasis on the "inner life." This is not to say that Paul rejects the body, humanity, or creation. But Paul definitely leans toward spirituality as the denial of self, as a mystical union with Christ, as an ascetic approach to life. Paul's emphasis is on the rejection of the powers of evil that rage in the creation. "For our struggle is not against flesh and blood," he reminds us, but against "authorities, against the powers" (Eph. 6:12).

Just as Christ is victor over the powers, so this victory extends to us. Spirituality is a union with Christ and his victory over the powers of evil. Spirituality is to engage in warfare with the powers and continually choose the defeat of the powers through Christ who dwells within.[2]

The Spirituality of Matthew

Matthew's spirituality is rooted in the Sermon on the Mount.[3] Here is the "new" law, the one that fulfills and completes the old. It calls, as did the Old Testament Law, for poverty of spirit, for mercy, for a desire for justice that practices the holiness of God. It is this spirit, this action, and this approach to life that will issue forth in the knowledge of God and peace.

The active aspect of spirituality is clearly indicated in the Sermon on the Mount, which takes up the commandments one after the other and stresses the need to go beyond a mere external act to the affirmation of a positive love—one that forgives and gives. The three essential practices of Jewish piety—almsgiving, prayer, and fasting—are urged on the believer. They are to be acts that come from the heart, not mere external acts done for show. Next, trust in the providential care of God emphasizes that trust in God, which begins in the inner self, must make itself real and visible in every aspect of life. Unless it does, it is faith built on sand, not on the rock. Consequently, we must choose one of two ways. The one is easy, the other is hard. If we commit ourselves to the ascent, then everything must be left behind.

The unmistakable emphasis of the Sermon on the Mount is an active spirituality—a spirituality that reflects the Jewish past, especially the emphasis of the prophets on creative love, justice, and mercy. Matthew's spirituality is one that works in the world, causing the new creation to appear everywhere as a sign of the redemption of all things.[4]

127

Inner and Outer Spirituality in the Early Church

We gain insight into the inner and outer approaches to spirituality in the early church in respect to preparation for baptism. On the inner side the person is to fast and "renounce the devil and all his work" before entering the waters. The stress on the outer is clearly seen in the testing of the new convert by the criterion of good works: "Have they lived good lives when they were catechumens? Have they honored the widows? Have they visited the sick? Have they done every kind of good work?"[5] For the most part, the early church maintained a good balance between a passive and an active spirituality.

An example of inner spirituality can be drawn from the Alexandrian monastics, beginning in the third century. These monastics carried on an important tradition within the religious community that goes back to Judaism. Theirs was a *desert* spirituality. It was a movement into the most desolate and forsaken part of God's creation, where, in solitude, they entered into an intense battle with God's enemy, Satan. It was in the desert that Moses, Jeremiah, John the Baptist, and Jesus wrestled with temptation and were instructed by God. In a sense it is in the desert where one goes, not to flee the world, but to go into its very heart, where, in its center, a victory over evil may be gained.

"The desert is," as John Meyendorff suggested in *St. Gregory Palamas and Orthodox Spirituality,* "the archetypal symbol of the world that is hostile to God, subject to Satan, the dead world to which the Messiah brought new life. And as his first coming was proclaimed by John the Baptist in the desert, so the Christian monks felt that their flight to the desert was an assault on the power of the Evil one, Heralding the second coming."[6]

Of course, there were excesses by the desert monks. In spending so much time alone, they failed to participate directly in the "building of the body of Christ" in the world. They paid little attention to the mission of the church. They were not active in evangelism, teaching, or reshaping the foundations of culture. Instead, they were involved in prayer—continual and fervent prayer on behalf of the church. Yet even in their self-imposed solitude, the church came to them for counsel and inspiration.

An example of outer spirituality can be seen in the legitimation of the Christian faith by Constantine. Christians began to assume roles of public responsibility that they had previously shunned because of the emperor worship it required. Now their attention was drawn toward an effort to master the world, to bring into focus a spirituality that emphasized involvement in human institutions. Augustine's *City of God* posited two cities, the city of God and the city of man, existing side by side. The struggle between these two cities is interpreted in view of the struggle between good and evil. The Augustinian vision was to view the task of the church in the world as a call to convert the world, to establish the city of God on earth. Spirituality, therefore, extended to the activities of the believers in church, society, and culture. Every aspect of life belongs to God the Creator, and is God's by right of redemption. Therefore, the fourth-century church felt called to redeem the structures of life, to Christianize the social order, to produce a culture that bears the stamp of its Creator.

But this approach to spirituality carried dangers. The temptation was to synthesize with culture, to accommodate to worldly materialistic goals, to lose sight of other-worldly spiritual values, to fail to negate or confront the secularization of the church. As a result the late medieval church became a bureaucracy, burdened with the management of land, susceptible to corruption, hungry for power and wealth. It lost a sense of its spiritual mission and stood in drastic need of reform and renewal.

Protest movements grew up within the church to bear witness against a worldly and secular church. The monastic movements, particularly those inspired by the Rule of Benedict, emphasized prayer and work. Here was a synthesis of inner and outer spirituality. They observed the hours of prayer, contemplation, meditation, and Scripture study, yet they were involved in the fields, in education, in preaching, and in works of charity. In this way monasticism sought for a balance between other-worldly and this-worldly spirituality and became a key factor not only in the reform of the church but also in the transmitting of education, culture, and works of charity.[7]

Mysticism emerged as another protest movement against a worldly church. It stood in the tradition of negation, emphasizing the cultivation of an inner relationship with God. It called for an abandonment of self and a purging of sin and selfishness as a means of probing through "the Divine Dark" to enter into an ecstatic union with the transcendent deity where a feeling and knowing of God can take place. Mystical experience cannot be confined to the early church, or to several writers, or to a single movement.[8]

Inner and Outer Spirituality Throughout Church History

Interestingly, in the history of the church the two differing emphases of Paul and Matthew have emerged in the *via negativa* (way of negative) and *via positiva* (way of affirmation).[9]

The *via negativa* has always affirmed the knowledge of God through some form of direct experience. Historically, the way of negation has received more attention than the way of affirmation, partly because it uses biblical language, especially Paul's, to describe the experience. The way of negation is a way of knowing God that has always been impressed with God's transcendence, "otherness," and "hiddenness." For this reason it always emphasizes the need for an experience that is supernatural, an experience that transcends the mundane, the business as usual, the humdrum.

On the other hand, the *via positiva* has always affirmed the knowledge and experience of God through indirect means. Historically, the way of affirmation has been less popular than the way of negation, partly because it demands greater attention to the spiritual significance of the mundane, the earthly, the usual, and partly because it requires action within the structures of life, which, in many cases, is more difficult and more demanding than the more passive approach of negation.

The way of affirmation has always been impressed with the doctrine of creation and subsequent emphasis on the immanence of God in the existing order of creation as well as in the ongoing creative activity of God in history. For this reason, it has always emphasized the "form" of things, the "imagery" of God in creation. The way of affirmation is the way of the artist, the poet, the social, moral, and political activist. It affirms humanity, the structures of life, history, and beauty. It calls for an affirmation of God within life and looks for the restoration of all things at the end of history.

The church, however, has always recognized the need for both affirmation and negation in the spiritual life. In brief, a study of early church spirituality seems to suggest that the spiritual norm is the balance between the divine and the human, the inner and the outer, the negative and the affirmative, the mystical and the practical, the monastic and the vocational.[10] Yet the attainment of this balance is a struggle. And frequently one group is a corrective for the other, a balance to an extreme. The early church helps us to see the balance, but it also leads us to recognize that this balance is difficult to achieve. Perhaps this accounts to some degree for the confusion that still exists regarding spirituality. So we continue to ask what kind of direction the early church may give us in our desire to have an authentic spirituality.

16

CHRISTIAN SPIRITUALITY
IN A POSTMODERN WORLD

The underlying classical assumption regarding Christian spirituality in the postmodern world is that, like the incarnation, an authentic spirituality brings together the divine and the human, negation and affirmation, the disciplines of the inner and outer life.

The current trend in evangelical spirituality is the recovery of the classic inner and outer disciplines. Richard Foster in *Celebration of Discipline* writes of the inner disciplines of mediation, prayer, fasting, and study and the outer disciplines of simplicity, solitude, submission, and service. He concludes with the corporate disciplines of confession, worship, guidance, and celebration. All of these disciplines are brought together in the closing words of his book:

> We have come to the end of this study but only to the beginning of our journey. We have seen how *meditation* heightens our spiritual sensitivity, which in turn leads us into prayer. Very soon we discover that prayer involves fasting as an accompanying means. Informed by these three Disciplines we can effectively move into study which gives us discernment about ourselves and the world in which we live. Through simplicity we live with others in integrity. Solitude allows us to be genuinely present to people when we are with them. Through submission we live with others without manipulation, and through service we are a blessing to them. Confession frees us from ourselves and releases us to worship. Worship opens the door to guidance. All the Disciplines freely exercised bring forth the doxology of celebration.[1]

Because much has been written on these disciplines I will not attempt to review them. Instead I will speak to the sources of spirituality that can communicate to postmoderns.

Christocentric Spirituality

Many people seem to think that spirituality is something that inheres within them as a result of what they do to be spiritual—that becoming spiritual is a matter of works. However, *Christ* is our spirituality. God in Christ has become humanity and has lifted humanity into a relationship with the divine. Spirituality is not a matter of works, but freedom to be in Christ.[2] Evangelical spirituality in a postmodern world needs to begin with the proclamation that *Jesus is our spirituality.* It is his life, death, and resurrection that make us acceptable to God. We cannot love God with our whole heart, soul, and mind, but Jesus can and has. We cannot love our neighbor as ourselves, but Jesus can and has. It is Jesus Christ, therefore, who presents us to the Father, and it is because of him and through him and in him that we are spiritual. Spirituality begins with simple yet profound trust in Jesus.

Athanasius, the great fourth-century theologian, captured the essence of an incarnational spirituality in his famous saying that "God became man in order that man may become God."[3] (By this he did not mean that we could become divine essence; rather, through the grace of God we can "participate in the divine nature" [2 Peter 1:4] and become heirs with Christ, sharing in the glory that is God's own glory.) We become incorporated in Christ through our conversion and identification with his death and resurrection in baptism. The pattern of spirituality is death and resurrection. We are to continually die to the old person and habitually be related to the new person. (See Romans 6; Galatians 5; Colossians 3.)

Ecclesial Spirituality

Spirituality is also related to the church because the church is the continuation of the incarnation, the place where the "other" is made "near." Because Christ is inextricably linked with the church, which is his body, the church is, as Stanley Hauerwas calls it, "a community of character."[4]

This community of character is the context in which our spirituality is formed. This is why the famous statement of Cyprian, "You cannot have God as your Father without the church as your mother,"[5] has been affirmed throughout history. Our life "in" Christ is a process that takes place within his body in transactional relationship with each other.

What takes place in the community is the handing down of the tradition through a kind of cultural transmission. Communication theory makes a distinction between discursive and cultural transmission. Discursive communication arose after the invention of the Gutenberg printing press. It is related to print, to logic, to broadcast and media. Cultural communication is the communication of oral communities. It happened in Scripture, it happens in tribes that are illiterate, and it happens in our culture today through the values that permeate our social institutions.

The church needs to recognize the role of cultural transmission. The society of the church views life differently, plays by the rules of Jesus, and signifies the future by making it present. In this way the church transmits its values. It hands down spirituality through interaction with authentic lives marked by integrity, honesty, faithfulness, and servanthood. Spirituality is not only taught, it is also caught.

Liturgical Spirituality: Baptism, Word, Eucharist

Because the liturgy continually enacts the story of Israel and Jesus, it forms and shapes the community by its content. While this is true of the entire liturgy in its singing, praying, and confessing, we will look in particular at the spirituality engendered by baptism, the Word, and the Eucharist.[6]

First, because Jesus is our spirituality the supreme image of the spiritual life is baptism into his death and resurrection. This is the pattern of spirituality: death to all that is sin and resurrection to all that is life-giving.[7]

Postmodernism has turned its back on the overly optimistic view of the human person that has dominated modernity. Rejecting the notion of the evolutionary progress of humanity toward a utopian outcome, postmoderns affirm a more realistic understanding of the human propensity toward evil. This new sensitivity to the conflict between the power of evil and the power of the good is fertile soil for the Christian proclamation of the Fall and the influence of sin in personal choices and in the various structures of society.

Baptism speaks to this human predicament. It says that there is only one person who is the solution to the problem. His name is Jesus. He was condemned for us all. By his death he has destroyed the consequence of sin (death), and by his resurrection he has begun a new humanity. We are called to a new life in the Spirit in this community, the church, his body in the world.

Second, Word spirituality derives from the way we handle Scripture in public worship and in our private lives.[8] The two sides of incarnational spirituality will show up in the contrast between the mystical and the reasonable interpretation of Scripture. Scripture is beyond full comprehension and therefore mystical, but also within the realm of understanding and therefore reasonable. In the history of Christian spiritual experience one or the other of these elements has often been denied. This error may be seen today. The current experience-oriented approach applies a mystical method to the interpreting of Scripture. The "what does it say to you" approach is often elevated over the interpretation that arises from the consensus of the church.

Often the interpretation of well-meant personal insights is regarded as authoritative simply because "it makes me feel good" or "it gives me a lift." This scriptural interpretation needs the corrective of the church's communal mind. The rejection of the mind, whether it be by the lay person in a home study circle or a preacher in the pulpit, is a denial of the human in the incarnation.

But the rejection of the mystical by those who overemphasize the mind is equally problematic.

Once Christian truth is grasped, intellectual apprehension becomes personal only as we act on it and live by it. Furthermore, intellectuals need to be characterized by a humility that recognizes that what is known is not fully known. Paul knew the limitations of reason, the frailty of the human, and could speak of seeing "through a glass darkly." We hold these truths in earthen vessels, and the failure to remember our intellectual limitations is a denial of what it means to be human, as well as a failure to recognize the mysterious nature of even that which is known. The postmodern world, with its emphasis on mystery and ambiguity, readily recognizes that our knowledge is not exhaustive. Certainty in spirituality is less important than the mystery of our union with Christ expressed in the worship of the church.

Third, Eucharistic spirituality is related to healing and nourishment. God does for us in the Eucharist what God did for us in the Christ event. The remembrance is not a mere intellectual recall, as in Enlightenment theology, but an *anamnesis* in which the divine action of God brings to us the forgiveness of our sins and the healing of our broken lives. There is a mysterious and nonunderstandable presence of Christ through the human materiality of bread and wine. Just as the promise of God is in the Word, so the promise of God is communicated to us through bread and wine. We are to receive the promise and ingest Jesus in our lives so that we may be continually shaped by the image of God for us in the Eucharistic bread and wine.[9]

Private Inner Spirituality: Spiritual Reading, Meditation, Discipleship

The private inner spirituality of the Christian in a postmodern world will be driven by a return to the reading of the spiritual classics, to personal quiet meditation, and to the spirituality of discipleship.[10]

First, Christians in a postmodern world are characterized by a rediscovery of the great treasury of spiritual resources in the history of the church. The primary source of spiritual reading is the Bible. But we now recognize that in our love of Scripture we dare not avoid the mystics and the activists. Exposure to the great devotional literature of the church is essential. More and more people are turning to the great work of the mystics. Richard Foster has called us to recover Augustine's *Confessions*, Bernard of Clairvaux's *The Steps of Humility*, the anonymous *Theologia Germanica*, and *The Cloud of Unknowing*, as well as *The Imitation of Christ* by Thomas à Kempis, the writings of Meister Eckhart and John Tauler, the works of the Spanish mystics such as Teresa of Avila and John of the Cross, the writings of Protestant mystics like George Fox and William Law, the Russian spiritual literature of Saint Theodosius, Saint Sergius, and *The Way of a Pilgrim*, and the contemporary writings of Thomas Merton. All these writings and more belong to each of us. To immerse ourselves in these great works is to allow our vision to be expanded by a great treasury of spirituality.[11]

Attention is also being paid to the less abundant but equally important social writings of the church: Augustine's *The City of God*, Thomas Aquinas's writings on church and society contained in his *Summa*, the *Social Gospel* by Rauschenbusch as well as more recent literature such as *The Politics of Jesus* by John Yoder and the work of Stanley Hauerwas, especially his books on the church in the world.[12]

The value of all these books as well as many not mentioned are indispensable to spirituality. Those who neglect these works do so to their harm, and those who read them do so for their inspiration and spiritual growth.

Second, a new interest has emerged in cultivating the art of meditation.[13] Meditation is not a contentless wandering of the mind, but a fixed attention on the object of faith, Jesus Christ. Meditation increases our awareness of Christ and his work for us. In turn, this awareness creates an identification with Christ, a love for him, and a desire to serve him. For example, the early church adopted the practice of Judaism: prayer three times a day at the third, sixth, and ninth hours. The prototype was Daniel. Of him we read, "three times a day he got down on his knees and prayed" (Dan. 6:10).

Hippolytus in *The Apostolic Tradition* provides a detailed picture of personal meditative prayer in the early church. It was the custom of Christians throughout the day to meditate on the successive phases of Christ's Passion. At the third hour, Christians meditated on the suffering of Christ, "For at that hour Christ was nailed to the tree."[14] Hippolytus compared Christ to the shewbread of the Old Covenant, which was to be offered at the third hour, and to the lamb that was slain. Christ, by contrast, is the living bread and the good shepherd who gave his life for the sheep. At noon, or the sixth hour, the Christian is to meditate on the last moments of Christ's life. *The Apostolic Tradition* had this to say:

> Pray likewise at the time of the sixth hour. For when Christ was nailed to the wood of the cross, the day was divided, darkness fell. And so at that hour let them pray a powerful prayer, imitating the voice of him who prayed and made all creation dark for the unbelieving Jews.[15]

The ninth hour is the moment of Christ's death. At this time the Christian is to "pray also a great prayer and a great blessing," for our Lord's death marks the beginning of the resurrection:

> For at that hour, Christ pierced in his side and poured out water and blood; giving light to the rest of time of the day he brought it to evening. Then, in the beginning to sleep and making the beginning of another day, he fulfilled the type of the resurrection.[16]

That a mere formal repetition of daily prayer may have little meaning is not disputed. On the other hand, a regular habit of prayer throughout the day (even if circumstances only permit silent prayer) is a means for continual spiritual nourishment. Alexander Schmemann, commenting on the Christian approach to time, which sees every hour of the day in respect to Jesus' death and resurrection, had this to say:

> And thus through that one day all days, all time were transformed into times of *remembrance* and expectation . . . all days, all hours were now referred to this *end* of all "natural" life, to the *beginning* of the new life.[17]

A number of people in the postmodern church are seeking to bring their consciousness of time up into the event of Christ, which gives time meaning. While it may be a minority of people who follow the instruction of Hippolytus for daily prayer, many more now seek to bring their yearly sense of time under the Lordship of Christ by adopting a prayer life relative to the church year.

Finally, there is a rediscovery of spiritual directors.[18] The office of a spiritual director emerged within monasticism in the early church among the monks who needed the direction of a wise and mature person. The principle was already evident in the personal relationship that existed between Paul and Timothy in New Testament times. Theologically, the idea was grounded in the New Testament notion that the church is the body of Christ, that Christians are "members" of each other, and that in this context growth occurs.

The office of spiritual director is not an actual church office but a function in the body. A mature Christian assumes responsibility toward one or more believers and guides them through regular counsel into a disciplined growth in Christ. The ultimate task of a spiritual director is to help younger Christians find the will of God. In the process, the director may help the person develop disciplined habits of prayer and spiritual reading, may listen to the confession of sins, and may encourage and counsel the growing Christian in many areas of life.[19]

Outer Spirituality

Social and ethical spirituality are inseparable from the fundamental conflict between good and evil. There are two powers at work in the world: the power of Satan and the powers of Christ. Spirituality recognizes, in the words of the Lausanne Covenant, "that we are engaged in constant spiritual warfare with the principalities and powers of evil, who are seeking to overthrow the church and frustrate its task."[20]

For this reason spirituality must take shape in the work of the local church in society. It may be expressed by the attempt to establish justice, feed the hungry, clothe the naked, heal the sick. It may concern itself with the disastrous effect of sin in the world, attempt to restore the ecological balance, resist war, fight greed, distribute the wealth, or bring reconciliation between people. In this struggle spirituality recognizes that it is not thereby bringing in the kingdom, but instead is acting out of love and obedience to Jesus Christ, caring for his creation, anticipating the return of Christ in the words of the Lord's Prayer: "thy kingdom come, thy will be done on *earth* as it is in heaven."

Conclusion

The classical incarnational view of spirituality recognizes the validity of both the divine and the human in our struggle to be a spiritual

137

people. There is both a negative and a positive side to spirituality. Through the negative, we assert the necessity of rising above life to encounter God through self-abandonment and quiet. In the positive, we meet God in the responsibility of life, in the process of history, in the issues of the day. One without the other is incomplete, although at times an individual or the church is called to place greater stress on one than on the other.

We must learn, then, not to *have* a spirituality, something we turn on at a particular place or time, but to *be* spiritual, as a habit of life, a continuous state of being. It is to this end that we seek after God in the stillness and hubbub of life, but always and everywhere in and through the church, where Christ is made present to us and, through us, to the world. It is this kind of spirituality that will challenge and motivate the people of the postmodern world. It is mystical yet reasonable, inner yet outer, ecclesial yet personal. Therefore, it is a point of contact for a culture already immersed in various kinds of spirituality.

Table I: Spirituality in the Paradigms of History

Ancient	Medieval	Reformation	Modern	Postmodern
Baptismal spirituality	*lectio divina*	Spirituality of the Word (witness of the Spirit)	Spirituality of knowledge	The return to mystery, to a supernatural worldview, and to baptismal, liturgical, and eucharistic spirituality
Eucharistic spirituality Liturgical spirituality Spirituality of the hours	Monastics pilgrimages Feasts and fasts	Vocational spirituality	Spirituality of the new birth Spirituality of rule keeping Spirituality of witnessing	
	Veneration of the saints Inner and outer discipleship			

A Classical/Post-modern Mission

What the soul is in the body,
That Christians are in
The world.
> —*Epistle to Diognetus,*
> c. A.D. 200

The first seven years of my life were spent in Africa, where my parents were missionaries. I still have vivid memories of our mission station, located in a clearing within the thick wilds of the jungle. All around us, as far as the eye could see, were the impenetrable forests of deepest Africa.

While it was the jungle that drew on my imagination as a child, it is the buildings of the clearing that come in view when I think of the mission of the church in the world. My thoughts turn to two buildings: the church and the barn.

First, I see the mud walls and the grass-thatched roof of the church as a symbol of evangelism. The Africans were able to look at that building and sense that Christ was calling them to enter into the new community of faith. And then during the week, the church doubled as a schoolhouse, where the Africans were taught how to read and write using the Bible. As I reflect on the double use of the building, I'm reminded of the union that exists between evangelism and education.

The other building on the compound that exercises my imagination is the barn. To me, the barn stands as the symbol of the social action of the church. Around the barn were the chickens, the goats, the pigs, and beyond, were fields of vegetables and sugarcane. Missionaries even then were concerned not only with the soul, but with the re-creation of the world. The work of teaching the nationals how to cultivate the ground, plant the seed, and care for the tender shoots was a work of redeeming the creation.

This threefold mission of evangelism, education, and social action is rooted in the victory of Christ over evil. When the church evangelizes, educates, and meets social needs, it continues the work of Christ in the world. For this reason the mission of the church in the postmodern world will stand in contradiction to the norms of society. The postmodern doctrine of pluralism affirms the validity of the religion of all cultures. No religion, postmoderns teach, is valid for all. According to Charles Jencks, "pluralism is the leading 'ism' of post modernity, and a condition which most critics agree underlies the period."[1] Christianity, however, is characterized by its universality and its mission mandate to convert others and bring them into the Christian faith and perspective. In a postmodern world of pluralism, this scandal of particularity will not be well received. Yet it is made necessary by the claim of Jesus that he is "the way, and the truth and the life" (John 14:6) and the mandate to make this message known throughout the world (Acts 1:8).

I do not start as I have, in previous sections, with the history of missions in the paradigms of Christian history. Because evangelism, education, and the place of the church in the world have their own histories, I deal with the historical paradigms at the beginning of each chapter.

EVANGELISM AS PROCESS

Evangelism is the hallmark of evangelical Christianity. In this century alone Christians have circled the globe and penetrated the obscure parts of the world to present Christ's saving message to millions of people. Recently, the Roman Catholic Church and the World Council of Churches have recognized the urgency of evangelism and are now giving greater attention to what has always consumed the energies of evangelical Christians.[1]

Evangelism Within the Paradigms of History[2]

In the later part of the first century and the opening decades of the second century there were many itinerant evangelists and prophets who roamed the Roman Empire preaching the gospel of Jesus. By the end of the second century the church had become established in nearly every city and evangelism shifted from the itinerant, independent evangelist to the local church. During the second and third centuries the church developed an elaborate form of evangelism, culminating in baptism. This form of evangelism consisted of four stages of threshold growth marked off by three passage rites celebrated in worship. This type of evangelism permeated the Roman world and resulted in numerous conversions to Christ and the church.[3]

The medieval paradigm of evangelism shifted more toward the institutional church. This institutional form of evangelism reaches back into the Constantinian period and to the Christianization of the empire by the end of the fourth century. The most notable change from the early church was the shift in baptism.[4] In the early church baptism was the culmination of a process of personal salvation, whereas in the medieval church baptism became the first act of conversion. In baptism original sin was forgiven. Then, through the sacraments God's grace was infused throughout the various stages of life. Baptism, it was argued, confers an indelible Christian character that cannot be denied. By virtue of baptism a person is made a true believer. For this reason, the medieval church used force by the sword as a way of evangelism: Holy wars were fought and heretics were punished, all in the name of bringing people under the jurisdiction of the church, the true source of salvation.[5]

A more personal form of evangelism was expressed in the monastic movement. Monasteries dotted the landscape of medieval Europe and became places where one could see and experience an authentic personal faith. For this reason many common people fled to the monastery, where they could experience personal conversion and a new life in Christ. By the end of the medieval period the doctrines of penance and works righteousness through which an angry God was placated so permeated the church and even the monasteries that there was a need for the reformulation of evangelism.

In many ways the Reformers' doctrine of salvation continued to reflect the convictions of the medieval era. While they broke with the use of force, Luther and Calvin as well as the Anglican reform still understood the church's role as redeeming the structures of society and accomplishing a Christianization of society. Against the medieval background, they sought to reform the understanding of salvation by deemphasizing the role of works and reemphasizing the role of faith. Their starting point was God. It was God who initiated salvation. God made salvation available through Jesus Christ, who took on himself the punishment for our sins on the cross. God in Jesus Christ has done for us what we cannot do for ourselves. Conversion means trusting in Christ alone. This trust sets a person free to live in the world under God boldly. It was the newness of this message, now proclaimed in the churches, that constituted the essence of evangelism. The Anabaptist community, however, differed radically from the Reformers and emphasized the church as the alternative society of true Christians. They called for a conversion to a Christian culture within the context of an otherwise pagan and heathen culture. For them, evangelism was a matter of a corporate lifestyle within a community separated from the surrounding world. Christianity was an alternative community of faith that differed radically from the non-Christian society.[6]

Evangelism of the modern era can be traced back to the emergence of the pietist movement and the epistemological shift from the Reformation doctrine of objective faith to the emergence of a more subjective faith.

For the Reformers salvation derived from the imputation of Christ's right-eousness which, when it was heard and acted on in faith, resulted in jus-tification. Sanctification then became the working out of the reality of justification in Christian living. This view was challenged by the pietists with their more subjective view of salvation. They shifted the experience of salvation to regeneration. A person became born again from within through faith in Christ. This was a dramatic, turnaround experience of justification. Sanctification then became the personal commitment to die to the world, to all its allurements and wicked ways. These convictions informed modern-day revivalism and missions. The goal of the church, expressed in the Great Commission, is to convert people to Christ. As Enlightenment individualism began to take root, it shaped evangelism in its own image and evangelism lost its ecclesial character and became evan-gelism into Christ alone. Unwittingly, a wedge was driven between Christ and the church. In the worst-case scenario of modern evangelism, a per-son can be a Christian without an active life in the church. This approach to evangelism contributed to the privatization of faith, to a personal, me-oriented gospel that undercut the role of the church.[7]

In the postmodern world evangelism is shifting away from Enlight-enment individualism to the more communal model of the early church, a model that will be explained in this chapter. Evangelism is therefore not only a conversion to Christ, who has won a victory over the powers of evil, but a conversion into a community. These are the people whose outlook and lifestyle are being reshaped by their participation in the alternative community of faith. Conversion is also shifting from the punctilinear, dramatic movement of faith to process: a faith nurtured by the church in whom the new convert finds his or her place in the world.[8]

Problems Inherited from the Enlightenment

The major problem of Enlightenment evangelism centers around its focus on individualism. Individualism resulted in an overemphasis on personal salvation and lost the larger message of the gospel. R. B. Kuiper offers this critique: "Too often the limelight is turned full upon the evan-gelist—his personality, his eloquence, his ability as an organizer, the story of his conversion, the hardships which he has endured, the num-ber of his converts, in some instances the miracles of healing allegedly performed by him. At other times attention is focused on those who are being evangelized—their large numbers, their sorry plight as exempli-fied by poverty, disease, and immorality, their supposed yearning for the gospel of salvation, and, worst of all, the good that is said to dwell in them and to enable men to exercise saving faith of their own free, although unregenerate, volition. And how often the welfare of man, whether temporal or eternal, is made the sole end of evangelism."[9]

Modern evangelism, grounded in the satisfaction theory of the atonement, has been primarily cross-centered evangelism. It emphasizes the substitutionary dimension of the gospel and the change that takes place in people when they trust in Christ. While this side of evangelism should not be neglected, it fails to say everything about the gospel that needs to be said. Its primary shortcoming is that it fails to move from the death of Christ to the victory of Christ over the powers of evil. Consequently, evangelism is reduced to personal and privatized Christianity and fails to express that Christ has bound, dethroned, and will destroy all evil at the end of history. The far-reaching implications of the recapitulation of all things by the work of the second Adam are reduced to "my new birth." The place of a community under the reign of God along with the eschatological destination of history are not part of the message. We need, as David Bosch has written, "an interpretation of salvation which operates within a *comprehensive* christological framework, which makes the *Totus Christus*—his incarnation, earthly life, death, resurrection, and parousia—indispensable for church and theology."[10]

This points to the second problem of a highly individualized approach to evangelism: It separates evangelism from the church. Enlightenment evangelism centers almost exclusively on the change accomplished in the individual. *You* are saved. *You* are a new person. *You* have been born again. Consequently, it does not adequately stress the role of the church in the nurturing process of salvation. At conversion, a convert has only begun the process of being saved. The church is the community in which this process is encouraged and brought to completion.

Individualistic evangelism also separates evangelism from baptism. In many cases new Christians are told to go to the church of their choice and be baptized. But in most evangelical churches of the Enlightenment, baptism is seen as *my witness* to *my salvation*. The divine action of God's work in baptism is often neglected. The biblical meaning of baptism is that through identification with Christ we are called to put to death everything that is sin in our lives and bring to life a new person shaped in the image of Christ by the power of the Holy Spirit. Baptism is not a once-for-all my-witness-to-the-world action. It is the ritual that initiates us into the body of Christ and begins our lifelong pursuit of holiness which takes place in the accountability of God's community on earth, the church.[11]

The separation of evangelism from the church has resulted in a separation of evangelism from obedience and introduced the cult of easy and attractive Christianity. All too often the faith is packaged through people who testify that Christianity has really been good for them: It has given meaning to their life, saved a marriage and a home, or made life great.

Others testify that they are now happy, acceptable, in control of things, popular, even rich. I do not mean to demean the positive effects of Christianity. Certainly, many lives have been given meaning and direction. Our major emphasis, however, must not be to make Christianity attractive, as attractive as it is, nor to make it a panacea for all ills, as much as it does give life meaning and purpose. Instead, we need to emphasize the cost of discipleship, the absolute claim of God over our entire life, the necessity of a faith that issues forth in obedience, and our belonging to an alternative culture shaped by the kingdom of Jesus.[12]

One reason modern evangelism may be divorced from obedience is due to the purpose of evangelists. Evangelists seek to elicit a response, to get someone to make a decision, to make a commitment to Christ. For this reason evangelistic services sometimes play on the emotions. The music, the testimonies, the sermon, the invitation are all geared so that people can be skillfully and psychologically guided toward a decision. (A friend of mine describes one manual for "soul-winning" that counseled the witnesser, at a critical moment of decision, to apply steady pressure with the hand to the back of the sinner's neck!)

Often such a heavy emphasis is put on the decision that the inquirer leaves with the false impression that the sum and substance of Christianity is making a decision. The result is an individualization of the Christian message. The need for preevangelism, for a return to the unity of *kerygma* (preaching) and *didache* (teaching), for a follow-up program in the local church is being increasingly recognized as a healthy corrective to emotional evangelism.

Another reason for the divorce between evangelism and obedience may be found in "cultural conversions." That is, a person may make a radical break from a former way of living into a particular form of Christianity. For example, a person may be persuaded to give up bad habits and join a group whose identity is strongly defined by the absence of smoking, drinking, dancing, gambling, and the like. The problem is that the new convert may confuse obedience to the forms of this "new culture" with obedience to Christ. The person may be told that obedience means giving up bad habits and taking on new habits, such as Bible reading, prayer, witnessing, attending church, and tithing.

As good as these new habits are, they do not get at the heart of Christian obedience, and the reduction of the Christian life to these few principles tends to obscure deeper issues as well as to lead the convert who obeys them to substitute a cultural change of habits for a more far-reaching, biblical change of lifestyle.

Another problem of Enlightenment evangelism is the way it has functioned in non-Western societies. Western Christianity embraced the Enlightenment idea of progress and viewed Western civilization as shaped by Christian values. For this reason, evangelism, particularly to other cultures, was not just the message of Christianity, but the message embedded in the cultural form of the Western Enlightenment. Evangelism was judged successful in other countries if people assumed Western civilization and sought to bring their personal, family, and tribal life into conformity with Western style of dress, Western values of thrift, work, and savings, and governmental principles of democracy and capitalism. The demise of Western civilization at the end of the twentieth century and the rise of third world Christianity has reduced the significance of Western culture. In the postmodern world evangelization will take place *within* the various cultures of the world[13] (see table J).

A Classical/Postmodern Evangelism

Aspects of Apostolic Preaching

Evangelism in the early church was associated with the victory of Christ over evil and the establishment of the kingdom of God (see chapter 2). There are three aspects of apostolic preaching and teaching that are important to keep in mind in evangelism. The first is that the apostles were not preaching mere facts, but an interpretation of an event. The message was that Jesus lived, died, and rose again *for their sins!* Salvation is no mere assent to the facts about the King, but repentance, faith, and obedience. This is the Good News that saves (1 Cor. 15:2).

The second aspect of apostolic preaching is that Christ is the inaugurator of a new era in the church. The special feature of this new era is that God has entered human history (John 1:15). It is the age in which the King of Glory has appeared in human flesh and lived out the rule of the King before the eyes of people. His rulership extends over all of life. What we do, say, and think must be executed under his rule. Our eating, sleeping, drinking, judging, and loving must all take place under the rule of the King. He is the Lord of life—all of life. Thus the inauguration of the new age is not merely some intrusion into the secular world, nor a spiritual component that runs alongside of life. Rather, it is the central dynamic to the whole of life and it involves the whole person in all his or her thinking, feeling, and living.

A third aspect of apostolic evangelism is that it always led to baptism and entrance into the church. Baptism was a physical sign and seal of conversion, of turning away from a wrong way of life, of trusting in Jesus. It was no empty symbol, but an act that was a *necessary* aspect of conversion. The message was repent *and* be baptized. The doctrine of justification and the doctrine of baptism were all of one piece, in a holistic sense. It is no accident, as Michael Green remarked in *Evangelism in the Early Church*, that Romans 6, the great chapter on baptism as an identification with Christ, comes after Romans 5, the great chapter on justification. They belong together and the pattern of the early church was always conversion, then baptism.[14]

The meaning of baptism in the New Testament period shows us how important baptism was regarded. Baptism implies repentance and renunciation; its form symbolizes the main facts of the gospel; its content signifies an entrance into the new community and a mark of the reception of the Spirit. In baptism one dies to the world with Christ and is raised with him to new life, is washed in the waters of regeneration from all guilt, is baptized into the body of Christ, and receives the Holy Spirit as Jesus did at his baptism. The cumulative evidence suggests that conversion and baptism were not mere emotional experiences, but were entered into on the basis of commitment. Take up your cross and follow after Christ.

The Method of Evangelism in the Early Church

From the very beginning of the faith, baptism was the primary symbol of coming into the church. By the fourth century the process of baptism was two or three years in length and was marked by four distinct periods of growth and three stages or passage rites. The first stage was that of the inquiry (seeker stage); the second was that of the catechumenate (hearer stage); the third was the period of purification and enlightenment (kneeler stage); and the fourth was entrance into the full life of the church (faithful stage). Each stage of development concluded with a passage rite that carried the person into the next stage. These passage rites are the rite of welcome, the rite of election, and the rite of initiation (baptism) (see table K).

This early church evangelism assumed four things. First, it was based on the *Christus Victor* understanding of the death of Christ. Second, it presupposed that the church plays a mothering role in the process of

147

salvation. Thus, the church was referred to as the "womb" in which the formation of the new convert was nourished. Third, the rituals of the church pertaining to salvation (passage rites) were treated as external means of organizing an internal experience. Fourth, conversion was understood as happening in various stages of development; a person was led through a maturation that led to baptism and entrance into the church as the culminating events of the converting process.[15]

In order to understand third-century evangelism more fully, let me ask you to use your imagination. Let's assume for a moment that you are a third-century neighbor to a devout Christian. Through that person's life and witness your desire to become a Christian grows in intensity, and you share this with your neighbor, who then evangelizes you third-century style (the roots of which are in the New Testament, but space does not permit that development here). What is the process through which you will be carried?

The answer to this question is fully described by Hippolytus in his work, *The Apostolic Tradition*.[16] This work, written around A.D. 215, provides us with a description of the life of the church in the early third century. This is not the only work that describes evangelism through worship, but it is the most complete and succinct.

First, you are a seeker and you will be taken to an *inquiry* conducted by the pastor or leaders of the church in what might be called a pre-evangelism screening. The purpose of the inquiry is to proclaim the gospel clearly and to determine whether your commitment to Christ is real.

Second, assuming you have made a firm commitment of faith, you are next brought into the life of the church through the *rite of welcome.* This simple ritual had as its central feature a verbal and symbolic repudiation of the devil and all his works along with words and symbols that indicate you are turning to Christ. First, the seeker is asked: "Do you renounce all false worship?" False worship touches many matters, but it is primarily a repudiation of Caesar as Lord. When the candidate says, "I do," the sign of the cross is made on the head, indicating that the seeker now wears the invisible tattoo of the Christian, the cross (many Roman occupations were identifiable by a special tattoo). After this and other symbols, the seeker is invited to walk down into the congregation and take his or her place among the faithful. The seeker is now a hearer.

Third, you then enter into a period of instruction known as the *catechumenate* (the word means instruction), which may last as long as three years. During this time you are a *hearer* and you are taught the faith and discipled in Christian living. The next and very powerful symbol is the passage rite from the time of instruction to the period of purification and enlightenment (a time for baptismal preparation). This passage rite, called the *rite of election*, invites the hearer to the front of the church to respond to the question, "Do you choose Jesus?" When the answer is given in the affirmative, the hearer walks to an open book standing before the pulpit and writes down his or her name in this book of life. The hearer now becomes a *kneeler* and spends the next six weeks preparing for baptism with an emphasis on personal holiness. This six-week period is a time for intense spiritual preparation for baptism. It is called *purification and enlightenment* and is a period of prayer and fasting in preparation for baptism.

The third cluster of symbols is found in the baptism itself. The baptismal service is part of the great paschal vigil service conducted on the Saturday night before Easter. Christians have gathered for an all-night service that includes the lighting of the fire (foreshadows the resurrection), readings of Scripture that begin with creation and end with re-creation, the baptismal rite, and the Easter Eucharist.

As the sun rises in the east and the cock begins to crow, the symbols of baptism into Jesus' death and resurrection begin. First, the bishop will breathe into the faces of the candidates to indicate the coming of the Holy Spirit into their lives. Then the sign of the cross is made over the water, setting it aside to be a special agent of God's bidding. The candidate takes off his clothing as a symbol of putting off the old man. He then walks into the water (usually pools in the early church) and proceeds with the ritual of renunciation. In this rite the minister asks, "Do you reject the devil and all his works?" The candidate replies with a strong "I do," turns to the west (symbol of darkness), and spits into the face of the devil. He then receives the oil of thanksgiving, followed by immersion into the water three times—in the name of the Father, the Son, and the Holy Spirit. Immediately after water baptism, the kneeler is anointed with oil, signifying reception of the Holy Spirit. The kneeler then for the first time since his journey began enters into the full worship of the church: prays with the faithful, passes the kiss of peace, and receives the Eucharist (the Christian is now a member of the *faithful*).

As one can see, the rite of baptism symbolically carries the converting Christian through the story of Jesus. Entrance into the story of Christ is not just a verbal communication, but *an immersed participation in the event itself.* Finally, after Easter in a period know as *mystogogy*, the newly baptized person is incorporated into the life of the faithful. During this time the convert is given a deeper appreciation of baptism and the Lord's Supper through a series of postbaptismal lectures.

Evangelism in the Postmodern World

In a postmodern world the content and method of evangelism may creatively draw on that of the early church, a time similar to that of our postmodern world. Craig Van Gelder summarized the issue for us. He writes: "The emerging paradigm of mission to North America must be able to respond to postmodernism and its accompanying relativity. To do so the following two issues will need to be addressed. Building communities of faith and addressing fragmentation and brokenness."[17] My own conviction is that the postmodern world is fertile ground for the Christian message, but it must be the full message and not a reductionism to a decision without an in-depth follow-up to Christian thought and practice. If we are to evangelize effectively, we must set about building community and providing healing to the hurts of life.

The Content of Evangelism

If evangelicals are to build communities and address the fragmentation and brokenness of life, we need to look back to the content of evangelism in the classical tradition. First, there is a need to recover the emphasis that Christ's death is a *victory over the powers of evil*. In the supernatural world of postmodernism there is a new understanding of the powers of evil. People wrestle with the brokenness of society, with the constant violence of our inner cities, which has now spread to the rich suburbs. Numerous people deal daily with broken marriages, broken relationships, financial hardships, and the inner struggle with evil. *Christus Victor* makes connection with churched and unchurched people. It says that God has won a battle for us that we ourselves can't win. This message is the point of contact with people frustrated by the powers.

Second, evangelism in a postmodern world needs to restore the sense that a relationship with Christ demands radical obedience. This obedience begins by demanding full identification of the believer with Christ through baptism. Baptism in many churches has lost its meaning. In many cases the gospel has been reduced to "something good for you." To be baptized into Christ means to identify with his suffering, to enter into his death, and to be raised to new life with him. In this way the Christian participates in the victory of Christ over evil. Salvation is not only in an individual sense, but also in the corporate sense of the church as a witness to the kingdom. Our message begins with the preaching of the kingdom, the future and ultimate reign of God. But the kingdom of God is more than an eschatological hope; it is a present reality as well.

150

It is found now in the church, among the people God has called out and formed into the community of Christ's body.[18]

Third, evangelism in a postmodern world will speak to all of human existence. "A Christianity which has lost its vertical dimension has lost its salt, and is not only insipid in itself, but useless to the world. But a Christianity which would use the vertical dimension as a means of escape from responsibility for and in the common life of men is a denial of the incarnation of God's life for the world manifested in Christ."[19] This statement contains in a nutshell the essence of kingdom evangelism. The whole person in all vertical and horizontal relationships is to be brought under the jurisdiction of Jesus Christ.

In summary, postmodern evangelism not only *announces* the kingdom but also seeks to *inaugurate* the kingdom in the biblical sense. Evangelism must stress obedience. True obedience is a call to forsake the false gods of culture. All too often we have identified false gods as personal sins only. There is no question that the Christian is called to flee the personal sins of immorality, impurity, passion, evil desires, greed, anger, wrath, malice, slander, abusive speech, lying, and the like. To live by these values is to live under the rule of Satan. But when we fail to recognize the controlling presence of these sins not only in our hearts but also in the very warp and woof of society, we miss both the depth of the biblical understanding of sin and the depth of the kingdom of God as the rule of Christ in every area of life.[20]

The Method of Evangelism

At the time of this writing, few Protestant churches are aware of the local church evangelism of the third century. This form of evangelism has been resurrected mainly among the renewing Catholic churches in the missional approach known as the RCIA (Rites for the Christian Initiation of Adults).[21] This third-century form of evangelism has unusual insight into the converting process and is characterized by high relevance to a postmodern world.

First, third-century evangelism is thoroughly evangelical. It preaches Christ. It calls people into the church. It demands radical obedience. Second, third-century evangelism is local church evangelism par excellence. It does not bring people to Christ at mass rallies on television and turn them loose to find their way in the faith. Rather, it emanates from the local church and manifests a personal, caring touch in which a person is taken by the hand and walked through the various stages of growth and development into conversion. The community of God's people in a local church, therefore, plays a supportive role, not only for the community that is evangelizing, but also for the person being evangelized. One is not subjected to an individualistic salvation, in which one stands alone, but is introduced to a community of people who provide social, moral, and psychological assistance to the converting person undergoing a radical change in life. Thus, a symbiosis between the evangelizer and the enangelizee is attained. Third, early church evangelism does not replace current forms of evangelism. Rather, it supplements them by providing a plan whereby converting persons can be brought into a deeper and lasting commitment to Christ and the church. Therefore, all the various forms of evangelism can be treated as the inquiry stage of evangelism. Evangelism brings people to the door of the church, where the process of continuing what has begun can be carried out. Finally, third-century evangelism meets the demands the postmodern world places on the church: It is personal, visual, developmental, communal, mystical, and thoroughly related to a person's life in the world.

18

EDUCATION AS WISDOM

Most mission models of the recent past are based on the concept that evangelism and education are two different functions of the church. This questionable view finds support in C. H. Dodd's *The Apostolic Preaching and Its Development*. Dodd's thesis is that "it was by Kerygma . . . not by didache that it pleased God to save men."[1] This loss of evangelism in education as well as the loss of education in evangelism is one of the root causes of superficiality in evangelism today. The message of Christianity is a *historical* message with *content*.

Whenever Christianity is preached without its history or content, it is reduced to a social or psychological panacea, or worse, a manipulation of feelings, moving the individual into a contentless response. On the other hand, whenever the content of Christianity is presented as factual or intellectual data without an accompanying call to commitment and change of life, Christian education loses its power to form character in the convert. Clearly, evangelism and education must stand together. There must be content in preaching and proclamation in teaching.

Although a number of scholars have questioned Dodd's conclusion, it wasn't until the publication of *Preaching and Teaching in the Earliest Church* by R. C. Worley that Dodd's conclusions were given a full-scale treatment. Worley showed, as Michael Green also suggested in *Evangelism in the Early Church,* that in both rabbinic Judaism and early Christianity there was no such clear-cut distinction between the work of the evangelist and the teacher.[2] Paul's example at Ephesus, where he "entered the synagogue and spoke boldly there for three months, arguing persuasively about the kingdom of God" (Acts 19:8), suggests that the mission of the church to the unconverted was accompanied by rigorous intellectual activity. Consequently, as we focus on education and nurture, we recognize the close connection between evangelism and education.

Education Within the Paradigms of History[3]

The era of the early church was based on the oral transmission of knowledge. In this setting liturgy played a key role in the communication of Christian thought and experience. A brief glance at the early Christian liturgies shows that they were full of Scripture (read to the community) and the theological imagery of baptism and the Eucharist. Converting Christians were allowed to stay with the community of the faithful through the sermon. They then went to a room where they were instructed in the faith as the faithful (the baptized) continued in worship with the prayers and the Eucharist. Because less than 2 percent of the population was able to read, education in the faith was conducted through an oral catechesis of preaching, explaining, and interpreting the faith.

The medieval era was also a period of illiteracy. In addition to the continuation of the oral form of communication in the liturgy and oral explanation, the church introduced participatory forms of communication. Faith was communicated through cultural transmission.

People were fully and completely immersed in the faith in every aspect of life. The church literally stood in the center of the town, where everything revolved around it. From the church proceeded philosophy, music, art, and literature. Consequently, people were initiated into the Christian faith in the same way that they learned their mother tongue.[4] Christianity was essentially a "religion of participation." In the thirteenth century education was related to the liturgy and parents were to teach their children clearly and make them remember, both in French and in Latin, the angelic salutation, the Lord's Prayer, the articles of faith, and God's commandments.[5] People were obliged to go to the parish church every Sunday to hear the Divine Office and the commandments, and to confess to the priest, who questioned penitents about knowledge of the *Pater Noster*, the creed, and the *Ave Maria*.[6]

Immersed participation in the faith also occurred through the ever-present visuals of the faith. The church was full of images of God, the works of Jesus, and the lives of the saints. The space and environment of the church was like a journey into the heavens and communicated the "otherness" of the Christian faith, the destiny toward which the church was moving.

This immersed form of communication changed drastically with the Renaissance and the invention of the printing press.[7] The Renaissance introduced education to the masses, and the printing press made knowledge available through print. This new shift from the visual to the verbal fueled the Protestant Reformation and introduced new approaches to education.

The Reformation introduced the written catechism. Luther's catechism, published in 1529, sold more than one hundred thousand copies by 1569. Considering the size of the population in the sixteenth century, this was an astonishing feat. The catechetical way became the new form of learning—even in the Catholic Church. Catechetical training from the Reformation to the present has been based on the notions of reading, writing, linear sequence, analysis, and memory. Since every church produced its own catechesis, the tendency has been to teach a strict understanding of the faith in the specific tradition of the church. While catechisms share what is common to the church, their special feature is an emphasis on the unique features of the denomination they represent. Consequently, a shift occurred away from a mystical view of the Christian faith experienced in the liturgy to an intellectual understanding of the faith. The liturgy of the Protestant church shifted from the faith handed down through proclamation and enactment to the didactic sermon. While the didactic approach to education has dominated the entire period of modernity, the new revolution in communications is shifting from didactic education toward a more immersed and participatory, audiovisual way of learning.[8]

In the postmodern world education will shift from the passing down of information to the passing down of wisdom through experience. Christian truth, which was regarded as propositional, intellectual, and rational, will be experienced as an embodied reality. Faith will be communicated through immersion into a community of people who truly live the Christian faith. This corporate community will communicate through its depth of commitment, through hospitality, and through images such as baptism, the importance of Scripture, the significance of Eucharist celebration, and the feasts and fasts of the Christian year. These events will shape the imagination of the believer and provide transcendent points of reference that bring meaning to the cycle of life. The meaning of the stories, symbols, cycles of time, and audiovisual experiences of faith may become the center for thoughtful discussion and application in the small group and stimulate both an intellectual and emotional knowing.[9]

Problems with Contemporary Christian Education

Evangelical educators generally agree that today's church education needs to overcome three specific problems: an overemphasis on moralism, a reduction of learning to factualism, and a failure to see things holistically.[10]

First, moralism resembles a do-goodism that neglects a more biblical understanding of Christian ethics as it grows out of the redemptive work of Christ. The moralistic teacher tends to find "the moral" in Bible stories and in the lives of biblical heroes. There is a tendency to emphasize how "doing good" and "being responsible" always pay off in the end. On this basis, the teacher urges the students to be helpful, kind, and sharing.

The problem with this kind of teaching is not with the behavior suggested by moralism, but with the misinterpretation of what Scripture *actually* says. Moralism fails to emphasize the redemptive nature of the Word. The stories of Scripture are often explained as isolated incidents, and not as examples of the way God is working to accomplish redemption. Thus the picture of Christianity as a superficial do-goodism is unconsciously presented. For example, if we treat the story of Abraham merely as an example of obedience without putting Abraham in the context of God's covenant to bring into existence a people through which the world will be blessed, we reduce his story to moralism. True morality is not based on this or that particular story, but on the story of Israel and Jesus and the calling to be a new person within the community of God's people on earth.

Second, factualism is similar to moralism in that it calls for the mere memorization of material apart from an understanding of the meaning of that material. It is good for a student to know the periods of biblical history and to know what happened in each period. But unless the student is able to interpret biblical facts the message is missed. Memorized names of the kings or of the important dates, events, places, and people of the Bible are mere trivia unless the role they play in the unfolding of the redemptive process is made clear. What is the redemptive meaning of Seth, Abraham, Moses, David, and Jeremiah? How is God working in history to bring Christ into the world? What does God's action mean in relation to the human predicament? What am I to do about it? Unless these questions are probed—along with the teaching of facts— the education given can make no claim to be really Christian at its root because it does not shape perception and impart wisdom.

Third, the failure to see the complete picture of the biblical framework on which to hang what is being taught provides only scattered information, bits and pieces of truth that never come together in a whole. For this reason it is imperative to teach a grasp of the entire Christian faith. Holistic education improves, deepens, and strengthens the learners' grasp of the claims Christ makes over the whole of life and imparts a Christian worldview.

The basic problem with moralism, factualism, and the failure to see the complete picture is that these approaches do not lend themselves to real growth in the Christian faith, to its understanding, and to the way it is lived out. It supports an individualistic approach to Christianity, fails to provide an adequate basis for faith, fails to deepen commitment to Christ, and does not show how the Christian faith relates to all of life. We turn, therefore, to the early church in search of guidelines for a post-modern agenda for education.

Education in the Early Church

Throughout this writing I have been emphasizing the communal nature of the classical church. And I have repeatedly suggested that the effective church in the postmodern world will be the church that becomes a community of hospitality and belonging. The huge and complex nature of the global world and the sense of lostness need to be offset by a small, intimate community of relationships. It is in this close setting that education and nurture occurred in the classical church, especially the smaller churches of the first three centuries.

In these churches people were integrated into the life of the church through the seven steps of evangelism and character formation discussed in the previous chapter. During this time a person traveled through four stages: seeker, hearer, kneeler, and the faithful. We turn to an examination of these stages of growth and development in the early church, looking for a clue to implementing education and nurture in the post-modern world[11] (see table K).

The Seeker

According to Hippolytus's *The Apostolic Tradition*, preevangelism education, which focused on the seeker, was practiced in Rome by the end of the second century. The seeking person was brought to the church for an inquiry with the leaders of the congregation, who communicated the demands the Christian faith makes on its converts (like an education in the cost of discipleship). For example, if a person was engaged in an occupation that involved idol worship or allegiance to the emperor as God, that job must be given up. If a person was involved in practices contrary to the gospel, such as astrology or immorality, these must be given up. The implications of repentance are not only on inner attitudes but on outer actions as well. More than likely many people were turned away from the faith when they discovered the kind of obedience it demanded.

157

However, once seekers made an initial choice to follow after Jesus, they passed through the rite of welcome and entered the hearer stage.[12]

The Hearer

The hearer stage is a more formal instruction in the faith, especially in the matters of orthodoxy and orthopraxis. Orthodoxy means *right praise*. Consequently, studies focused on the worship of the primitive church. This teaching appears to be basic: "I believe Jesus is Lord" (Rom. 10:9); or "I believe Jesus is the Christ, the Son of the living God" (Matt. 16:16); or the more expanded creed of Paul in 1 Corinthians 15:3–5, "that Christ died for our sins according to the Scriptures, and that he was buried, that he was raised on the third day according to the Scriptures, and that he appeared to Peter." These early hearers of the gospel were at first hearing the message of the Christian church, not delving into the depth of doctrine. This message was clearly oriented around baptism. In Romans 6 Paul indicates that the form of baptism itself speaks to the content of the Christian faith. As Christ died, was buried, and rose from the dead, so converts who confess Jesus recognize their identification with Jesus by their own symbolic act of death, burial, and resurrection in baptism. It is clear, then, that to confess Christ is to acknowledge the truth of the gospel about him. The convert confesses faith in the person of Jesus, but not apart from who that person is and what that person has done.

While initial instruction had to do with an identification with Christ in baptism, the instruction over the next three years gave the hearer a firm basis in the thought patterns of Christianity and in the Scriptures.

An indication of the actual content of early Christian education has been preserved for us in a number of catechetical lectures. One of the most important of these is *The Catechetical Lectures* of Cyril of Jerusalem (d. 386).

In lectures 1–3 Cyril speaks of the frame of mind necessary for baptism. He writes of sin, the devil, repentance, remission of sin, and the meaning of baptism. In lecture 4 he speaks of the ten Christian dogmas: belief about God, Christ, the virgin birth, Christ's crucifixion and burial, the resurrection, the second coming and judgment, the Holy Spirit, the cross, and human nature and its end. He then lectures on the subject of faith, followed by thirteen lessons on the creed. Here, in a most interesting manner, is set forth the content of the Christian faith that a convert should know before baptism. We are well justified in concluding that evangelism, education, and nurture were characterized by depth.[13]

The second aspect of early Christian instruction had to do with *ortho-praxis,* or living the right way.

The orthopraxis of the early church followed the method of Jewish teaching. For example, Jewish teaching began with Leviticus, a cate-chetical summary of religious duties. The central chapters of this cate-chism are chapters 19–20, the so-called Holiness Code. And within this code two verses are of supreme importance: The first is Leviticus 19:2, "Be holy because I, the LORD your God, am holy," and the second is Leviticus 19:34, "Love [your neighbor] as yourself." These two verses constitute the key to Jewish catechaetical instruction. The theme of their instruction—the holiness of God and love for neighbor—appear fre-quently and with some apparent organization in the New Testament lit-erature, suggesting that parts of the New Testament are the actual mate-rial of the earliest catechetical instruction of the church. (Be holy: Matt. 5:48; 1 Thess. 4:7; 1 Peter 1:16; 1 John 3:3. For love: Matt. 5:43; 1 Thess. 4:9; 1 Peter 1:22; 1 John 3:10.)

The earliest catechetical document of the church is the *Didache,* a short, sixteen-chapter document that some date as early as A.D. 50 and others as late as A.D. 130. The *Didache* begins, "There are two ways, one of life, one of death; and between the two ways there is a great differ-ence."[14] The way of life (wisdom) consists of a number of instructions on how to live, drawn mainly from the teachings of Jesus, particularly the Sermon on the Mount. The "way of death," which begins in chapter 5, is a catalogue of evils similar to those found in the New Testament letters. An interesting point about the use of "the two ways" is the thor-oughly Jewish nature of the approach. Much of the material included in "the two ways" is found in Leviticus 17–19.[15]

The origin of "the two ways" is in the Wisdom Literature. Proverbs 4:18–19 refers to the "path of the righteous" and "the way of the wicked." We know that the term *way* was used of Christianity in the New Testa-ment as well. In Acts 19:23, the apostle Paul caused much disturbance to Ephesus through his teaching the "Way." This emphasis on the "two ways" was necessary to teach Christian morality to the Gentile converts who had a pagan amoral upbringing. Teaching through the "two ways" is apparent in Paul's writings. In Galatians 5, Paul lists the sins that char-acterize those who live according to the flesh and the virtues that result from walking in the Spirit. In Colossians 3 he lists what the new person is to "put off" and what he or she is "to put on." In Romans 6 he urges converts to yield to God and not to sin. This comparison between the way of life and the way of death is found in the practical portions of all the New Testament writings.[16]

The evidence is that Christians coming for baptism had to attest to a good character, that indeed they did live by the way of life. Justin pointed out that only those who "promise they can live accordingly" we baptized.[17] Hippolytus wrote, "And when those who are to receive baptism are chosen, let their life be examined. Have they lived good lives when they were catechumens? Have they honored the widows? Have they visited the sick? Have they done every kind of good work?" Again, Hippolytus stated, "Let catechumens spend three years as hearers of the word. But if a man is zealous and perseveres well in the work, *it is not time but his character that is decisive.*"[18] Clearly, Christian growth in the early church is not just the accumulation of knowledge, *but the pursuit of wisdom.*

The Kneeler

The third stage for spiritual growth in the early church was developed in connection with the six and one half weeks of Lent. During this time those who were preparing for baptism (as well as their sponsors and, in some cases, the whole church) went through an intense time of personal repentance and cleansing. The theme of this period is Ephesians 6:12, "our struggle is not against flesh and blood, but against the rulers, against the authorities, against the powers of this dark world and against the spiritual forces of evil in the heavenly realms." The *Christus Victor* theme was being put to the test. Kneelers were to examine themselves to find those impurities that needed to be put off by the power of the Spirit so that they could grow into Christian maturity. The symbol of this period was the practice of the laying on of hands with the anointing of oil and a prayer for cleansing.

During three years of passing through the seeker, hearer, and kneeler stages, the converting person was given a firm basis in the structure of Christian orthodoxy over against the teaching and practice of opposing religions, especially the mythologies of Rome. And when the time for baptism came, the convert confessed Christ as he or she had been instructed. According to Hippolytus, the convert renounced Satan and all his works and then was taken to the water, where the following confession was made with the baptism:

"Dost thou believe in God, the Father almighty?" And he who is being baptized shall say:

"I believe."

Then holding his hand placed on his head, he shall baptize him at once. And then he shall say:

"Dost thou believe in Christ Jesus, the Son of God, who was born of the virgin Mary and was crucified under Pontius Pilate, and was dead and buried, and rose again the third day, alive from the dead, and ascended into heaven and sat at the right hand of the Father, and will come to judge the quick and the dead?" And when he says:

"I believe."

He is baptized again. And again he shall say:

"Dost thou believe in (the) Holy Ghost, and the holy church, and the resurrection of the flesh?" He who is being baptized shall say accordingly:

"I believe."

And so baptized a third time.[19]

The Faithful

The fourth and final stage of development was the baptized person's integration into the full life of the community. Prior to baptism, the candidates were dismissed from worship after the sermon. They were taken to a room where instruction in the faith was conducted as the faithful engaged in prayer, the passing of the peace, and the Eucharist. After baptism the baptized became members of the faithful with a participation in the prayers, the peace, and the Eucharist. The newly baptized were taught once again about a life that is honoring to God and they were given instruction on the mystery of the Eucharist.[20]

In sum, early church education and nurture was oriented toward baptismal identification and character. The central image of baptism spoke to the content and the practice of the Christian faith. In baptism the Christian died to sin and was raised to newness of life. To live in the reality of putting off the old and putting on the new was to live in wisdom.

Education and Nurture in the Postmodern World

Parker J. Palmer has summarized the most appropriate approach to education and nurture in a postmodern world. "It must be," he states, "a slow, subtle, nearly unconscious process of formation, something like the way a moving stream shapes the rocks over the long passage of time."[21]

The first and most crucial task of the church is to become a living model of a community that seeks to live out Christian belief and practice. There are several sources through which this growth may occur, sources previously discussed in this work: the recovery of a *Christus Victor* view of the gospel, the restoration of worship as praise for God's saving deeds in history, the recovery of the healing and nurturing ministry of the Eucharist, and the ordering of the church's life around the great feasts and fasts of the Christian year. All these sources for the communication of faith need to be characterized by creativity and interactive involvement on the part of the people. As involvement of the people in the memory of the church is intensified, the people's progress in understanding and wisdom will be that of continual growth.

Assuming the church is a living community, continually rehearsing its fundamental meaning in worship, the next commitment of the church is to emphasize growth in knowledge and wisdom through the image of baptism. Postmodern people learn through images. Because baptism is the image of an identification with Christ (knowledge) and a pattern for living (spiritual wisdom), the classical approach to evangelism and education around the image of baptism will capture the imagination of the postmodern mind (see table L).

In the early church baptism was always on Easter Sunday, an image that reinforced the pattern of dying to sin and rising to new life. During the Easter season the newly baptized were integrated into the full life of the church. In future years they reaffirmed their baptismal vows by washing their faces and hands in a gesture of continued commitment to Christ in the fresh baptismal waters of Easter.[22]

In a postmodern church this form of evangelism, education, and nurture needs to be recovered. Consider this: On Pentecost Sunday commission the church to be an evangelizing community (the entire church or those especially called and trained for evangelism). Then from Pentecost to Advent (about a six-month period from May or June to late November), have the church concentrate on contacting seekers and bringing them to a commitment to become hearers of the Word. Celebrate the rite of welcome on the first Sunday of Advent. Now the *hearer* is taught during Advent, Christmas, and Epiphany. Concentrate on the basics of the Christian faith such as the message of Christ, the church, and worship. On the first Sunday of Lent, take the hearers through the rite of election into the kneeler stage. Concentrate on baptismal spirituality as it calls kneelers to put off the old and put on the new. On Easter Sunday baptize the kneelers into their identification with Jesus' death and resurrection. Follow the baptism with an Easter time of teaching them the mysteries of the Christian faith, particularly the meaning of the Eucharist and its implication to help those in need.

Once people have been through this yearly cycle, they can progress once again, but on a deeper level. While a seeker may have been introduced to Christianity 101, the second year teaching can be developed that is Christianity 102, and so on. In this model everyone is taking a similar journey, but within different levels of knowledge and intensity.

This fits the postmodern model of individuals finding a personal center in community. However, in order for this model to work and to be effective in the local church, it will require a deep sense of commitment on the part of nearly all the active members because it is a corporate education that occurs within the church as a community. The spiritual journey coincides not only with the life of Christ (in the Christian year), but also with *each other.*

In a postmodern world this interactive approach to Christian education and nurture must happen in a dynamic, integral, and transactional way. In this context orthodoxy and orthopraxis are being brought together in the relational way in which they were originally understood and practiced. Furthermore, if there is one thing, among others, that the biblical concept of the church teaches us, it is that the church is to be seen as a whole. To be in Christ means to be in the church. If the whole church is present in every local congregation, then education and nurture cannot be divorced from the life of the whole church. The entire congregation together seeks to become Christlike.

The discovery that orthodox belief and orthodox living are not to be separated, but constitute the two sides of a single reality, makes it clear that growth in these two aspects can take place only in the church. It is the church that has received the faith of the apostles. Consequently, the church is called to pass down the faith not just in creeds but as a living example. The church models the truth, it incarnates the truth, it has "this mind in you which was Christ Jesus." As the church corporately knows and loves God, so its members corporately know and love one another. In this context education is not mere moralism, a bare fact, or a partial insight, but a holistic experience of learning to love God and fellow persons in the context of a loving community. This is the kind of community that will attract the seeker in a postmodern world.[23]

19

THE CHURCH IN THE WORLD

The third area of mission is the role of the church in the postmodern world. It arises out of the mission of Jesus to the world, is rooted in his death and resurrection, and is related to the recapitulation of all things in the eschaton. So the question is: How does the church function in the world between the time of the Christ event and the consummation of history?

Church and World Within the Paradigms of History

We have seen that the self-understanding of the church in the ancient period of history is incarnational. The church as the body of Christ is the continuing presence of Jesus in and to the world. As Christ suffered for the sake of the world, overcame the powers of evil, and left an example of love for all to follow, so the church expresses itself in the world through the politics of Jesus.[1] In Jesus' politics, the early church was a counterculture movement that did not align itself with worldly politics. The early church was seen as a politically subversive movement, a threat to the Roman government and its gods, especially the notion that the emperor is a son of god. Christians refused to say, "Caesar is Lord." Instead, they cried, "Jesus is Lord." In this central cry of faith, they looked for the coming of Christ and the establishment of his kingdom over the face of the earth.

The vision of the church as a sign of the other world present in this world was modified after the conversion of Constantine.[2] A shift in eschatological thought suggested that since Christ had not returned, and since the empire through Constantine became Christian, perhaps it was God's intent to establish heaven on earth. This idea was confirmed by Augustine, who asserted that we now live in the millennium, that the church is the kingdom, and that God intends to rule in the world through the church. It was Gregory the Great (A.D. 600) who took these ideas and wrote the script for the medieval era. The church shifted its self-understanding from the sign of the kingdom to the idea that God rules the world through the presence of his divine institution within the world. Thus the pope became the vicar of Christ over the world and claimed authority over both the church and the state. While this view of the church seemed to work well in the thirteenth century, it resulted in the corruption of the church in the fourteenth and fifteenth centuries and necessitated the Reformation.[3]

For Luther God had ordained two "spheres" of life: the state and the church. Christians were to live in both worlds simultaneously. In the church God rules by the Spirit; in the world God rules by the sword. The ideal was to inform the rule of the state by the church. Calvin replaced the rule of the pope with the rule of the Bible. Both church and state were under the Bible, but the church held the right to interpret the Bible for the state. The Anabaptists of the Reformation era broke with the union between church and state which had been modeled by the Catholics throughout the medieval era and modified by the Reformers. Anabaptists insisted that the church was in antithesis to society and had no business making alignments with societal politics. The church was, they insisted, about the politics of Jesus, which put the church in conflict with society. The church, they argued, was a brotherhood, an alternative culture to the culture of the world.

In the modern era the church has become separated from state control in America and most other places around the world. However, the evangelical church has become an institution that has sought to fulfill its moral mission in the world through legislation and control and has functioned as the chaplain to society. Thus the church is present in civil ceremonies and orients itself toward patriotism in various ways such as celebrating Independence Day and Memorial Day and offering prayer at crucial historical moments such as the inauguration of presidents. The church has therefore lost its radical nature as a counterculture driven by the politics of Jesus and has made itself the watch dog for morality[4] and a chaplain to society.

Problems Inherited from the Enlightenment

The primary problem regarding the church in the world is the notion that the church works in the world through the political structure of government. The church, rather than being the politics of Jesus and his kingdom, becomes enslaved by worldly politics and compromises its true role in culture.[5]

This is an acute problem in the United States in particular. Conservative Christians are working hand in hand with the Republican Party to establish a Christian morality through Republican politics. On the other hand liberal Christians support the Democratic Party, hoping through their influence to establish justice and alleviate poverty. In both cases the unique nature of the church and its mission to the world is compromised. The church is not to complete its work in the world through worldly politics. The church is a political order of a different kind. It is to be about the politics of the kingdom—the politics of forming and nurturing a society in the world that images the new creation through forming a people with Christian virtues and a Christian view of life.

The second problem inherited from the Enlightenment is the failure to develop a redemption of creation. The more detailed emphasis on rationally proving or disproving the faith has resulted in the loss of the grand overview of the Christian faith that sees God's work in Jesus Christ as the restoration of the entire created order. For example, the "creationists," who insist on a literal seven-day act of creation, locate the battle with science on the wrong issue. By arguing for a scientifically based interpretation of Genesis they miss the point of the passage and fail to come to grips with the theological connection between creation and re-creation. The privatization of sin ignores how sin has permeated all the structures of society and the works of culture. The reduction of salvation to individualism fails to see that Christ will liberate the entire created order from its "bondage to decay." The spiritualization of the incarnation prevents a wrestling with the Christ event as the inauguration of a new beginning in history. An individualized view of the church stands in the way of understanding what it means to be the presence of new creation in the midst of the old.

There are several unfortunate results of this failure to come to grips with a biblical worldview that sweeps from creation to re-creation. First, it creates a split between the so-called secular and sacred aspects of life. Therefore, it is sacred to pray, to read the Bible, to witness, and to go to church. But work, play, and cultural activities are secular. This dichotomy is an "other-worldly–this-worldly" conflict. It fosters a superspirituality, a private ethic, a Christianity that can successfully withdraw from the conflicts of the world. It supports loving God with the "heart," but shrinks from loving God by actions in the social order or in the public aspects of life. Piety becomes exclusively private—something practiced at home, during quiet time, at church, or in the private decisions of life.

The second result of the failure to have a biblical worldview is a retreat from the cosmic battle in which the church is really engaged. Because Christ's death is cosmic, having to do with the whole of creation, the battle in which the church is now engaged in the period between Pentecost and the second coming must be one that *recalls* Christ's victory over sin through the resurrection and *anticipates* the consummation of his victory over evil in his return. This means that although evil permeates every area of life, the hope of the church is the reign of Christ in all of life. And the task of the church is to realize that reign in the life of the church.

In the postmodern world the place of the church in the world has become a matter of utmost importance due to the collapse of Christian values that have dominated Western society.

Charles Colson has called our attention not only to the collapse of Christian values, but to the far-reaching implications of this cultural shift. In *Against the Night* he rightly states, "The barbarians of the new dark age are pleasant and articulate men and women. They carry briefcases, not spears. But their assault on culture is every bit as devastating as the barbarian invasion of Rome. We have bred them in our families and trained them in our schools. Their ideas are persuasive and subtle, and very often they undermine the pillars upon which our civilization was founded."[6] In a response to the dissolution of objective truth Colson and others think we have entered a new "dark ages."[7]

We will not win the war of returning America to pre-postmodern values. Nor should we. Our goal is to focus on the church as a community of light, an alternative to a relativistic society.

The social and political work of evangelicals is countercultural. However, the calling of the church is not to "clean up America for God," but to be the church, a radical countercultural communal presence in society. The ultimate question is not "How is America?" but "How is the church?"[8]

Church and World in the Classical Era

While there is a considerable amount of commentary in the early Fathers on Christians and how they should relate to the world, none summarized it better than the anonymous author of the second-century *Epistle to Diognetus:*

For Christians cannot be distinguished from the rest of the human race by country or language or customs. They do not live in cities of their own;

they do not use a peculiar form of speech; they do not follow an eccentric manner of life . . . [they] follow the customs of the country in clothing and food and other matters of daily living. . . . They marry, like everyone else, and they beget children, but they do not cast out their offspring. They share their bread with each other, but not their marriage bed. It is true that they are "in the flesh," but they do not live "according to the flesh." They busy themselves on earth, but their citizenship is in heaven. . . . To put it simply: What the soul is in the body, the Christians are in the world.[9]

The essential teaching of the early church regarding how Christians live in the world is captured in this threefold tension: (1) the church is separate from the world; (2) the church is nevertheless identified with the world; and (3) the church seeks to transform the world. These three motifs are especially helpful to our understanding of the place of the church in the postmodern world.

The Church Is Separate from the World

The separation of the church from the world is rooted in those Scripture passages that stress the otherworldliness of the Christian life. Its Christ-model is the crucified Lord, the suffering servant, and the one whose power is in the weakness of the cross. Its ethos is that of a people who are "strangers and pilgrims in an alien land," a people who do good to all but "especially to those who are of the household of faith," a people who firmly believe that it is possible and indeed necessary to live by the Sermon on the Mount. Its patron saint is Peter, who reminds them that they are "a chosen race, a royal priesthood, a holy nation, God's own people" (1 Peter 2:9–10).

For all this Christians expect to suffer, to be misunderstood, to be reviled, to be persecuted for righteousness' sake. But that is not of ultimate importance because separationists look to the city "whose builder and maker is God." Furthermore, seeing that "all these things are to be dissolved" they concern themselves with "what sort of persons they ought to be in lives of holiness and godliness" (2 Peter 3:11).

One of the earliest Christian thinkers to espouse the separational model was Tertullian, the great third-century theologian of North Africa.[10] In his pre-Constantinian world, paganism permeated all of life. Consequently, Tertullian admonished Christians to shun much of life, especially any association with the Roman gods and lack of ethical values. The principle to derive from Tertullian is that Christianity is anti-establishment, and that it contains the seeds of a countercultural movement. The Christian community is a counterculture that stands *against the powers of evil wher-*

ever they may be found. Tertullian admonishes the Christian, "It is not asked who is ready to follow the broad way, but who the narrow."[11] Charles Colson expresses the same sentiment in these words: "The church is to be the community, reflecting God's passion for righteousness, justice and mercy. When we are that holy community, we make an impact on an unholy world, no matter how desperate the circumstances."[12]

The Church Is Identified with the World

The concept of identification stands in the tradition of Scripture that stresses the this-worldly character of the Christian faith. Its Christ-model is the incarnate Lord, the one who through living in the world can identify with the struggles and tensions of life. Its ethos revolves around Jesus who ate and drank with the "tax collectors and sinners," with the tension of Paul who, when he wanted to do right, found that "evil lies close at hand." Its concern is to affirm the abundant life declared by Jesus and recognized by Paul, who insisted that "all things are lawful." It wishes to "render unto Caesar those things that are Caesar's," to uphold the state, to pray for kings and emperors, and to admonish slaves and servants to be obedient to their masters.

The *Epistle to Diognetus* clearly states that Christians are not a revolutionary society attempting to overthrow the governments of the world. They are good, upright citizens going about the normal business of working, raising a family, and participating in those aspects of society that do not require a compromise with Christian values. Consequently, Hippolytus urges the Christian to "be zealous to perform good works, and to please God, living righteously, devoting himself to the church, performing the things which he has learnt, advancing in the service of God."[13]

The Church Seeks to Transform the World

The church as a transforming presence in the world stands in the tradition of those Scripture passages that emphasize the power of the gospel to change not only the life of an individual but also the life of culture. Its Christ-model is the resurrected Christ, who reigns in power and glory over the entire cosmos. Its ethos is based on the assertion that God was pleased to dwell in Christ "and through him to reconcile to himself all things, whether things on earth or things in heaven, by making peace through his blood shed on the cross" (Col. 1:20). Its vision is like that of the prophets who demanded, "let justice roll on like a river, righteousness like a never-failing stream" (Amos 5:24). Like Isaiah it sees that

169

"heaven is my throne, and the earth is my footstool. Where is the house that you will build me? Where will my resting place be? Has not my hand made all these things, so they came into being?" (Isa. 66:1–2). The church's responsibility on earth is to witness the transformation of the world so that "your will be done, on earth as it is in heaven" (Matt. 6:10) may become a reality.

One of the earliest figures to espouse the transformational model was Augustine who, in his vision of society, saw two cities existing side by side, the city of man under a secular rule and the city of God under a sacred rule.[14] Augustine saw Christ as the transformer of culture, and had a strong sense of the church as the city of God, or at least prefigured it in many ways. Christ, Augustine argued, had come to convert and redirect humanity, who, in turn, should influence culture to redirect, reshape, and transform the world to the glory of God. The author of the *Epistle to Diognetus* captured this theme in the statement, "What the soul is in the body, that Christians are in the world."

These three contrasts provide us with a key to the role of the church in a postmodern world. We are identified with the everyday pattern of existence, we create an alternative community, and, acting as the soul to the body, we generate a transforming presence in the world.

The Church in the Postmodern World

The church in a postmodern world must acknowledge the influence of the powers of evil. Recognizing that the powers act through political, social, and economic structures the church needs to take a stand against those powers that rule this world; the gods of materialism, sensualism, greed, war, hate, oppression, and injustice are no longer to rule the Christian. The church in a postmodern world brings the Christian into a new community and, as a new being, it teaches believers to live by the standards of the kingdom. The church is a community that does not embrace relativism, abortion, apartheid, pornography, drugs, and alcoholism. It is called to be a counterculture that witnesses to the politics of Jesus as it lives by the ethics of the kingdom. In brief, the church is an alternative society.

Nevertheless, the church recognizes the reality of belonging to the structures of existence. This world is not Satan's world. It is God's, and, as such, is the arena in which redemptive activity takes place. While the church in a postmodern world recognizes the sinful nature of humanity, it does not commit the error of identifying sin with physical nature or creatureliness. Therefore, like the people of the early church, Christians in a postmodern world will not reject the many basic customs of the general culture. They marry, bring children into the world, pursue education, work in industry, banking, health care, and the like. They are normal, life-pursuing people.

But the church in a postmodern world seeks to transform the world. It affirms the new order in the midst of the old. It calls the old to repentance and renewal. It recognizes that redeemed persons are to influence their culture by being a counterculture. This witness will result in more equitable economic patterns, more just laws, and less oppression and dehumanization.[15]

Those who believe in a Christian responsibility to the world are sensitive to their calling to be "salt" and "light." They want to witness not only privately but also publicly through their lives and the values they express in every situation. Like Christ, the church will identify with the world, speak prophetically to the world, and minister to the world in a priestly fashion. It will do so by recognizing that Jesus is Lord over all systems, ideologies, and institutions. In this way our confession that "Jesus is Lord" looks to the day when Christ will have put all evil away forever, the day when swords will be turned into plowshares, the day when the lion and the lamb will lie down together.

Consequently, the work of the church in the world, as in the early church, will be done with the ultimate vision of a restored universe in mind. The result is a new kind of activism motivated not only by *Christus Victor* but also by the vision of the recapitulation of all things in the new heavens and the new earth. And this activism will be primarily expressed in the church as an alternative culture that expresses the new corporate humanity that functions within the societies of the world.

Conclusion

I began this section by recalling the church and the barn in the mission compound where my parents served Christ in Africa. I suggested these two buildings symbolized the mission of the church, which is to evangelize, educate, and make an impact on the world. In the church of the postmodern era the sense of this threefold mission will need to include the following: In evangelism there will be an increasing shift away from mass rallies to evangelism by the local church. Believers will bring friends and neighbors to the church, where people will be brought into the church through conversion and baptism. The process of evangelism will be connected with worship, and the emphasis on education will be on gaining wisdom.

Finally, the church in the postmodern world will play a prophetic and priestly ministry in society. Believing that the gospel applies to every area of personal, social, moral, and national life, it will seek to exert an influence on society by being an alternative culture within society. Many congregations will recognize that the Christian vision of reality, informed by the politics of the kingdom, will keep the church free of particular political agendas so that it may speak to and serve the whole society as an alternative community.[16]

Consequently, the church around the world and in various denominations and cultures will be united through the sense of task. Thus, the sense of competition between the churches in their tasks of evangelism, education, and social action will decrease in proportion to their realization that there is only one Christ, one church, and one task. To borrow a phrase from Stanley Hauerwas, our concern should be "not only for the church that does exist but for the church that should exist."[17]

Table J: Evangelism within the Paradigms of History

Ancient	Medieval	Reformation	Modern	Postmodern
A process of incorporation into Christ through the church and adult baptism	Living into and out of infant baptism	Justification by faith	The "experience" of being born again Mass evangelism	A return to an evangelism that incorporates a person into Christ through baptism and in the context of community

The postmodern emphasis on community is a point of contact for an evangelical witness. However, much work needs to be done to wean evangelicals from modern individualism, to restore the communal nature of the church, and to develop a process by which the converting person is incorporated into Christ and the church.

Table K: The Seven Steps of Evangelism and Nurture in the Early Church

Seeker	Rite of Welcome	Hearer	Rite of Election	Kneeler	Baptism	Faithful
A time for pre-evangelism and the awakening of faith	A *preliminal* rite of separation from sin	A time for the study of the Christian faith: orthodoxy and orthopraxis	A *liminal* rite of transition toward full participation in the church	A period of intense spiritual preparation for baptism	A *postliminal* rite that completes the process of conversion through the ritual of baptism and the anointing of oil—the rite of *incorporation*	Continues to explore the responsibilities of the new Christian and unpacks the mystery of the Eucharist

172

Table L: Education within the Paradigms of History

Ancient and Medieval	Reformation and Modern	Postmodern
Immersed participation in the event of worship, baptism, Eucharist, Christian year, visual	Shift to education through print	Shift back to "immersed participation" with a new emphasis on the audio-visual experience
	Introduction of catechism, Sunday school, intellectual verbal communication of faith	

Table M: The Church in the World within the Paradigms of History

Ancient	Medieval	Reformation	Modern	Postmodern
Antithesis; identification; transformation	Transformation; the emergence of Christendom	Luther and Calvin: continuation of Christendom idea but under the word, not the pope and territorial, not universal	Church achieves its mission in the world through collusion with government	Return to church as antithesis to evil, yet identified with culture, making a transforming impact on culture by its very existence as a counter-culture community
		Anabaptist: church in antithesis		

A CLASSICAL/POSTMODERN AUTHORITY

> Get the Apostolic epistles for your constant
> teachers . . . dive into them as into a chest of
> medicines . . . keep them in your mind.
> —St. John Chrysostom, A.D. 380

> All possible care must be taken, that we
> hold that faith which has been believed
> everywhere, always, by all.
> —Vincent of Lerins, A.D. 450

I live in Wheaton, Illinois, a place that many people jokingly call the "evangelical Vatican." The presence of Wheaton College with its large administration, faculty, and staff as well as numerous Christian organizations such as *Christianity Today* and Tyndale House Publishers means that there is a decided Christian influence in this town.

It's nearly impossible to sit in a local restaurant without overhearing a conversation about the church or shop locally without bumping into a fellow Christian or drive a few blocks without passing a church. Christians are in every area of life—doctors, dentists, lawyers, artists, grocers, store managers, and laborers.

For example, my dentist is a Christian. Recently, I was sitting in his dental chair with my mouth packed with the usual equipment while he drilled away at a tooth in need of attention. As usual, he was carrying on a monologue with me, a monologue that I desperately wanted to turn into a dialogue. But under the circumstances I could only grunt a few incoherent sounds, wag my head, or flutter my eyes.

Usually, the subject of the monologue isn't dealing with ultimate realities. But on this occasion my dentist was giving his opinions about theology and theologians, an opinion that is probably shared by many.

"Well, Bob," my dentist said, "I'll tell you something about you guys who teach Bible and theology." My ears pricked up, wondering what he was going to say. "I don't think you have any better understanding of truth than I do," he blurted out. Since I couldn't respond, I sat helplessly silent as he continued. "You fellows learn all that Greek and Hebrew; you study the background to the Old and New Testaments; you read all that theology; but I tell you that I think I know just as much as you do. I pick up the English text of the Bible and God reveals the same truth to me directly."

Unfortunately, I'm one of those persons who comes up with a great response about two hours after the fact. So, after my dentist was finished with his discourse on theology and my tooth was restored, I politely paid my bill and left. But I kept thinking about what he had said. My thoughts shifted back and forth between amusement and the urge to give him an appropriate response. Finally the answer came.

I wish I had said to him, "Well, I agree with you. God indeed reveals the truth to all of us. Now, why don't you sit in the chair and hand me your drill. I don't need an education in dentistry, I'll just let the Lord guide my hand and tell me what to do. I'm sure your teeth will be fine. I can do dentistry just as well as you can, so long as I depend on God."

Of course the analogy breaks down, because all Christians are, in a sense, armchair theologians, while not all Christians are armchair dentists. Nevertheless, the point is clear. I wouldn't dare do dentistry, because I have neither an education nor a skill in that area. In other words I have no authority in that field.

Authority is a major question of every field of human thought and work. We depend on authorities not only in dentistry and the medical profession in general, but also in science, technology, foreign affairs, and many other spheres of life.

However, postmodernism is by its very nature an assault against the idea of a single, all-encompassing authority. Charles Jencks clearly makes this point: "Post-modernism means the end of a single world view and, by extension, a war on totality, a resistance to single explanations, a respect for difference and a celebration of the regional, local and particular."[1] This more relativistic approach needs to be taken by evangelicals toward Catholic, Orthodox, and other Christians, but breaks down when it comes to an acceptance of the cults or other religions of the world.

Because this is such an important issue, I want to end this book with a discussion of the development of authority in the early church. Early

Christians lived in a highly pluralistic world like ours. It was no more popular in the early church to make Christianity exclusive than it is today. In the Roman world, there were numerous religions, each of which was tolerated as long as they were willing to confess Caesar as Lord. The Christian faith confessed Jesus alone as Lord. In the post-modern world tolerance of all religions is sacrosanct. Any suggestion that Christianity is a universal faith, and not just one of the many faiths, requires a new apologetic. Because the early church forged out its apologetic in a pluralistic world, its approach may very well be beneficial to an evangelical apologetic in the postmodern world.

Authority within the Paradigms of History

Authority in the early church is located in the apostles. These original interpreters of the faith passed the faith down through oral preaching and teaching, through the written gospel accounts and letters, and through the appointment of their successors, the bishops. Consequently, apostolic tradition and succession emerged in the late second century as the apologetic for the preservation and the handing down of truth. About the same time the "rule of faith" emerged in cities all over the empire. This "rule" was regarded as a summary of the salient features of the Christian faith, a framework for the essential truths confessed by those who stood in the tradition of apostolic teachings. During this time the writings of the apostles were collected and affirmed as authoritative by the Council of Carthage in A.D. 457. These books had been recognized over a long period of time and affirmed in the church because of their apostolic origins (either written by an apostle or under the authority of an apostle) and because of *consensus fideum*, their acceptance in worship by the faithful.[2]

Once the canon of Scripture had been declared, the church began its search for an authoritative interpretation. There were three schools of interpretation: the literalists from the Antiochene school, who used the grammatical-historical and theological method; the allegorists from the Alexandrian school of thought, who looked for a literal, moral, and spiritual meaning in each passage; and the typologists, who represented the approach of most church fathers. The typologists emphasized the types and shadows of the Old Testament that were fulfilled in the New Testament, particularly those that clustered around the exodus event as a type of the Christ event. Then, in A.D. 450, Vincent of Lérins suggested in his *Commonitory* that those interpretations are valid that meet the criteria of antiquity, universality, and consensus: the classical view of authority was established—apostolic authority expressed in the rule of faith, in the apostolic writings, and in the interpretation that was characterized by antiquity, universality, and consensus.[3]

Authority in the early medieval era, like in the ancient church, was rooted in the apostolic tradition and succession. Their understanding of the authoritative sources of truth did not separate church, tradition, Scripture, and interpretation into a series of categories with one taking preference over the other. Instead, they viewed authority in a somewhat ambiguous but dynamic way. Any writing of a Father of the church, or any council or assembly of the church that stood in the apostolic tradition, was an extension of the principle of inspiration. Therefore, while the apostles were the original authority in the church, a writing of Augustine or another Father of the church, or a creed or council that extended or expounded an idea in keeping with apostolic teaching enjoyed a kind of apostolic authority. Because the church was viewed as the one true interpreter of the faith, the authority of the church grew greater and greater through time as more and more Fathers and councils were regarded as espousing teachings in line with the apostles. Finally, the church established a magisterium for the proper interpretation of truth and positioned the pope as the true spokesperson of truth. This idea reached its zenith in Pope Boniface VIII (1303), who declared that to be saved one needed to be under the pope's authority. His *Unam Sanctum* turned out to be a turning point in medieval authority. The idea of papal authority was the subject of much discussion for the next two hundred years. Various alternatives were proposed, such as the authority of a council, the authority of tradition, the authority of Scripture, or the authority of Scripture and tradition.[4]

The debate of the fourteenth and fifteenth centuries paved the way for the Reformers who chose the doctrine of *sola scriptura*. The Reformers pulled Scripture away from the church, separated it from tradition, set it over against popes and councils, and made it stand on its own. However, the Reformers began another cycle of tradition within their churches (Lutheran, Reformed, Anglican) in which the Reformers themselves were viewed as authoritative interpreters of Scripture. Each Reformation tradition was marked by a particular confession that functioned in an authoritative consensus on the teaching of Scripture. Thus confessionalism was born: the Lutherans wrote the Augsburg Confession of faith; the Presbyterians, the Westminster Confession; the Anglicans, the Thirty-Nine Articles; the Anabaptists, the Schleitheim Confession of faith. These confessions functioned as the "Authoritative Rule" for the interpretation of faith in each confessing tradition. Consequently, the various Protestant traditions defined themselves by the differences that existed between them as opposed to the unity underlying their various confessions.[5]

The modern era of authority reflects the rationalism and individualism of the period. The rise of rationalism in the hands of modern liberals relocated authority from Scripture to reason. Consequently, Scripture was removed from its context in the church and tradition. Scripture was subjected to a critical analysis of its origins and its distinctive character as the Word of God was lost. Conservatives continued to affirm the authority of the Bible, but defended its apostolic origins and truthfulness through reason and evidential apologetics.[6]

A dispute also arose over the value of the various creeds and confessions of the church. The liberals dismissed the creeds and confessions as pious expressions of a believer's experience with God and argued they have no correspondence with reality (what Lindbeck calls the "Experiential-Expressive" model). On the other hand, the conservatives argued that creeds and confessions were to be understood literally as corresponding exactly with the reality they represent (what Lindbeck calls "Propositionalism"). By the end of the modern era liberals and conservatives were locked into a hopeless debate with no way out because of their commitment to the rationalist method. The liberals' "mythical" view of Scripture and doctrine and the conservatives' "propositionalism" view of Scripture and doctrine remain at an impasse.[7]

In the postmodern world the impasse between liberals and evangelicals will be broken as both abandon rationalism for a canonical reading of Scripture. This postcritical approach to Scripture will allow it to be read as a narrative rooted in God's inspiration and recognized by the communal authority of the church. Likewise, the issue over the validity of the creeds will fall into the background as liberals and evangelicals find common ground in the "cultural linguistic" model suggested by Lindbeck.

The Problem of Authority Inherited from the Enlightenment

The primary problem inherited from the Enlightenment for both liberals and evangelicals is the authority given to reason. Rationalism shows up in two areas: the authority of reason over Scripture; and the authority of reason over the creeds of the church and theology in general.[8]

THE AUTHORITY OF REASON OVER SCRIPTURE

Throughout the history of the church, Scripture has always been regarded as the inspired and revealed Word of God. Therefore, its trustworthiness has been an assumed rather than debated aspect of faith. However, the Enlightenment with its emphasis on truth as known through reason rather than faith introduced a watershed event in the attitude toward Scripture. Modernity reversed the dominant and long-standing principle that faith precedes understanding and taught that understanding precedes faith. Christians now asked, "How do we know the Bible is true?" This question introduced the critical method of biblical studies, which investigated Scripture for its origin in the primitive communities of faith.[9]

The liberal insistence that the Bible emerged from various schools of thought, that it is full of contradictions, that much of it was written at a later time and was redacted into the text, and that it was mythical wherever it touched on the supernatural, eroded confidence in Scripture as the Word of God. On the other hand, the conservative and evangelical attempt to develop a response to biblical criticism never succeeded in answering the issues and resulted in a distancing of Scripture from experience. The evangelical insistence on discovering authorial intent made the reading of Scripture suspect by the lay person and placed the authority of Scripture in the work of the scholars who had allegedly recovered the intention of the author.

The lay person was put under the burden of reading the Bible with an open commentary written by an evangelical scholar who rightly attested to the meaning of Scripture. The Bible, removed from a subjective experience of the Spirit, became instead an objective book to be studied quite apart from subjective experience. The problem of the Bible as a book of objective knowledge that can be determined by reason is the issue that postliberals and postconservatives seek to address in our postmodern world.[10]

THE AUTHORITY OF REASON OVER CREEDS AND CONFESSIONS

A second problem inherited from the Enlightenment is the liberal and conservative attitude toward the creeds. Until the modern era the creeds were accepted as authoritative rules of faith. They defined the perimeters of our thinking about the faith in general (the Apostles' Creed), the Trinity (Nicene Creed), and Christology (Chalcedon Creed) in particular. These creeds, being attested by antiquity, universality, and consensus, were included in the confession of Reformation Christianity.[11]

Liberals placed the creeds and confessions under the authority of reason. They argued against any regulative authority of the creeds by dis-
missing them as statements of faith reflecting a Hellenistic worldview.
They concluded that creeds have no authority in the church and are to
be dismissed as curious theological reflections of a bygone era. On the
other hand Reformational evangelicals held fast to their particular confession as a universal standard of doctrinal truth over against the confession of other reformational groups. The conflict of authority continued among Calvinists, Lutherans, Arminians, Anabaptists, and others,
as each asserted they had the right interpretation.

Evangelicals who are not rooted in any creedal tradition tended to
dismiss the creeds in favor of a biblicism. They argue that Scripture
alone is the source of all Christian knowledge and that the creeds of the
church are of little, if any, value.

These are the problems that must be addressed in a postmodern world
by both postliberal and postconservative thinkers. How are we to read
the Bible in a postcritical era? What attitude should we adopt toward
creeds and confessions in a postdenominational era? We will explore
these issues as we look at the authoritative source of truth, the authoritative rule of faith, the authority of Scripture, and the quest for an
authoritative interpretation (see table N).

The Authoritative Source of Truth

One of the major fears people have about the early church movement
is expressed in the question: Do those who are returning to the early
church elevate tradition over Scripture? This question cannot be
answered without looking at the biblical view of tradition.[12] The original meaning of the word *tradition* is a key to understanding the relationship between Scripture and tradition. The Greek word *paradosis* is
used throughout the New Testament to mean "hand over" (see, for example, Matt. 25:14; Luke 4:6; Acts 15:26, 40; 16:4; 1 Cor. 15:24; Eph. 4:19;
5:2). In terms of Christian belief it is used by Paul when he directed the
Thessalonians to retain hold of the "traditions" that he had taught them
by word or pen (2 Thess. 2:15) and it refers to the faith summary (1 Cor.
11:2, 23; 15:3) he had "handed over" to the Corinthians. Further, according to Luke, original eyewitnesses had "handed over" information to
him (Luke 1:2); according to Jude, the faith could be described as that
which had been "handed over" to the saints. Finally, the notion of "handing over" the faith through the centuries was expressed by Paul when
he admonished Timothy to "hand over" the tradition of faith he had

received from Paul's teaching (2 Tim. 2:2). This sense of "handing over" the truth which had been passed down from the apostles became prominent in the second-century battle with the gnostics. It accounts for the development of the earliest form of apostolic tradition and succession among the early church fathers. Here, for example, is a telling quote from Tertullian (c. A.D. 200):

> the ruling which we lay down; that since Jesus Christ
> sent out the Apostles to preach, no others are to be
> accepted as preachers but those whom Christ appointed. . . .
> Now the substance of their preaching, that is, Christ's
> revelation to them, must be approved, on my ruling, only
> through the testimony of those churches which the Apostles
> founded by preaching to them both *viva voce* and afterwards
> by their letters. If this is so, it is likewise clear that all doctrine
> which accords with these apostolic churches, the sources and
> origins of the faith, must be reckoned as truth, since it maintains
> without doubt what the churches received from the Apostles, the
> Apostles from Christ, and Christ from God. . . . We are in communion
> with the apostolic churches because there is no differences of
> doctrine. This is our guarantee of truth.[13]

In doing a postmodern apologetic, it is important to develop a phenomenological description of the way in which a Christian truth or practice may have developed in the primitive Christian community and on into the second century and beyond. Part of the apologetic task is to reconstruct this development in search of the apostolic faith and practice which was "handed over" to the next generation. In broad strokes the unfolding of authority may be outlined as follows:

1. The authority of the Christian faith is the revelation of God in Jesus Christ.
2. The church was given the responsibility of handing Jesus Christ over from generation to generation.
3. The apostles were faced with the immediate responsibility of interpreting Christ and handing down the truth about Jesus accurately.
4. The context in which Jesus was interpreted was in the worship of the church. The primitive Christian hymns, creeds, doxologies, benedictions, catechetical literature, and apostolic interpretations contained the recognized apostolic traditions (liturgical epistemology).
5. The Scriptures were written for the church and were to be read in worship. They contain the authoritative accounts of Christ

together with the apostolic interpretation of Christ. Thus, Scripture is tradition; that is, it hands over Jesus Christ.

6. Summaries of faith such as the rule of faith and the ecumenical creeds are more specific reflections on apostolic teaching and practice. The church fathers were not creating something new. Rather, they were writing summaries of the faith that were true to the apostolic interpretation. Athanasius summarized the process: "The actual original tradition, teaching, and faith of the Catholic church, which the Lord conferred, the apostles proclaimed, and the Fathers guarded."[14]

What may be observed here is a process of the development of authority within the developing tradition of the church. Jesus Christ the ultimate authority is authoritatively interpreted by the apostles. The Bible is authoritative because it preserves and hands down this witness. The rule of faith and the creeds enjoy a kind of authority because they remain faithful to the apostolic tradition. The Holy Spirit "oversaw" this process so we can speak of Scripture as the revealed and inspired Word of God and the ecumenical creeds as authoritative summaries of the biblical faith.[15]

The Authoritative Rule of Faith

The faith of the church, from the earliest times, has been characterized by a specific content. It is a recognizable body of truth. What was true in the New Testament period was equally true in the second century. The picture of the church at the end of the second century is that of a number of churches clustered around the major cities of Rome, Carthage, Alexandria, Jerusalem, and Antioch united under their bishops, similar in worship, and grounded in the teachings of the apostles as summarized in the "rule of faith." Hegesippus, a church historian, part of whose work is preserved in Eusebius's *Ecclesiastical History*, made a trip from Jerusalem to Rome and found that "in every succession . . . and in every city, the doctrine prevails according to what is declared by the law and the prophets and the Lord."[16]

The doctrine which Hegesippus referred to was not something that was the private possession of a few scholars. Instead, his reference was to the contents of apostolic preaching, to the *rule of faith*, to the summary of Christian teaching that had been passed down from the apostles.

This summary of the Christian faith that emerged with clarity in the second century is not theology but what we can aptly term "a biblical framework of thought." That is to say, the contents of biblical or historic Christianity set forth the necessary presuppositions from which Christian thinking proceeds. Consequently, the content of the rule of faith was a summary of revelation: the apostles had summarized the essence of revelation and had passed it on. This "biblical framework" defined the perimeters within which the Christian church did its thinking. It was the *regula fidei* (regulation for faith).[17]

The Origin of the Rule of Faith

Christianity had already begun to be tested in the New Testament period by Judaism and esoteric religious ideas from Egypt and Persia. The acid test of the substance of its faith came, however, when the gnostics began to claim to have a superior knowledge handed down in a secret tradition. This knowledge, while it varied somewhat from sect to sect, basically taught the existence of two Gods—the Spirit God who was responsible for the good and the Creator God (often identified with Yahweh in the Old Testament) who was responsible for evil.

Because the evil God was the creator, matter was regarded as evil. Naturally then, the human body was looked upon as the prison of a person's soul. Salvation was the release of the soul from the body so it could ultimately unite with the good Spirit God. To accomplish this, the spirit God sent Christ, an emanation, to bring knowledge *(gnosis)* that would free the soul from the body. This knowledge, which Christ gave to the disciples, the gnostics declared, was what one needed to know to be saved[18] (see table O).

It is obvious that the teaching of the gnostics was diametrically opposed to apostolic teaching. What was needed therefore to combat this perversion of Christian truth was a summary of the Christian faith, an authoritative answer to the gnostic threat. Consequently, summaries of apostolic Christianity began to emerge independently of one another in various parts of the Roman Empire. The similarity of content among these statements, which came to be known as "rules of faith," is remarkable. Here is the rule of faith written by Tertullian about A.D. 200:

We believe one only God. . . , who has a Son, his Word,
who proceeded from himself, by whom all things were
made; he was sent by the Father into a virgin, and was
born of her, man and God, Son of man and Son of God,
named Jesus Christ; he suffered, died, was buried, according
to the Scriptures; was raised again by the Father; and taken
back to heaven; and sits at the Father's right hand; who
will come to judge living and dead; who thereafter, according
to his promises, has sent from the Father the Holy Spirit, the

Paraclete, the sanctifier of the faith of those who believe in the Father, the Son and the Holy Spirit.[19]

The issue that the gnostics had raised by their teachings was simply this: What is the substance of Christian teachings? And the second-century church responded with a resounding affirmation of the faith that came from the apostles.

It is important to recognize that the existence of these rules of faith represents a strong case that the substance of the church's belief and teaching was widely understood in the second century. Theologians like Irenaeus and Tertullian did not pull their doctrine out of the air or invent a counter-doctrine to the gnostic point of view. Irenaeus stated that his doctrine was no novelty, that it was, in fact, widely known, received, and confessed throughout the church universal:

> As I have already observed, the Church, having received this preaching and this faith, although scattered throughout the whole world, yet, as if occupying but one house, carefully preserves it. She also believes these points (of doctrine) just as if she had but one soul, and one and the same heart, and she proclaims them, and teaches them, and hands them down, with perfect harmony, as if she possessed only one mouth. For, although the languages of the world are dissimilar, yet the import of the tradition is one and the same.[20]

In summary, then, by the end of the second century the church had an *authoritative source* and an *authoritative summary* of what the church believed and taught. The authoritative source was the apostles. They had received their message from Christ and passed it on in the church. Both the oral and written traditions of the apostles, which they had transmitted to the church and which the church had received and guarded and passed on, were the authoritative "rule of faith." This rule was regarded as key to the interpretation of the Christian faith, a framework of thought for all to follow. Eventually, the rule of faith became universally summarized in the Apostles' Creed.

The "Rule of Faith" in a Postmodern World

In today's postmodern and postcritical Christianity, Christian leaders are searching for a faith that is common to the whole church. The "rule of faith" in the early church holds out the promise of a framework of faith for the church in a postmodern world. It is a rule that functions for us in what Lindbeck refers to as those "communally authoritative rules of discourse, attitude and action."[21]

In modernity we always sought for truth that could be somehow verified outside the community of faith. Lindbeck refers to this quest as "extratextual." That is, using reason and logic we expected to prove that the framework of faith could be demonstrated to be true through historical or scientific research. Both liberals and conservatives wanted statements of faith to have a proven correspondence with reality.[22]

This led liberals to the process of demythologizing Christian doctrine and relegating doctrines to pious experiential expressions of faith. On the other hand, conservatives attempted to prove the factual nature of their doctrines through evidential apologetics and argued for propositions of faith.

Lindbeck identifies the ancient *regula fidei* as "intratextual."[23] That is, it makes sense within its own story. Its sense is not determined by outside factors, but by the system of thought it intends to communicate. The point is that Christianity is not provable outside itself through the scientific method. One must come to the Christian faith believing that it is true and embrace it as such without any dependence on data outside the faith. Christianity requires trust, a believing embrace, a willingness to step inside its story apart from any dependence on historical, scientific, or rational persuasion. Once a person steps into the stream of faith, the community introduces that person to the rules of discussion. The rule of faith is the rule, the perimeter within which the community talks about its belief system. What stands at the very center of Christian faith is Jesus Christ, God incarnate for our salvation. This conviction regulates all discussions of faith and functions as the primary rule of the Christian community. For this rule derives not from human invention, but from the inspiration of the Holy Spirit given to the apostles who have handed these truths down to the church. Because the rule of faith was formed at the same time that the apostolic writings were being collected, it precedes the scriptural canon in time and functions as the key to the interpretation of Scripture. Anyone, for example, who espouses a doctrine that conflicts with the rule of faith, misinterprets Scripture.

The Authoritative Writings

Because the church regarded the apostles as authoritative interpreters of the Christian faith, the oral and written teachings of the apostles were regarded with an enormous amount of respect. From the very beginning of the Christian faith, the Fathers always wanted to know what the apostles taught. Justin, for example, speaks of "following God and the teaching derived from Him."[24] Athanasius wrote "the actual original tradition, teaching and faith of the catholic church, which the Lord bestowed, the apostles proclaimed, and the fathers safeguard."[25]

As we have seen, this teaching derived from Jesus was entrusted to the apostles, who preserved it in both oral tradition (especially in the liturgy) and writing (meant to be read in the liturgical assembly). For this reason the number of citations from the apostles contained in the writings of the Fathers is impressive. Scripture was never separated from oral tradition as if the apostles had two mouths. Both the oral and the written tradition came from the same source and were not perceived as contradictory. The oral tradition was primarily the interpretation of Jesus summarized in the "rule of faith." This rule stands behind the more precisely developed creeds of the church such as the Apostles' Creed, the Nicene Creed, and the Chalcedon Creed. Because the interpretation of Scripture was influenced by the presuppositions brought to it, the early church fathers insisted that the outline of Christian truth regarding God, creation, the fall, incarnation, and re-creation found in the rule of faith was the key to apostolic interpretation.

Therefore, apostolic epistemology includes the oral tradition, reflected in the liturgy and in the rule of faith, and the written tradition, in which the liturgy and the rule are embedded. To separate these sources of authority from one another is a mistake. The liturgy celebrates the apostolic tradition; the Scriptures are the authoritative apostolic writings. There is one truth, Jesus Christ, one source of truthful interpretation, the apostles. The work of the church is to preserve and hand down this apostolic witness. In this sense, Scripture, tradition, and authority are not three distinct subjects, but the intertwining of the grand tapestry of faith rooted in Christ and the authority of apostolic interpretation.[26]

Beginnings of Canonical Authority

The conflict of the church with Marcion resulted in a clearer understanding of the authoritative writings.[27] Although Marcion, who came to Rome around A.D. 140, was influenced by gnosticism, it is not entirely correct to call him a gnostic. He rejected the basic gnostic myths about the aeons that had supposedly come forth from an original divine being. But he accepted the gnostic premise that the Old Testament was the product of an inferior God.

Irenaeus informs us that Marcion accepted the teaching of Cerdo, a gnostic whose chief doctrine was that "the God proclaimed by the law and the prophets was not the Father of our Lord Jesus Christ."[28] For this reason Marcion wanted to rid the church of any connection with the

Old Testament or Jewish practices. The issue Marcion raised was simply this: Does the Old Testament belong to the Christian tradition?

The answer to that question was determined by the tradition that had already been established by the apostles. The apostles understood the Jewish past in terms of Christ's coming. This is evident in their attitude toward the Old Testament. They regarded the Law and the Prophets as well as the events and worship of Israel as part of the Christian tradition because they believed them to testify to Jesus Christ. Paul, for example, in 1 Corinthians 15:3–4, insisted that everything regarding Christ took place "according to the Scriptures."

Soon, a typological interpretation of the Old Testament as reflected in the Book of Hebrews became a standard way of interpreting the Hebrew Scriptures in the church. This is evident in the so-called *Epistle of Barnabas,* written around A.D. 135 in Alexandria, Egypt, in which the author wrote: "The prophets, having obtained grace from Him, prophesied concerning Him."[29] In the *Homily on the Passover* by Melito of Sardis, written around A.D. 170, Melito's explanation of the paschal lamb in Exodus 12 is that it typologically points to Christ, the true Paschal Lamb.[30] And Justin Martyr in his *Dialogue with Trypho the Jew* argued that the entire Old Testament points to Jesus Christ.[31] Therefore, the Old Testament Scriptures were regarded as the Scriptures of the New Testament church because the apostles had received this precedent from Jesus.

Marcion's opposition to the Old Testament and his concern that Christians were too Jewish led him to form his own canon. He took the Gospel of Luke and the Epistles of Paul, with the exception of those written to Timothy and Titus, and edited out everything that came from the Old Testament. As Irenaeus wrote:

> He dismembered the Epistles of Paul, removing all that is said by the apostle respecting that God who made the world, to the effect that he is the Father of our Lord Jesus Christ, and also those passages from the prophetical writings which the apostle quotes, in order to teach us that they announced beforehand the coming of the Lord.[32]

Marcion was convinced that Paul's doctrine of grace stood in absolute antithesis to the Old Testament. He saw the Old Testament God as just, vengeful, and demanding. Salvation in the Old Testament was by Law, keeping the commands, and doing good. But the New Testament God was loving and kind, practicing mercy and forgiveness, giving salvation in Christ, and making no demands.

187

Consequently, Marcion would have nothing to do with the Old Testament. For him, it represented another God, another salvation, another way of life. His conviction was that if Christianity continued to mix with the doctrines of this inferior religion, it would lose its distinctiveness.

Marcion's attitude toward the Old Testament and his deconstruction of the apostolic writings created a crucial situation for the young church. For one thing, the apostles themselves had already set a precedent by interpreting the Old Testament through the death and resurrection of Christ. Were they right? The second-century church had already received the writings of the apostles as authoritative. Was the church right in doing so?

As a result of these issues, the young church was motivated to clarify the *authoritative writings* of Christian teaching. Before the end of the second century the church affirmed the Old Testament, the four Gospels, and the letters of Paul as authoritative in their entirety. (The canonicity of some of the Catholic Epistles and the Book of Revelation remained controversial for some time.)[33]

The first collection of the New Testament canonical books as we have them today was listed by Athanasius's Easter letter for the year 367. But, "the process was not everywhere complete until at least a century and a half later."[34] The church witnessed to the apostolic norm as authoritative. For example, the attitude toward the apostolic writings is clearly seen in the literature of the early church. For example, Clement, bishop of Rome in A.D. 96, wrote: "The Apostles have preached the gospel to us from the Lord Jesus Christ; Jesus Christ (has done so) from God. Christ therefore was sent forth by God and the Apostles by Christ."[35] Irenaeus tells us that Polycarp "always taught the things which he had learned from the Apostles, which the church has handed down, and which alone are true."[36] H. E. W. Turner, in *The Pattern of Christian Truth,* has successfully demonstrated the reverence of the Fathers toward Holy Scripture. They were not, as Adolf von Harnack once suggested, metaphysical theologians but *biblical* theologians. Any reading of Justin Martyr, Irenaeus, Tertullian, Clement, Origen, Athanasius, Basil, Jerome, or Augustine shows that the Fathers are steeped in the Scriptures and that they agree with the judgment of Saint John Chrysostom:

> Tarry not, I entreat, for another to teach thee; thou hast the oracles of God. No man teacheth thee as they; for he indeed oft grudgeth much for vainglory's sake and envy. Hearken, I entreat you, all ye that are careful for this life, and procure books that will be medicines for the soul. If ye will not any other, yet get you at least the New Testament, the *Apostolic Epistles* [italics mine], the Acts, the Gospels, for your constant teachers. If grief befall thee, dive into them as into a chest of medicines; take thence com-

fort of thy trouble, be it loss, or death, or bereavement of relations; or rather dive not into them merely, but take them wholly to thee; keep them in thy mind.[37]

Scripture in the Postmodern Church: The Church's Book

Throughout this book I have attempted to demonstrate that the tapestry of faith begins with the person and work of Christ. I have tried to make it clear that we trust in Christ for our salvation. Christ, the Word, became incarnate, died, and rose again to destroy the power of the evil one and to renew the world. This principle is the *regula fidei*, the controlling rule of our approach toward Scripture.

In some circles, faith in Christ appears to be replaced by faith in the Bible. To make this point I sometimes say to my students, "You would think the Bible became incarnate, was crucified, and rose again for our salvation." By this statement I do not intend to demean the Bible. Instead, I want to put the Bible in its proper place. It is not the object of our faith or belief. We do not believe in the Bible for our salvation. We believe in Christ.

A new feature of evangelicals in the postmodern world is the growing awareness that the Bible, which takes us to Christ, belongs to the church. The church preceded Scripture in time. The writings of the apostles were intended for the church. Therefore, Scripture is the church's tradition, the possession of the church, and as such, the church is responsible to guard it, preserve it, pass it down, and interpret it. Here then lies the apologetic for Christianity in a postmodern world. It is not the Bible standing alone, but Scripture as the product of apostolic interpretation handed down in the church for generations.[38]

One of the major problems for postmodern evangelicals is to find a way to affirm the claim to Christian truth. In the past the claim has been made on the authority of Scripture alone. However, in the modern era biblical criticism has eroded the authority of Scripture. Instead of rational arguments, the postmodern will turn to tradition and continuity.[39] Consequently, the authority of Scripture will be best served by putting it back into its historical setting in the church, in its apostolic origin in both the oral and written tradition that resulted in the canon and its summary in the rule of faith. This is the received tradition, the archives of historic Christianity which cannot be violated and must be maintained to preserve the integrity of the Christian faith. This is the kind of language and imagery that will speak authentically in the postmodern world.[40]

189

This postcritical reading of the text holds a greater affinity to the Bible of precritical times than it has to the critical reading of the text by both the liberals and conservatives of modernity. A postcritical reading of the text approaches Scripture with the realization that it is God who formed the canon and the church who recognized its formation. Consequently, the text is read theologically. The ultimate meaning of the text is not found in its historical origins but in its theological meaning. We want to know how this book, this passage, this verse has been used in the history of the church. What is its life-giving element? How has it formed the people of God and transformed their lives from one age to the next? In this approach to the Bible we are allowing the original presentation to cross into the horizons of other paradigms. Drawing from Hans Georg Gadamer's "fusion of horizons" we recognize that each generation of readers will bring their own presuppositions, their own cultural formation, and their own issues to the text. How has God spoken to the church through the text in each paradigm of history? in times of suffering? in times of plenty? in times of glory? This is what we want to know as we put ourselves under the text and allow the text to speak to us and from us in our time and place and in our condition of life. This kind of reading is consistent with the "canonical intentionality" of Paul Ricoeur which, as Charles Scalise has stated, "points to the theologically authoritative shape of scripture through which God has spoken and continues to speak to the lives of those who listen to the word of God."[41]

I am reminded of an example of this kind of thinking that occurred a number of years ago. Michael Ramsey, the hundredth archbishop of Canterbury and a well-known figure worldwide, was being interviewed on the Johnny Carson "Late Night Show." As soon as he was introduced and sat in the chair near the host of the show, the person who had been interviewed previously blurted out, "You know what I don't like about your religion?" Looking somewhat stunned, the archbishop turned and asked "What?" "I don't like your exclusiveness. You say Christ is the only way to God." "Oh, oh," I thought. "How's the archbishop going to respond to *this* one?" The archbishop, without any defensiveness in his body language or voice, simply said, "Well, really, I never said that. Jesus was the one who made that claim. As a Christian I work with the documents of the faith handed down in the church. I'm not really free to disagree or reinterpret Jesus. I am committed as his follower to teach what he has taught."[42]

In a postmodern world this is the answer that will speak to the claims of Christ. We will have to learn to trust more in the work of the Holy Spirit to make this truth claim real and trust less in our attempts to either reexplain or argue rationally for its rightness.

We turn now to the next set of problems we have inherited from the past: the claim of this or that group to have an extensive and all encompassing authoritative interpretation of the apostolic interpretation—the only right theology.

Quest for an Authoritative Interpretation

Early Christians were familiar with such terms as *belief, doctrine,* and *confession* but not with the term *theology.* Theology comes from the Greek word *theologia* and means *study of God.* But it was not used by the church as a technical term until the eleventh century, when Abelard used it to apply to the whole of Christian teaching. However, it was primarily Thomas Aquinas in the thirteenth century who worked out a theory of theology as a science of revealed truths. Ever since Aquinas, the term has been used to refer to the analysis, application, and presentation of Christian beliefs, doctrines, and confessions.

Today we can use the word *theology* in an inclusive or exclusive way. We can speak of the common theology of the church expressed in the universally accepted creeds, or we can use the term in an exclusive manner and speak of the theology of Calvin, Luther, Arminius, or our local pastor. Therefore, as we approach the quest to find an authoritative theology, it will be helpful for us to make distinctions among "the faith of the church," a "creed," a "confession," and a "personal conviction."

The phrase "faith of the church" is not being used here in the sense of subjective response to truth *(fiducia)* or relationship *(fides),* but in the sense of the summary of faith, the corpus of Christian doctrine, the convictions that are a necessary part of the Christian view of things *(credentia).* That is, we are speaking of the *faith* (noun), not the act of faith (verb). Paul referred to this body of doctrine as the "gospel," the "pattern of sound words," the "truth" (2 Tim. 1:11–18). This is the truth taught by Jesus, transmitted by the apostles, and received in the church. While there are summaries of the truth in the New Testament, such as the sermons in Acts, Paul's creedal statement in 1 Corinthians 15:3–5, and the confessional hymn of Philippians 2:1–11, the full-orbed truth became more specifically developed in the classical era by the year 600. While the rule of faith affirmed the Trinity and that Jesus is both God and man, the rule did not clarify in any detail how this affirmation was to be expressed linguistically. As the church confronted Hellenistic culture with its particular language and categories of thought, it met in universal councils to clarify in creeds what language needed to be used to re-present the faith in a different age in a way consistent with its orig-

191

inal presentation in the rule of faith. These creeds, particularly the Nicene Creed of 325 (ratified in 381) and the Chalcedon Creed of 451 have been unanimously received by the church as communally author-itative "witnesses"[43] to the truth summarized in the rule of faith and expressed in the apostolic writings. They therefore bear a 'culturally lin-guistic' authority in the church.[44] The church throughout history is allowed to think and rethink these creeds, but always with a faithful-ness to the way the creeds have been received and interpreted for the church throughout history.

In the third century the task of *theoretical thinking* became increas-ingly important to the church. Between A.D. 300 and 600 the church was engaged in the task of formulating creeds to explain what it already believed. An examination of these debates and the creeds they produced leads to three observations:

First, the church formulates its creed in conformity to the apostolic faith. For example, Irenaeus's rule expressed faith in "one God . . . the Father Almighty; one Christ Jesus, the Son of God; and in the Holy Spirit." In similar fashion the rule speaks of the full humanity and divin-ity of the Son—"The Son of God who was made flesh." And it refers to the sinful state of humanity "in the godless and wicked and lawless and blasphemers among men," as well as to the fact that the incarnation, death, and resurrection of Jesus were "for our salvation."[45] The point is that the trinitarian, Christological, and soteriological controversies revolved around the explanation of the rule of faith. The church was engaged in a reflective exercise, thinking about the truths, which had always been accepted, as *given* by God, *transmitted* by the apostles, and *received* by the church.

The second observation is that the church articulates its faith within the context of its culture. For example, the creedal controversies must be understood against the background of the cultural, geographical, and philosophical setting of the early church. Both the trinitarian and the Christological controversies were, at their center, exercises in commu-nicating biblical truth in a Hellenistic frame of reference. The genius of both the Nicene Creed and the Chalcedonian definition is that the Fathers recognized the inadequacy of human language to capture the mystery of God as one yet three and the mystery of Jesus as fully human yet fully divine.

The Fathers rejected the dualistic notions that tended to separate the Son from the Father and the human from the divine and affirmed, within a culture that was dualistically inclined, the holistic faith of the church. In this way the church succeeded in remaining faithful to apostolic Chris-tianity while communicating the faith in a cultural form different from that in which the truth had been originally received and understood. While this can be said generally of the Nicene Creed and the Chalcedon Creed, it cannot be said of soteriology, where no universal creed has been written.

The soteriological controversy, which has to do with the nature of human beings, of sin and grace, of election and free will, and of the means of receiving the benefits of the death of Christ, has resulted in a number of different confessions. Although the entire church is united in its belief that all are sinners and that Jesus Christ's death and resurrection procure salvation, there exists a number of explanations about our sinful nature and the means of receiving the benefits of Christ's death. The diversity on the soteriological question accounts for much of the diversity in the church. An examination of these differences reveals the variety of influences that have given them shape—both cultural and philosophical. In other words, the church is not divided over whether humans are sinners whose only hope is in the death and resurrection of Christ, but in its disagreement on *how* this is to be explained.[46]

A third observation is that the existence of disagreement forces the church to face the issue of private judgment. How can we determine which of the many interpretations we should follow? If there are many explanations, many theologies, many formulations, is the church left in a sea of relativity or is there a criterion by which these various interpretations may be judged? The answer to this question was provided by Vincent of Lerins (d. 450) in his *Commonitory:*

> In the Catholic Church, all possible care must be taken, that we hold that faith which has been believed everywhere, always, by all. For that is truly and in the strictest sense "Catholic," which, as the name itself and the reason of the thing declare, comprehends all universally. *This rule we shall observe if we follow universality, antiquity, consent.* We shall follow universality if we confess that one faith to be true which the whole Church throughout the world confesses; antiquity, if we in no wise depart from those interpretations which it is manifest were notoriously held by our holy ancestors and fathers; consent, in like manner, if in antiquity itself we adhere to the consentient definitions and determinations of all, or at least of almost all priests and doctors.[47] (italics mine)

Vincent of Lérins held a high view of the church. For him, the church was not a mere human organization of people who believe, but the body of Christ inseparably united with the Holy Spirit. Thus, the Holy Spirit who is truly within the church brings consensus.

Although the suggestion of Vincent does not represent a doctrine as such, it does offer a helpful way to look at much of the theological diversity within the church. In essence it suggests that the church in the fifth century was united in its affirmation of the biblical framework of thought, but sought to sort out which theology stood in the tradition of the apostles.

This brief summary suggests that the content of the Christian faith is basic to and even prior to the creeds. The content of the church's teaching, which is based on the apostolic preaching and writings, is common to the whole church, belonging to the simple believer, the theologian, the philosopher, or any other Christian thinker. It is the basic framework of truth from which all Christians live and think.

Creeds, on the other hand, speak the faith through various cultural or philosophic forms in such a way that the biblical framework of truth is not violated. And the guide to Christian thinking, the means by which Christians hold their subjective interpretations in check, is the rule of universality, antiquity, and consensus.

It is the recognition of the universal nature of the creeds that helps us to reflect on the emergence of the confessions of the Reformation. We need to recognize that confessions do not meet the criteria of universality, antiquity, and consensus. They are parochial; they define one movement within Christianity that emerged in a particular geographical area, in a particular culture, and at a particular time. Their value is not for the whole church, but for a part of the church. They do not define what it means to be Christian in the broadest sense, but what it means to be Lutheran, Presbyterian, Anglican, Anabaptist, or one of the many other groups. Their value is in distinguishing one group from another, in explaining the differences that separate Christians. These confessions are all secondary to the creeds and are not binding upon the whole church.

The distinctions among the rule of faith, the universal creeds, and the particular denominational confessions obviously make personal theological opinion highly tentative. We are to hold our opinions up against the universal faith of the church and test them by the witness of the Holy Spirit in the church. Any personal opinion that does not stand the test of universality, antiquity, and consensus must be set forth with the greatest of humility and be described for what it is—a personal opinion. We do not stand in judgment over the church and its thinking. We submit ourselves to the communal authority of the church's teachings. A commendable example of this kind of approach is found in the *Ancient Christian Commentary on Scripture* (InterVarsity Press). This twenty-seven-volume series is explained as a series "encompassing all of scripture and offering contemporary readers the opportunity to study for themselves the key writings of the early church Fathers." The series therefore "invites us to listen with appreciative ears and sympathetic minds as our ancient ancestors in the faith describe and interpret the scriptural vistas as they see them."[48]

Theological Thinking in a Postmodern World

The most helpful way to deal with creeds, confessions, and personal opinion in a postmodern world is to distinguish among them. The authority of the rule of faith and the universal creeds of the church is primary, while the particular teaching of a branch of the church is secondary, and personal opinion is just that, opinion.

In the thinking of various denominations, all denominations originally confessed the apostolic tradition, the authority of Scripture, and the rightness of the universal creeds. But in their confessions, they went beyond the thinking of the universal church to speak authoritatively in areas where the universal church allowed for the freedom of disagreement. Luther, for example, developed his entire theology around justification by faith; Calvin, around the sovereignty of God; and Menno Simons, around the theme of discipleship. In our postmodern world we recognize that no one denomination is able to write a comprehensive, all-embracing theology for everybody.

Theology in a postmodern world recognizes that all interpretations of the truth must be understood in their cultural context. For example, the confessions of Luther and Calvin are best understood against the background of the late medieval interpretations of Christianity, which they regarded as perverse. In that context, as they broke from the Roman Church, they accented the Word so strongly that a weakened view of the church, ministry, and sacraments resulted. What they did, although a "tragic necessity," as Jaraslov Pelikan describes it, was indeed a necessary corrective for that time and place. Nevertheless, it set in motion divisions and differences in the church which to this day have not been healed and which have multiplied a hundredfold.

There are several important guidelines for evangelicals as we think about the difference among creed, confession, and personal opinion. First, our theological thinking should not do violence to the essential truth of Christianity. In the case of a modern theological formulation, where the historic faith is regarded as untenable but the language of faith is retained, the formulation cannot be said to stand in continuity with the truth, for it denies the historic deposit, the apostolic testimony to the content of truth. However, where there is an honest acceptance of the historic content of the faith, the thinking church is responsible to investigate the sources or attempt to articulate the faith within the context of a modern system of thought. But this thinking must always be brought under the judgment of the Scriptures and the testimony of history.

Second, the freedom to think theologically raises a certain cautionary note about the so-called doctrine of the private judgment of Scripture. The careless, subjective approach to Scripture has been abused. In the New Testament those who became converted were expected to submit to the teaching of Christ and his apostles. For this reason it is important for Christians to make sure that their personal ideas are tested by Scripture and the history of interpretation in the church. With so many subjective and ill-informed opinions filling the air, especially those coming from group discussions and sharing sessions, it is a good idea to test our insights by asking, "What has the church said?" This is a surer and safer test for truth than the personal insights that are being passed around in gatherings of well-intentioned believers.

Third, it would be well for all of us to hold our denominational and personal theological formulations with a degree of tentativeness. Of course, we should not be tentative about the gospel or the deposit of faith. The truth which has been revealed and passed down in history is unchangeable. Our conviction about it, our adherence to it, our propagation of it, is to be executed with firm conviction that it is true. But our formulation of that truth into a *system*, whether it be Calvinism, Arminianism, Dispensationalism, or whatever, must be expressed with tentativeness, even hesitancy.

We must learn to say, "It seems to me," or "My interpretation of Scripture seems to suggest," or "Our church follows the interpretation of so-and-so who saw it this way." Here in the area of formulation we must learn to be inclusive, not exclusive. Obviously, such an approach serves the gospel in a postmodern era for it accents what the universal church teaches and makes what has been passed down in history unmistakably clear. It avoids making nonessentials essential and sets forth an attitude of Christian humility and graciousness that makes us accepting of and open to other Christians who also stand in the historic faith, but who articulate it through a different frame of reference.

Fourth, thinking about the truth is the ongoing task of the church. To think about the truth and to articulate it in human form is consistent with the incarnation. Mere biblicism is a denial of the human container through which truth is always known. The task of the church is to articulate truth within the context of history and culture. Such a task demands the critical use of human methods of thought—be they philosophical, psychological, anthropological, economic, or whatever. We need to learn to communicate truth in human garb in such a way that truth is not lost.

Communicating Truth in Human Garb

As the church faces the task of doing theology in a postmodern world the inevitable problem is that of communicating truth in human garb without accommodating it to the garb through which it is being presented.

Because we interpret our faith through the glasses of the culture in which we find ourselves, we tend to impose cultural categories of thought on the faith, articulate our faith through these categories, and create an expression of Christianity peculiar to those cultural forms. Consequently, the faith becomes inextricably interwoven with a particular view of life or method. This is true even when an interpretation arises in protest to the surrounding culture. In this case, too, the culture sets the categories, whether one agrees or disagrees with them. Our orthodoxy becomes not only believing the faith but also believing it within the life-view or by the method through which it has been expressed; the "grid" through which we are seeing theologically becomes a matter of belief just as much as the faith itself.

Helmut Thielicke addressed this problem in *The Evangelical Faith* by making a distinction between a theology of *actualization* and a theology of *accommodation*.[49] A theology of actualization "always consists in a new interpretation of truth . . . the truth remains intact. It means that the hearer is summoned and called 'under the truth' in his own name and situation."[50] On the other hand, a theology of accommodation takes a different approach. It calls truth "under me" and lets me be its noun. It is pragmatic to the extent that it "assigns truth the function of being the means whereby *I master* life" (italics mine).[51]

Thielicke termed accommodation theology the "Cartesian" approach after René Descartes, the seventeenth-century philosopher who insisted that the starting point for truth was the individual person: "I think, therefore I am." According to Thielicke there are, broadly speaking, two approaches in which Cartesian theology may be expressed—rationalism and experientialism. In both systems the receiving I is primary. We might paraphrase it like this: "The Christian faith is a perfectly rational system about life. When *you* accept it and live by it *you* will really have life by the tail. *You* will be able to stand up strong and really face life"; or, "What *you* need is an experience of Jesus Christ. When *you* let him come into *your* life and take over, *you* will feel much better. Everything will fall in place for *you* and life will be beautiful." The emphasis is on the person, what the person does, how much better it is for the person, how much more in control of life the person will be.

On the other hand, actualization theology comes at a person's lost situation in an entirely different way. Because the person is "under the truth," an appeal is not made to a Christianity that is "good for you." Instead, the truth is spoken in such a way that the person stands under God.

Through this proclamation the person is confronted by truth—the truth about the human situation, the truth about personal involvement and participation in that situation, and the truth about the way Jesus Christ has met that situation and overcome it by his death and resurrection. Such an approach is a return to the kerygmatic preaching of the apostles.

The theology of actualization is the historic approach to communicating the gospel. The emphasis is on the biblical proclamation as truth and not the explanation that is often reliant on current philosophical categories of thought as well as subject to creaturely limitations. Final truth, it says, is always deeper and much more complex, more mysterious, than the best explanations we can offer.

This was the task of the church in the creedal era. How could it take the biblical concepts and articulate them within the framework of a Hellenistic mind-set, a Platonic or Neo-Platonic philosophy? For example, the trinitarian controversy employed Greek words like *homoousion* and *hypostasis* to communicate the unity and diversity of the Godhead. The Christological controversy, as well, was settled through the use of Greek language and Hellenistic thought forms.

However, the genius of the creedal formulations is *that they did not elevate the methodology or the final theological form as truth in and of itself. Instead, the Nicene Creed and the Chalcedonian definition pointed to the truth contained in Scriptures and summarized in the rule of faith as ultimately beyond the possibility of being captured in a comprehensive form.* In other words, the creeds wrote a negative theology: Jesus is not a creature as Arius taught; Jesus' humanity is not lost into divinity as Apollinarius taught; nor is his divinity a mere appendage to his humanity as Nestorius taught. The Chalcedonian definition, in particular, can be seen as an attempt to set the limits of thinking about the union of the divine and human natures in the person of Christ and not to offer a final and complete formulation of this truth. This is evident in the central statement of the definition: "One and the same Christ, Son, Lord, Only-begotten, recognized in two natures, *without confusion, without change, without division, without separation.*"[52] The phrases emphasized here tell us at least how *not* to think of the union of Christ's divinity and humanity.

No, instead of allowing Jesus Christ to be defined as some wanted, the creeds affirmed the mystery of the unity of the Son with the Father and the completeness of full humanity and full divinity in the person of Jesus Christ. The creeds did not propagate a system, but affirmed the ultimate mystery of Christ through the thought patterns of the day. They "spoke" the biblical framework through a language and thought form different from the biblical language and thought forms without accommodating the truth to those forms.

The use of cultural forms as channels for truth has always been an issue in Christianity. In the early church much theology was done through a Platonic grid. Aquinas expressed the Christian faith through the Aristotelian system of philosophy. Reformation thought was filtered through nominalism. Modern thought has been filtered through rationalism. And now we face postmodern thought. We create problems for ourselves when the method of thinking is made authoritative. That's why the appeal for evangelicals in the postmodern world is not to change the faith, but to recognize the need for the presentation of the historic faith in a new culture situation.

The theology of the early church didn't try to explain everything through a system. Instead, it developed creeds and theologies as *means* to communicate truth, not as *ends* in themselves. In the process of its thinking, it maintained a healthy, even joyous, regard for *mystery*—the fact that the truth about God and Jesus Christ and salvation and even life itself is beyond comprehension. As we learn to articulate an actualization theology in a postmodern world, we will become more tolerant of people we disagree with, more open to the mysterious character of the faith, and more able to see the complexity of doing theological study.

Actualization theology will free us to do theology within the framework of our own culture. The task of doing an evangelical theology will not be that of arriving at a fixed explanation, which we forever freeze, but rather the calling to bring biblical thought to bear on the ultimate questions asked by a postmodern world.

Consequently, we will always allow our systematic theology to become historical theology as the church remains alive to the truth of Jesus Christ. This more biblical approach to theological thinking will free us to make mistakes and to take the risk of thinking out loud—a risk that no one who is a slave to a system can take. Above all, this open-ended theology will free us to be related to Jesus Christ in a real way by allowing him and the truth about him in the Scriptures to be our final point of reference and our primary message to a postmodern culture.

Conclusion

I began this section with a story about my dentist and his well-meaning assertion that he had as much truth as people who do biblical exegesis and theology. There is, of course, a certain degree of truth in his statement. What is important, though, for him and other Christians like him, is to recognize that he has truth because it has been handed down from the apostles in the church through the Scriptures and summarized in the creeds. What we hold in common is the truth that we all have received from the church through its work of *paradosis* (the act of handing over).

Beyond this, the church has to face the difficult task of interpreting this truth in a particular time and place. But the task of theology, which is the reflective and ongoing task of the church, is usually done not by the dentists of the church, but by its theologians. And the theologian's work gets passed down to the people in the pew. Here, as they say, the rubber meets the pavement. It may be that part of the theologian's work is to test the interpretation in the context of the body of believers. This is to suggest that theology is properly the work of the church and belongs to the church. As in Christian living, a test of theology may be whether it bears fruit.

I sense that evangelicals in the postmodern world need to affirm what the church has always believed, everywhere and by all, and give greater authority to the common tradition and less weight to the theology of a particular tradition.

Therefore, what we can expect is this: Evangelical emphasis in the postmodern world will fall on the biblical teachings about the basic issues of faith and life. What is the message of the Bible? What does it mean to follow Jesus? What is the common theology of the church? Little interest will be focused on the differences between denominations. Denominational walls will continue to fall in a postmodern world where Christians are concerned with their common identity. And a new identity will grow around the common creeds of the church.

Theology as a system of truth that distinguishes "us" from "them" will make little sense to postmoderns. Theological systems will be studied from historical and sociological points of view. The emphasis will be on the cultural factors that lie behind a particular system. This attitude will continuously free evangelicals from a slavery to a particular system of thought to emphasize the authority that lies behind the common tradition, the authority that brings the church together around the tapestry of Christ, church, worship, spirituality, and mission to the world.

In this way the rule of faith, Scripture, the creeds, and theological reflection will function more as they did in the early church than they have in the more recent past. They will be viewed as a witness to the truth, placing Christ as the center with Scripture as the authoritative interpretation, with the rule of faith as an authoritative summary and the universal creeds as the common theology that unites all Christians everywhere. This kind of Christianity will speak convincingly to the postmodern world.

Table N: Authority within the Paradigms of History

Ancient	Medieval	Reformation	Modern	Postmodern
Apostolic authority; rule of faith; Scripture	Scripture and tradition regulated by the magesterium of the church	*Sola scriptura*	Reason over Scripture resulting in liberal criticism and conservative biblical apologetics	Relativism of all authorities suggests a return to the ancient understanding of apostolic authority, the rule of faith, and the ecumenical creeds as authoritative summaries and Scripture as the revealed Word of God. This is the possession of the church handed down by the apostles.
All guaranteed in the church who "interprets, guards, and hands down"				

The postmodern challenge to authority is best met, not by returning to *sola scriptura*, nor by the modern evangelical defense of the Bible, but by returning to the origins of authority in the Christian faith. The church possesses, interprets, guards, and hands down truth.

Table O: A Comparison of Gnostic Thought and Christian Thought

The Doctrine	Gnostic	Christian
God	Dualism (two Gods)	One: Father, Son, Holy Spirit
Authority	Secret tradition	Tradition passed down from the apostles and their disciples; Holy Spirit through prophets
Creation	An evil god made matter; thus matter is evil	The Father, the Almighty, who made the heavens and the earth
Jesus Christ	An appearance: Jesus could not partake of flesh because flesh is matter and matter is evil (known as Docetism—"to seem"); Jesus is the great teacher.	Son of God made flesh Born of a virgin Suffered and died Resurrected, ascended Will come again to restore all things
Eschatology	Absorption into divine; no resurrection of the flesh	Raise up all flesh Judgment
Salvation	Knowledge	Participation in Christ

EPILOGUE

From time to time faculty members take courses from their colleagues to learn something from a different field to integrate into their own studies. Recently, a colleague of mine who teaches physics took a graduate course from me in which we were dealing with classical Christian thought.

During the course he kept calling attention to the fact that scientists are concerned to find a unifying principle. He reminded us of the old Newtonian world-machine, which treated things as if they stood alone. He emphasized how the old scientific view had influenced all areas of life and study. Nothing seemed to be interrelated. All of life looked like the alphabet lined up in a row, with each letter independent of the other.

My colleague explained more of what science is doing in its quest for a single unifying theory of everything. Scientists are looking for a link that ties together the four basic forces of nature—electromagnetism, gravity, the strong force, and the weak force. Currently, scientists think in terms of "superstrings" that bind together the four forces of nature. These superstrings are described as infinitesimally small, winding, curling one-dimensional strings that account for the unity of the four forces of nature and thus bring life together in a single whole.

This scientific quest for the unity of all things reminds me of the Pauline assertion that Christ is the one who unifies everything in himself. In Colossians Paul tells us that Christ is the creator of all "things [that are] in heaven and that are on earth, visible and invisible" (1:16); that "in him all things hold together" (1:17), and that "God was pleased to have all his fullness dwell in him, and through him to reconcile to himself all things" (1:19–20). The unifying principle of all things is Christ.

I cannot comprehend the meaning of this sweeping proclamation. But I do know this: The early church fathers who sought to work out in a more comprehensive manner the meaning of Paul's teaching have guided me into a view of life and faith that is significantly different from my old view.

I am no longer an atomist. The things of faith do not stand alone nor do they stand still. The Fathers of the church have taken me back into a dynamic worldview, an understanding of the interrelationship of all things. The faith, which once looked like an alphabet with everything standing independently and in a row, now looks like a majestic tapestry.

In this book I have made several observations about this phenomenon—observations that I have not attempted to prove in a scientific or statistical way. For example, I have suggested that the shift in thought from a static view of the universe to a more dynamic view has affected the people of this country in ways that most cannot articulate. In the religious realm it has made the modern, static views of the faith that were like the alphabet suspect. The postmodern church is in quest of a more dynamic faith, a faith that has shifted away from the old debates that once divided Christians. Instead, the postmodern church seeks unity, spirituality, worship, and involvement in the lives of other people.

My argument has been that the evangelicals will do well to affirm a Christianity that has a deep kinship with the faith of the early church. What I sense is that many contemporary Christians who have been affected by the cultural change toward a more integrated and dynamic view of life are in search of a faith that corresponds with their experience in general. For this reason an increasing amount of dissatisfaction is being expressed over a rationalistic and divided Christianity. The challenge for us is to return to the Christian tradition. For here is a faith that, like a tapestry, weaves everything in and out of the main thread—Christ. My own experience with this rediscovered tapestry is a renewed and enriched faith. And I have talked with countless others who have experienced the same sense of newness in commitment through the insights of the early Christian tradition. Here, I believe, is a faith for our time, a faith that finds in the ancient Christian tradition a power to speak to the postmodern world.

NOTES

Part 1

1. See Yvonna S. Lincoln and Egon G. Guba, *Naturalistic Inquiry* (Newbury Park, Calif.: Sage, 1985), especially the first four chapters; and Norman K. Denzin and Yvonna S. Lincoln, eds., *The Landscape of Qualitative Research Theories and Issues* (Thousand Oaks, Calif.: Sage, 1995).

2. See Hans-Georg Gadamer, *Truth and Method* (London: Sheed & Ward, 1995).

3. Martin Buber, *I and Thou* (New York: Charles Scribner's Sons, 1970); Paulo Freire, *Pedagogy of Hope* (New York: Continuum, 1990).

Chapter 1: Paradigm Thinking

1. See Paul Hiebert, *Anthropological Reflection on Missiological Issues* (Grand Rapids: Baker, 1994); and Lesslie Newbigin, *Proper Confidence: Faith, Doubt and Certainty in Christian Discipleship* (Grand Rapids: Eerdmans, 1995).

2. Paradigm thinking was introduced by Thomas S. Kuhn, *The Structure of Scientific Revolutions*, 2nd ed. (Chicago: University of Chicago Press, 1970).

3. See Alasdair MacIntyre, *After Virtue* (Notre Dame, Ind.: University of Notre Dame Press, 1984), 204–25.

4. See Robert Schreiter, *Constructing Local Theologies* (Maryknoll, N.Y.: Orbis, 1985); and Andrew F. Walls, *The Missionary Movement in Christian History: Study in the Transmission of Faith* (Maryknoll, N.Y.: Orbis, 1996).

5. See Talal Asad, *Genealogies of Religion* (Baltimore: Johns Hopkins University Press, 1993), especially "The Construct of Religion as an Anthropological Category"; and Meredeth B. McGuire, *Religion: The Social Context*, 3rd ed. (Belmont, Calif.: Wadsworth, 1992), especially "The Dynamics of Religious Collectivity."

6. See Steven Best and Douglas Kellner, *Postmodern Theory: Critical Interrogations* (New York: Guilford, 1991), especially "In Search of Postmodernism."

7. David Wells, *No Place for Truth or Whatever Happened to Evangelical Theology* (Grand Rapids: Eerdmans, 1993).

8. See C. David Grant, *Thinking through Our Faith: Theology for the Twenty-First Century Christian* (Nashville: Abingdon, 1988).

9. See Henry H. Knight III, *A Future for Truth: Evangelical Theology in a Postmodern World* (Nashville: Abingdon, 1997).

10. Paul Lakeland in *Postmodernity: Christian Identity in a Postmodern Age* (Minneapolis: Fortress, 1997) distinguishes three groups: radical postmodernists like Mark C. Taylor, who follow Friedrich Nietzsche and Jacques Derrida in "Serious Combat" with traditional faith; a second group of "nostalgics" like Hans Frei, George Lindbeck, and John Milbank, who call for a continuance in one way or another with traditional faith; and a group in the middle made up of people Lakeland calls "pragmatic theologians," like

James Gustafson, who want to preserve some sense of God. Evangelicals will identify most closely with the "nostalgics."

11. See W. D. Ross, *Plato's Theory of Ideas* (Oxford: Oxford University Press, 1951); *Plato and the Republic,* trans. Allan Bloom (New York: Basic Books, 1968); and *Tinaeus,* trans. Francis Cornford (Indianapolis: Bobbs-Merrill, 1959).

12. See Thomas Bokenkotter, *A Concise History of the Catholic Church* (New York: Image Books, 1990).

13. See Louis Bouyer, *The Spirit and Forms of Protestantism* (London: Harvill, 1956).

14. See Charles Taylor, *Sources of the Self* (Cambridge, Mass.: Harvard University Press, 1989), especially chapter 8, "Descartes' Disengaged Reason."

15. See Nancey Murphy, *Beyond Liberalism and Fundamentalism* (Valley Forge, Pa.: Trinity Press International, 1996), especially chapter 1, "Experience or Scripture: How Do We Know God?"

16. See Timothy R. Phillips and Dennis Okholm, *Welcome to the Family* (Wheaton, Ill.: Victor/BridgePoint, 1996), especially chapter 16, "We Are Family: American Evangelicalism and Its Roots."

17. See Robert Webber and Donald Bloesch, *The Orthodox Evangelicals* (Nashville: Nelson, 1979).

Chapter 2: From a Modern to a Postmodern Paradigm

1. See Stephen Toulman, *Cosmopolis: The Hidden Agenda of Modernity* (New York: The Free Press, 1990; Chicago: University of Chicago Press, 1992).

2. Norman Hampson, *The Enlightenment* (Baltimore: Penguin, 1968; New York: Penguin, 1982; London: Penguin, 1968, 1990).

3. For a discussion of Enlightenment theology and its impact on Christian thought, see Stanley J. Grenz and Roger E. Olson, *Twentieth Century Theology: God and the World in a Transitional Age* (Downers Grove, Ill.: InterVarsity, 1992).

4. See Friedrich Schleiermacher, *The Christian Faith,* ed. H. R. Mackintosh and J. S. Stewart, 2nd ed. (Philadelphia: Fortress, 1928).

5. George A. Lindbeck, *The Nature of Doctrine: Religion and Theology in a Post Liberal Age* (Philadelphia: Westminster, 1984), 16.

6. Ibid.

7. See John E. Thiel, *Nonfoundationalism* (Minneapolis: Fortress, 1994). The quote is from Lakeland, ibid., 125.

8. See Claude Levi-Strauss, *Structural Anthropology* (New York: Basic Books, 1958).

9. See J. Richard Middleton and Brian J. Walsh, *Truth Is Stranger Than It Used to Be* (Downers Grove, Ill.: InterVarsity, 1995).

10. See Robert Wright, *The Moral Animal: Why We Are the Way We Are: The New Science of Evolution Psychology* (New York: Pantheon, 1994).

11. See Shailer Matthews, *The Faith of Modernism* (New York: Macmillan, 1924).

12. Mark A. Noll, *The Scandal of the Evangelical Mind* (Grand Rapids: Eerdmans, 1994), especially chapter 4, "The Evangelical Enlightenment" and chapter 5, "The Intellectual Disaster of Fundamentalism."

13. For an interesting exchange from both sides, see Steven Weinberg, "Sokals Hoax," *The New York Review,* 8 August 1996, 11–15.

14. See Michael Polanyi, *Personal Knowledge: Towards a Post Critical Philosophy* (Chicago: University of Chicago Press, 1958).

15. See David Ray Griffin, *The Reenchantment with Science* (Albany, N.Y.: State University of New York Press, 1988), especially the introduction, "The Reenchantment of Science."

16. See Nancey Murphy, *Reconciling Theology and Science: A Radical Reformation Principle* (Kitchner, Ontario: Pandora, 1997).

17. See the writings of Thomas C. Oden, especially his work *After Modernity . . . What?* (Grand Rapids: Zondervan, 1990); and the writings of Stanley Hauerwas, especially *After Christendom?* (Nashville: Abingdon, 1991).

18. For primary sources, see Charles Jencks, ed., *The Postmodern Reader* (New York: St. Martin's, 1992). For a good summary of the philosophical revolution that replaced the philosophy of the Enlightenment, see Stanley J. Grenz, *A Primer on Postmodernism* (Grand Rapids: Eerdmans, 1996). For this section I have drawn from my colleague Bruce Benson in an unpublished paper, "Postmodernism."

19. See Mikhail M. Bakhtin, *The Dialogic Imagination,* ed. Michael Holquist, trans. Caryl Emerson and Michael Holquist (Austin: University of Texas Press, 1981).

20. See Jerome Bruner, *Actual Minds, Possible Worlds* (Cambridge, Mass.: Harvard University Press, 1986); and Kenneth Gergen, *The Saturated Self: Dilemmas of Identity in Contemporary Life* (San Francisco: Bantam Books, 1991).

21. See Jacques Derrida, *Of Grammotology,* trans. Gayatn Chakvavovty Spivak (Baltimore: Johns Hopkins University Press, 1997, 1998; Delhi: Motilal Banarsidass, 1994).

22. See John McGowan, *Postmodernism and Its Critics* (Ithaca, N.Y.: Cornell University Press,), especially chapter 3, "The Problem of Freedom in Post Modern Theory."

23. Richard Rorty, *Philosophy and the Mirror of Nature* (Princeton, N.J.: Princeton University Press, 1980).

24. See Richard Rorty, *Objectivity, Relativism and Truth* (Cambridge: Cambridge University Press, 1991), especially "Solidarity and Objectivity?"

25. See Millard J. Erickson, *The Evangelical Left: Encountering Postconservative Evangelical Theology* (Grand Rapids: Baker, 1997).

26. Pierre Babin and Mercedes Iannone, trans. David Smith, *The New Era of Religious Communication* (Minneapolis: Fortress, 1991).

Chapter 3: The Return to Classical Christianity

1. A good introduction to the communications revolution and its impact on the Christian faith is found in Pierre Babin and Mercedes Iannone, trans. David Smith, *The New Era of Religious Communication* (Minneapolis: Fortress, 1991).

2. See Glanmor Williams, *Reformation Views of Church History* (Richmond: John Knox, 1970); and Philip Schaff, *The Principle of Protestantism,* vol. 1, Lancaster Series on the Mercersburg Theology, ed. Bard Thompson and George H. Bricker (Boston: United Church Press, 1964).

3. Keith Fournier, *Evangelical Catholics* (Nashville: Nelson, 1990), 19.

4. Quoted in *Christianity Today,* 24 September 1990, 29.

5. See Robert Webber and Donald Bloesch, *The Chicago Call* (Nashville: Nelson, 1979).

6. Charles Colson and Richard John Neuhaus, *Evangelicals and Catholics Together: Toward a Common Mission* (Dallas: Word, 1995).

7. *Asbury Theological Journal* 45, no. 2 (1990).

8. *Reclaiming the Great Tradition: Evangelicals, Catholics and Orthodox in Dialogue* (Downers Grove, Ill.: InterVarsity, 1997), 8.

9. Paul Lakeland, *Post Modernity: Christian Identity in a Fragmented Age* (Minneapolis: Fortress, 1997), 46.

10. For an excellent volume of primary sources from early Christianity, see Eberhard Arnold, *The Early Christians in Their Own Words* (Farmington, Pa.: Plough, 1997). The classic secondary source of the interpretation of the Fathers is J. N. D. Kelly, *Early Christian Doctrine,* 2nd ed. (New York: Harper & Row, 1960).

11. See Bradey Nassif, *New Perspectives on Historical Theology: Essays in Memory of John Meyendorff* (Grand Rapids: Eerdmans, 1996).

12. See especially Hans-Georg Gadamer, *Truth and Method* (London: Sheed & Ward, 1995, 1998).

13. George A. Lindbeck, *The Nature of Doctrine: Religion and Theology in a Postliberal Age* (Philadelphia: Westminster, 1984).

14. Ibid.

15. Ibid.

16. Philipp Jacob Spener, *Pia Desderia* (Philadelphia: Fortress, 1964), 81–85.

Part 2

1. See David Ray Griffin, "The Reenchantment of Science," in Charles Jencks, ed., *The Postmodern Reader* (New York: St. Martin's, 1992), 367.

2. Jencks, *Postmodern Reader,* 35.

3. Ibid., 36.

4. For explorations into science, see Philip D. Clayton, *God and Contemporary Science* (Grand Rapids: Eerdmans, 1998).

Chapter 4: Christ Within the Paradigms of History

1. See Gustav Aulen, *Christus Victor: A Historical Study of the Three Main Types of the Idea of Atonement* (New York: Macmillan, 1969).

2. See, for example, the Nicene Creed.

3. Anselm of Canterbury, *Why God Became Man: The Virgin Conception and Original Sin* (Albany, N.Y.: Magi Books, 1969).

4. See the treatment of Abelard in the text on historical theology in Alan Johnson and Robert Webber, *What Christians Believe* (Grand Rapids: Zondervan, 1993), 266–70.

5. Ibid., 265ff.

6. See Alois Grillmeier, *Christ in Christian Tradition,* vol. 1, *From the Apostolic Age to Chalcedon (451),* trans. John Bowden (Atlanta: John Knox, 1975).

7. See Diogenes Allen, *Philosophy for Understanding Theology* (Atlanta: John Knox, 1985), chapters 7 and 8; and James C. Livingston, *Modern Christian Thought: From the Enlightenment to Vatican II* (New York: Macmillan, 1971).

8. See Avery Dulles, *Models of Revelation* (New York: Image Books, 1985), chapter 3.

9. See Charles J. Scalise, *From Scripture to Theology: A Canonical Journey into the Hermeneutics* (Downers Grove, Ill.: InterVarsity, 1996).

10. For a discussion of the differences between event- and book-oriented methodologies, see John H. Sailhamer, *Introduction to Old Testament Theology: A Canonical Approach* (Grand Rapids: Zondervan, 1995), especially chapter 3. I contend that the event is revelatory and that the interpretation of the event is the written Scripture. The place to start, however, is with the event.

11. See Walter Wink, *Unmasking the Powers: The Invisible Forces That Determine Human Existence,* vol. 2 (Philadelphia: Fortress, 1986).

12. See Hendrikus Berkhof, *Christ and the Powers,* trans. John Howard Yoder (Scottdale, Pa.: Herald, 1977).

13. See Max Thurian and Geoffery Wainwright, eds., *Baptism and Eucharist: Ecumenical Convergence in Celebration* (Grand Rapids: Eerdmans, 1983), especially chapters 1–3, "The Baptism of the Early Church," "I Hippolytus," "The Eastern Orthodox Church and the Western Catholic Church."

Chapter 5: *Christus Victor* in the Apostolic Writings

1. See Robert Webber, *The Church in the World* (Grand Rapids: Zondervan, 1994).

2. For a systematic development of these ideas, see Thomas N. Finger, *Christian Theology: An Eschatological Approach* (Scottdale, Pa.: Herald, 1987), 317–24, 331–38.

3. For a thorough historical discussion of kingdom theology, see Gösta Lunström, *The Kingdom of God in the Teaching of Jesus* (London: Oliver and Boyd, 1963). For an updated discussion, see Wendell Willis, ed., *The Kingdom of God in Twentieth Century Interpretation* (Peabody, Mass.: Hendrickson, 1987), especially chapter 14, Everett Ferguson, "The Kingdom of God in Early Patristic Literature," 191–208.

Chapter 6: The Theology of Recapitulation

1. See R. C. D. Jasper and G. J. Cummings, eds., *Prayers of the Eucharist: Early and Reformed*, 2nd ed. (New York: Oxford University Press, 1980; 3rd ed., Collegeville, Minn.: Liturgical, 1990), 22–23.

2. G. F. Hawthorne, ed., *Current Issues in Biblical and Patristic Interpretation* (Grand Rapids: Eerdmans, 1975), 173.

3. *Service Book of the Holy Orthodox—Catholic Apostolic Church* (Englewood Cliffs, N.J.: Antiochian Orthodox Christian Archdiocese, 1983), 583.

4. For Irenaeus, see *Against Heresies* and for Tertullian, see *The Prescription against Heretics*, *The Five Books against Marcion*, *Against Hermogenes*, *Against the Valentinians*, *On the Flesh of Christ*, and *Against Praxeas*. These writings are found in *The Pre-Nicene Fathers*, vols. 1, 3, 4 (Grand Rapids: Eerdmans, 1973).

5. I am quoting from the shortened version of *Against Heresies* in Cyril Richardson, *The Early Church Fathers* (Philadelphia: Westminster, 1943).

6. Ibid.

7. For a discussion of Irenaeus and a thoughtful presentation of *Christus Victor*, see Gustav Aulen, *Christus Victor* (New York: Macmillan, 1969). Read also *The Scandal of the Incarnation: Irenaeus against the Heresies* (San Francisco: Ignatius, 1981); and Christopher Schönborn, *The Mystery of the Incarnation* (San Francisco: Ignatius, 1992).

Chapter 7: Christ, the Center

1. For an interesting discussion, see Dermot A. Lane, *Christ at the Centre: Selected Issues in Christology* (New York: Paulist, 1990).

2. Orthodox theologians draw from the Eastern church fathers to present the relationship between Christ and creation. The best book on the subject is Georgii Florovskii, *Creation and Redemption* (Belmont, Mass.: Nordland, 1976). Florovskii deals at length with Irenaeus.

3. Athanasius, *On the Incarnation* (Crestwood, N.Y.: St. Vladimir Orthodox Theological Seminary Press, 1993).

4. For a discussion of the Creed, see Berard Marthaler, *The Creed: The Apostolic Faith in Contemporary Theology* (Mystic, Conn.: Twenty Third Publications, 1996).

5. See William G. Rusch, ed., *The Trinitarian Controversy* (Philadelphia: Fortress, 1980); and Basil Studer, *Trinity and Incarnation: The Faith of the Early Church* (Collegeville, Minn.: Liturgical, 1993).

6. This is the fundamental question of the Christological controversy. See Richard A. Norris Jr., *The Christological Controversy* (Philadelphia: Fortress, 1980); and Paul R. Fries, *Christ in East and West* (Macon, Ga.: Mercer University Press, 1987).

7. See Studer, *Trinity and Incarnation*, 203–7.

8. Lindbeck, *The Nature of Doctrine*, 74.

9. Paul Lakeland, *Postmodernity: Christian Identity in a Postmodern Age* (Minneapolis: Fortress, 1997), 46.

Part 3

1. See *The Seven Letters of Ignatius*, in Cyril Richardson, *The Early Church Fathers* (Philadelphia: Westminster, 1953), 87–120.

2. Daniel Bell, "The Coming of the Post-Industrial Society," in Charles Jencks, ed., *The Postmodern Reader* (New York: St. Martin's, 1992), 264.

3. Robert Webber and Rodney Clapp, *People of the Truth* (San Francisco: Harper & Row, 1988; reprint, Harrisburg, Pa.: Morehouse, 1993).

Chapter 8: Christ Within the Paradigms of History

1. For a helpful history of the church in the various paradigms, see Eric G. Jay, *The Church* (Atlanta: John Knox, 1978).

2. This point of view is generally espoused by our fundamentalist brothers and sisters. See, for example, Jerry Falwell, *The Fundmentalist Phenomena: The Resurgence of Conservative Christianity* (Garden City, N.Y.: Doubleday, 1981).

3. Homily 16, Everett Ferguson, *The Encyclopedia of Early Christianity* (New York: Garland, 1990), s.v. "church," 208.

4. H. de Lubac, *Catholicism* (London: Burns, Oates and Washbourne, 1950), 29. See also Michael J. Hines, *Ongoing Incarnation* (New York: Crossroads, 1997).

5. See Cyprian, *On the Unity of the Church*, trans. Maurice Bevenot (Westminster, Md.: Newman, 1957).

6. The seeds of this idea are in Augustine, *The City of God*, trans. Marcus Dods (Edinburgh: T. & T. Clark, 1872).

7. See Avery Dulles, *Models of the Church* (Garden City, N.Y.: Doubleday, 1978), chapter 1, "The Church as Institution."

8. Ibid., chapter 5, "The Church as Herald."

9. See "On the Councils and the Churches," in *A Compend of Luther's Theology*, ed. Hugh T. Kerr (Philadelphia: Fortress, 1953), vol. 5, 126–33.

10. Ibid., 125.

11. Dulles, *Models of the Church*, chapter 6, "The Church as Servant," 89–102.

12. See John Howard Yoder, *The Royal Priesthood* (Grand Rapids: Eerdmans, 1994; Scottdale, Pa.: Herald, 1998) and his comments about the otherness of the church.

13. See Rodney Clapp, *A Peculiar People: The Church as Culture in a Post-Christian Society* (Downers Grove, Ill.: InterVarsity, 1996).

14. See Philip Kenneson and James Street, *Selling Out the Church* (Nashville: Abingdon, 1997).

15. Note, for example, the work of the Christian Coalition in the United States.

16. Rodney Clapp, personal note on review of this manuscript, January 1999.

Chapter 9: Restoring the Theology of the Church

1. Statement of faith, Wheaton College, Wheaton, Ill., 1995.

2. See James F. Cobble Jr., *The Church and the Powers: A Theology of Church Structure* (Peabody, Mass.: Hendrickson, 1988).

3. Paul Minear, *Images of the Church in the New Testament* (Philadelphia: Westminster, 1960).

4. The image of the church as the people of God is the primary one given to the church in *The Documents of Vatican II*. See "The Church" in *The Documents of Vatican II* (New York: America Press, 1966). This image has become primary in Protestant writings as well.

5. Cyril Richardson, ed., "The Teaching of the Twelve Apostles, Commonly called the *Didache*," ch. 9; in *Early Christian Fathers* [Library of Christian Classics, 1] (Philadelphia: Westminster, 1953), 175.

6. *The Epistle of Ignatius to the Smyrneans,* 1:6. *The Ante-Nicene Fathers,* 1950 ed. by A. C. Coxe (Grand Rapids: Eerdmans, 1960), 86.

7. From Cyprian, *The Unity of the Catholic Church,* trans. Maurice Bevenot (Westminster, Md.: Newman Press, 1956; London: Longmans, Green and Co., 1957).

8. John Calvin, *Institutes of the Christian Religion,* book 4, chapter 2, trans. John Allen (Philadelphia: Presbyterian Board of Christian Education, 1813), 273–74.

9. Ignatius, Ephesians 4:1, see Cyril Richardson, *Early Christian Fathers* (Philadelphia: Westminster, 1963), 89.

10. Ibid., Ephesians 4:2.

11. Barry Spencer, personal correspondence, 1998.

Chapter 10: Recovering Our Historical Connection

1. See Francis A. Sullivan, *The Church We Believe In: One Holy, Catholic, and Apostolic* (Mahwah, N.J.: Paulist, 1988).

2. *Clement's First Letter,* chapter 47, Richardson, *Early Christian Fathers.*

3. *The Teaching of the Twelve Disciples,* ibid., 9.

4. *On the Unity of the Church,* 5.

5. For a vigorous and thoughtful discussion of the church as community, see Miroslav Volf, *After Our Likeness: The Church as the Image of the Trinity* (Grand Rapids: Eerdmans, 1998).

6. Epistle of Ignatius to the *Smyrnaeans.*

7. XVIII, 3 *The Ante-Nicene Fathers.*

8. For a thoughtful discussion of catholicity, see John Meyendorff, *Catholicity and the Church* (Crestwood, N.Y.: St. Vladimir Orthodox Theological Seminary Press, 1983).

9. "What Is the Essence of Apostolic Succession?" in *Apostolic Succession: Rethinking a Barrier to Unity,* ed. Hans Küng (New York: Paulist, 1968).

Part 4

1. Catherine Pickstock, *After Writing: On the Liturgical Consummation of Philosophy* (Oxford: Blackwell, 1998), xii.

2. See Babin, *The New Era of Religious Communication,* 35.

Chapter 11: Worship Within the Paradigms of History

1. See especially Frank Senn, *Christian Liturgy: Catholic and Evangelical* (Minneapolis: Fortress, 1997); Robert Webber, ed., *Twenty Centuries of Christian Worship* (Peabody, Mass.: Hendrickson, 1993); James F. White, *Documents of Christian Worship: Descriptive and Interpretive Sources* (Louisville, Ky.: Westminster/John Knox).

2. See Ralph Martin, *Early Christian Worship* (Grand Rapids: Eerdmans, XXX).

3. See Aidan Kavanagh, *On Liturgical Theology* (New York: Pueblo, 1984).

4. See D. M. Hope, *The Medieval Western Rites,* in *The Study of Liturgy,* ed. Cheslyn Jones, Geoffrey Wainwright, and Edward Yarnold (New York: Oxford University Press, 1978), 220–40.

5. See Eamon Duffy, *The Stripping of the Altars: Traditional Religion in England 1400–1580* (New Haven, Conn.: Yale University Press, 1992).

6. For Reformation liturgies, see Webber, *Twenty Centuries of Christian Worship,* chapter 5, 75–78, and chapter 9, 188–225.

7. See Doug Adams, *Meeting House to Camp Meeting: Toward a History of American Free Church Worship from 1620 to 1835* (Austin, Tex.: Modern Liturgy—Resource Publications, 1981).

8. See Robert Webber, *Worship Old and New* (Grand Rapids: Zondervan, 1994), 109–19.

9. See Robert Webber, *Blended Worship: Achieving Substance and Relevance* (Peabody, Mass.: Hendrickson, 1995).

10. See Robert Jensen, *Visible Words* (Philadelphia: Fortress, 1978).

Chapter 12: Recovering the Theology and Order of Worship

1. See Carmine Di Sante, *Jewish Prayer: The Origins of Christian Liturgy* (New York: Paulist, 1985); and Paul F. Bradshaw and Lawrence A. Hoffman, eds., *The Making of Jewish and Christian Worship* (Notre Dame, Ind.: University of Notre Dame Press, 1994).

2. For a theology of worship, see Aidan Kavanagh, *On Liturgical Theology* (New York: Pueblo, 1984); T. F. Torrance, *Worship, Community, and the Triune God* (Downers Grove, Ill.: InterVarsity, 1997); Gordon Lathrop, *Holy Things: An Ecumenical Liturgical Theology* (Philadelphia: Fortress, 1993); and Alexander Schmemann, *Introduction to Liturgical Theology* (Crestwood, N.Y.: St. Vladimir Orthodox Theological Seminary Press, 1966).

3. Ibid.

4. The classical discussion of word and table is found in Gregory Dix, *The Shape of the Liturgy* (London: Dacre Press, 1945).

5. See R. C. D. Jasper and G. J. Cummings, eds., *Prayers of the Eucharist: Early and Reformed,* 2nd ed. (New York: Oxford University Press, 1980).

6. See Robert Webber, *Planning Blended Worship: The Creative Mixture of the Old and New* (Nashville: Abingdon, 1998). See also the fourfold pattern in Justin Martyr, *The First Apology of Justin,* in Cyril Richardson, *Early Christian Fathers* (Philadelphia: Westminster, 1943), 66.

Chapter 13: Recovering Symbolic Communication

1. See Peter Roche de Coppens, *The Nature and Use of Ritual* (Washington, D.C.: University Press of America, 1979), 137.

2. Ibid., 137–42.

3. See Pierre Babin, "The Symbolic Way," in ibid., 146–67.

4. See Marcheta Mauck, *Shaping a House for the Church* (Chicago: Liturgy Training Publication, 1990).

5. For more information on the relational nature of the fourfold pattern of worship, see Webber, *Planning Blended Worship.*

6. See Babin, "The Symbolic Way," 58–62.

7. See Michael Green, *Baptism: Its Practice and Power* (Downers Grove, Ill.: InterVarsity, 1987).

8. See C. W. Dugmore, *The Influence of the Synagogue in the Divine Office* (London: Oxford University Press, 1944), 11–15.

9. Justin Martyr, *The First Apology of Justin,* 66.

10. See Mark A. Pearson, *Christian Healing* (Grand Rapids: Baker, 1995), especially chapter 9, "The Sacraments as Vehicles of Healing."

11. Gregory Dix, *The Shape of the Liturgy* (London: Dacre, 1945), xii.

12. See Thomas J. Talley, *The Origins of Liturgical Year* (Collegeville, Minn.: Liturgical, 1986); and Adolf Adam, *The Liturgical Year* (Collegeville, Minn.: Liturgical, 1981).

13. Abraham Kuyper, *Lectures on Calvinism* (Grand Rapids: Eerdmans, 1931), 146–47.

14. See Robert Webber, *Music and the Arts in Worship,* vol. 4, A and B of *The Complete Library of Christian Worship* (Peabody, Mass.: Hendrickson, 1995). Volume 4, part B, is entirely on the arts.

Part 5

1. See Douglas Groothuis, *Confronting the New Age* (Downers Grove, Ill.: InterVarsity, 1988).

Chapter 14: Spirituality Within the Paradigms of History

1. See Nicodemus of the Holy Mountain, revised by Theophan the Recluse, *Unseen Warfare* (Crestwood, N.Y.: St. Vladimir Orthodox Theological Seminary Press).

2. See Susan Annette Muto, *A Practical Guide to Spiritual Reading*, rev. ed. (Peterson, Mass.: St. Bede's, 1944).

3. See Herbert B. Workman, *The Evolution of the Monastic Ideal* (Boston: Beacon, 1913). For a primary source, see Timothy Fry, ed., *The Rule of St. Benedict in English* (Collegeville, Minn.: Liturgical, 1982).

4. See Eamon Duffy, *The Stripping of the Altars: Traditional Religion in England 1400–1580* (New Haven, Conn.: Yale University Press, 1992).

5. John Calvin, *Institutes of the Christian Religion*, 1st Amer. ed. (Philadelphia: Presbyterian Board of Publication [PBP], 1813; New Haven, Conn.: Hezekiah Howe, 1816; Philadelphia: Nicklin & Fry, 1816; New York: S. Huestis & C.S. van Winkle, 1919); 5th Amer. ed. (PBP: 1844, 1909, 1930); 6th Amer. ed. (PBP: 1911, 1921; Philadelphia: Presbyterian Board of Christian Education [PBCE], 1928, 1932); 7th Amer. ed. (PBCE, 1936, 1949); 8th Amer. ed. (Grand Rapids: Eerdmans, 1949); (London: S.C.M., 1961); published as *Young-Hahn Gidokyo gangyo* (Seoul: Sungmoon Publication, 1993).

6. See *The Scheitheim Confession of Faith*, in Robert Ferm, *Readings in the History of Christian Thought* (New York: Holt, Rinehart, & Winston, 1964), 528–35.

7. See Stephen Sykes, *The Identification of Christianity* (Philadelphia: Fortress, 1984), especially chapter 11, "Worship, Commitment and Identity."

8. See Philipp Jacob Spener, *Pia Desderia* (Philadelphia: Fortress, 1964); Ronald Knox, *Enthusiasm: A Chapter in the History of Religion with Special Reference to the Seventeenth and Eighteenth Centuries* (New York: Oxford University Press, 1961).

9. See Walter Rauschenbusch, *A Theology of the Social Gospel* (New York: Macmillan, 1917; New York: Abingdon, 1971, 1978, 1987; Louisville: Westminster/John Knox, 1997).

10. See Ronald J. Sider, ed., *The Chicago Declaration* (Carol Stream, Ill.: Creation House, 1974).

11. See Richard Foster, *Celebration of Discipline: The Path to Spiritual Growth* (San Francisco: Harper & Row, 1978).

12. See Cheslyn Jones, Geoffrey Wainwright, and Edward Yarnold, eds., *The Story of Spirituality* (Oxford: Oxford University Press, 1986).

13. See Duffy, *The Stripping of the Altar*.

14. See Mark A. Noll, *The Scandal of the Evangelical Mind* (Grand Rapids: Eerdmans, 1996).

15. Harry Blamires, *The Christian Mind* (Ann Arbor: Vine Books, 1963, 1987).

16. See Daniel Stevick, *Beyond Fundamentalism* (Philadelphia: Westminster, 1963).

17. See Marva Dawn, *Reaching Out without Dumbing Down* (Grand Rapids: Eerdmans, 1995).

18. See Kenneth Leech, *Experiencing God: Theology as Spirituality* (San Francisco: Harper & Row, 1985).

Chapter 15: Classical Spirituality

1. See C. P. M. Jones, "The New Testament," in *The Study of Spirituality*; see also John Stott, *The Message of the Sermon on the Mount* (Downers Grove, Ill.: InterVarsity, 1978).

2. See Timothy Warner, *Spiritual Warfare: Victory over the Powers of Evil* (Wheaton, Ill.: Crossway, 1991); and Scott Moreau, *Essentials of Spiritual Warfare: Equipped to Win the Battle* (Wheaton, Ill.: Harold Shaw, 1997).

3. Jones, "The New Testament."

4. See Christoph Blumhardt, *Action in Waiting* (Farmington, Pa.: Plough, 1969; 2nd ed., 1979, 1998).

5. See Hippolytus, *The Apostolic Tradition of Hippolytus: A Text for Students,* 2nd ed., ed. G. J. Cuming (Brameote, England: Grove, 1987).

6. John Meyendorff, *St. Gregory Palamas and Orthodox Spirituality* (Crestwood, N.Y.: St. Vladimir Orthodox Theological Seminary Press, 1974), 14.

7. Ibid., The Rule of St. Benedict.

8. See Georgia Harkness, *Mysticism: Its Meaning and Message* (Nashville: Abingdon, 1973).

9. See Robin Maas and Gabriel O'Donnell, *Spiritual Traditions for the Contemporary Church* (Nashville: Abingdon, 1990).

10. Jones, "The New Testament."

Chapter 16: Christian Spirituality in a Postmodern World

1. Richard Foster, *Celebration of Discipline*, rev. ed. (San Francisco: Harper & Row, 1988).

2. Athanasius, *On the Incarnation* (Crestwood, N.Y.: St. Vladimir Orthodox Theological Seminary Press, 1993).

3. Athanasius, *On the Incarnation;* in *Nicene and Post-Nicene Fathers,* second series (Grand Rapids: Eerdmans, 1978), IV, 36–67.

4. *On the Unity of the Church,* in Robert Ferm, *Readings in the History of Christian Thought* (New York: Holt, Rinehart, & Winston, 1964).

5. See Vigen Guronian, *Ethics after Christendom: Toward an Ecclesial Christian Ethic* (Grand Rapids: Eerdmans, 1994).

6. Numerous books have been written on liturgy and spirituality. See Philip H. P. Fatteicher, *Liturgical Spirituality* (Valley Forge, Pa.: Trinity Press International, 1997); Gabriel Braso, *Liturgy and Spirituality* (Collegeville, Minn.: Liturgical, 1971); Louis Bouyer, *Liturgical Piety* (Notre Dame, Ind.: University of Notre Dame Press, 1995); Don E. Saliers, *Worship and Spirituality* (Philadelphia: Westminster, 1984); Kevin W. Irwin, *Liturgy, Prayer and Spirituality* (New York: Paulist, 1984); Joyce Ann Zimmerman, *Liturgy as Living Faith: A Liturgical Spirituality* (Scranton, Pa.: University of Scranton, 1993).

7. See P. Fatteicher, "Baptism, Hallowing Life and Death," 226–45.

8. See Irwin, "Proclamation of the Word of God," 99–126.

9. See P. Fattsicher, "The Holy Eucharist: Hallowing Sustenance," 174–204.

10. See Dallas Willard, *The Spirit of the Disciplines: Understanding How God Changes Lives* (San Francisco: Harper San Francisco, 1988).

11. For an introduction to the various spiritual traditions in history, see Richard J. Foster, *Streams of Living Water: Celebrating the Great Traditions of Christian Faith* (San Francisco: Harper San Francisco, 1998).

12. John Howard Yoder, *The Politics of Jesus* (Grand Rapids: Eerdmans, 1972); Stanley Hauerwas, *After Christendom* (Nashville: Abingdon, 1991).

13. See Foster, *Streams of Living Water*, especially chapter 2, "The Contemplative Tradition," 23–58; and Richard J. Foster and James Bryan Smith, eds., *Devotional Classics: Selected Readings for Individuals and Groups* (San Francisco: Harper San Francisco, 1993).

14. Hippolytus, *The Apostolic Tradition*, 41.

15. Ibid.

16. Ibid.

17. Ibid.

18. See Joseph J. Allen, *Inner Way: Toward a Rebirth of Eastern Christian Spiritual Direction* (Grand Rapids: Eerdmans, 1994); and Aelred Squire, *Asking the Fathers: A Lively Look at the Oldest and Longest Christian Tradition of Spiritual Living* (Westminster, Md.: Christian Classics, 1993).

19. L. Gregory Jones, *Embodying Forgiveness: A Theological Analysis* (Grand Rapids: Eerdmans, 1995).

20. J. D. Douglas, ed., *Let the Earth Hear His Voice* (Minneapolis: Worldwide, 1975), 7, article 6.

Part 6

1. Jencks, *The Postmodern Reader*, 11.

Chapter 17: Evangelism as Process

1. See Kenneth Boyack, *Catholic Evangelization Today: A New Pentecost for the United States* (New York: Paulist, 1987).

2. For a history of evangelism, see David J. Bosch, *Transforming Mission: Paradigm Shifts in Theology of Mission* (Maryknoll, N.Y.: Orbis, 1994).

3. See Michael Dujarier, *The Rites of Christian Initiation* (New York: Sadlier, 1979). See also Michel Green, *Evangelism in the Early Church* (Grand Rapids: Eerdmans, 1970).

4. See The Murphy Center for Liturgical Studies, *Made, Not Born: New Perspectives on Christian Initiation and the Catechumenate* (Notre Dame, Ind.: University of Notre Dame Press, 1976), especially chapter 3, "Dissolution of the Rite of Christian Initiation."

5. David J. Bosch, *Transforming Mission* (Maryknoll, N.Y.: Orbis, 1991) "The Medieval Roman Catholic Paradigm," *Made, Not Born*, chapter 7.

6. Ibid., "The Missionary Paradigm of the Protestant Reformation," *Transforming Mission*, chapter 8.

7. Ibid., "Mission in the Wake of the Enlightenment," *Transforming Mission*, chapter 9.

8. Ibid., "The Emergence of a Post Modern Paradigm," *Transforming Mission*, chapter 10.

9. R. B. Kuiper, *God-Centered Evangelism* (Grand Rapids: Baker, 1961), 80.

10. Bosch, "The Medieval Roman Catholic Paradigm," 399.

11. See Michael Green, *Baptism: Its Purpose and Power* (Downers Grove, Ill.: InterVarsity, 1987), especially chapter 4, "Baptism: What Does It Mean and What Does It Do?"

12. See Dietrich Bonhoeffer, *The Cost of Discipleship* (New York: Macmillan, 1976).

13. See George Hunsberger and Craig Van Gelder, *Church: Between Gospel and Culture: The Emerging Mission in North America* (Grand Rapids: Eerdmans, 1996).

14. Green, *Baptism*, 152–53.

15. Arnold Van Gennep, *The Rites of Passage*, trans. Monika B. Vizedom and Gabrielle L. Caffe (Chicago: University of Chicago Press, 1960), 189–90.

16. See Robert Webber, *Liturgical Evangelism* (Harrisburg, Pa.: Morehouse, 1994).

17. Craig Van Gelder, "Defining the Center—Finding the Boundaries," in Hunsberger and Van Gelder, *Church*, 32.

18. See Paul D. Hanson, *The People Called: The Growth of Community in the Bible* (San Francisco: Harper & Row, 1986).

19. A statement made by William Visserit Hooft in his retiring speech as general secretary of the World Council of Churches. Quoted by George Hoffman in "The Social Responsibilities of Evangelization," in *Let the Earth Hear His Voice*, ed. J. D. Douglas (Minneapolis: Worldwide, 1975), 698.

20. See especially Darrell L. Gruder, ed., *Missional Church: A Vision for the Sending of the Church in North America* (Grand Rapids: Eerdmans, 1998).

21. See *Christian Initiation Resources Reader,* vol. 1, *Precatechumenate;* vol. 2, *Catechumenate;* vol. 3, *Purification and Enlightenment;* vol. 4, *Mystagogia and Ministries* (New York: Sadlier, 1984).

Chapter 18: Education as Wisdom

1. See Craig Van Gelder, *Confident Witness—Changing World* (Grand Rapids: Eerdmans, 1999).

2. C. H. Dodd, *The Apostolic Preaching and Its Development* (New York: Harper & Row, 1939), 8.

3. Green, *Evangelism in the Early Church,* 204.

4. See Thomas H. Groome, *Christian Religious Education: Sharing Our Story and Vision* (San Francisco: Harper & Row, 1980); and Babin, *The New Era in Religious Communication,* particularly chapter 1, "Religious Education from Gutenberg to the Electronic Age."

5. Babin, *The New Era in Religious Communication,* 21.

6. Ibid.

7. Ibid., 21–22.

8. See Eamon Duffy, *The Stripping of the Altars: Traditional Religion in England 1400–1580* (New Haven, Conn.: Yale University Press, 1992).

9. See Babin, *Religious Communication.*

10. See Van Gelder, especially chapter 6, "Missional Community: Cultivating Communities of the Holy Spirit."

11. See the classic work on education as a process, Horace Bushnell, *Christian Nurture* (Cleveland: Pilgrim, 1994).

12. For primary sources, see Edward Yarnold, *The Awe Inspiring Rites of Initiation: Baptismal Homilies of the Fourth Century* (Middlegreen, Slough , England: St. Paul, 1971).

13. See Hippolytus, *The Apostolic Tradition.*

14. See *The Library of Christian Classics,* vol. 2, *Cyril of Jerusalem and Nemesius of Emessa* (Philadelphia: Westminster, 1960).

15. See, for example, *The Didache,* chapters 1–6, *The Library of Christian Classics,* vol. 1, *The Early Christian Fathers* (Philadelphia: Westminster, 1963), 171–74.

16. See Philip Carrington, *The Primitive Christian Catechism* (Cambridge: University, 1940).

17. Justin, *Apology,* 61.

18. Hippolytus, *The Apostolic Tradition,* 20.

19. Ibid., 21.

20. See George E. Gingras, tr., *Egeria: Diary of a Pilgrimage* (New York: Newman, 1970).

21. Parker J. Palmer, *To Know as We Are Known: Education as a Spiritual Journey* (San Francisco: Harper San Francisco, 1993).

22. See Dujarier, *The Rites of Christian Initiation* (New York: Sadlier, 1979), chapter 6, "The Sacred Triduum."

23. See Hunsberger and Van Gelder, *Church,* section 3, "Defining the Church."

Chapter 19: The Church in the World

1. John Howder Yoder in his classic book, *The Politics of Jesus* (Grand Rapids: Eerdman, 1972), views the Sermon on the Mount as the politics of Jesus.

2. See Stanley Hauerwas, *After Christendom* (Nashville: Abingdon, 1991).

3. For a history of the church in the world, see Robert Webber, *The Church in the World* (Grand Rapids: Zondervan, 1994).

4. This is true of the Moral Majority and its successor, the Christian Coalition.

5. See Robert Webber, *The Moral Majority: Right or Wrong* (Wheaton, Ill.: Crossway, 1980).

6. Charles Colson, *Against the Night: Living in the New Dark Ages* (Ann Arbor, Mich.: Servant/Vine, 1989, 1999), from the front flap of the jacket.

7. Ibid. Note the subtitle to Colson's book—*Living in the New Dark Ages*.

8. See Robert Webber and Rodney Clapp, *The People of the Truth* (Harrisburg, Pa.: Morehouse, 1993).

9. *Epistle to Diognetus*, 5 and 6 in Cyril Richardson, *Early Christian Fathers* (Philadelphia: Westminster, 1943).

10. See the following writings of Tertullian in *The Antenicene Fathers* (Grand Rapids: Eerdmans, 1972): *On the Apparel of Women, On the Veiling of Virgins, To His Wife, On Exhortation to Chastity, On Monogamy, On Modesty, On Fasting,* and *Defuga in Persecutione.*

11. Tertullian, *Defuga in Persecutione.*

12. Colson, *Against the Night*, 156.

13. Hippolytus, *The Apostolic Tradition,* in Jasper and Cummings, *Eucharistric Prayers: Early & Reformed* (Collegeville: Liturgical, 1993), 23.

14. See Augustine, *The City of God.*

15. See Timothy R. Phillips and Dennis L. Okholm, *Welcome to the Family* (Wheaton, Ill.: Victor/BridgePoint, 1996), especially chapters 12, 13, and 14.

16. See Stanley Hauerwas, *A Community of Character: Toward a Constructive Christian Social Ethic* (Notre Dame, Ind.: University of Notre Dame Press, 1986).

17. Ibid., 6.

Appendix

1. Charles Jencks, ed., *The Postmodern Reader* (New York: St. Martin's, 1992).

2. Hans von Campenhausen, *Tradition and Life in the Church* (New York: Collins, 1968).

3. See Ephraim Radner, *The End of the Church* (Grand Rapids: Eerdmans, 1998), chapter 1.

4. George Tavard, *Holy Writ or Holy Church* (New York: Harper and Brothers, 1959).

5. See just about any history of the Reformation. A good study is found in Clyde Manschreck, ed., *A History of Christianity: Readings in the History of the Church*, vol. 2, *The Church from the Reformation to the Present* (Grand Rapids: Baker, 1964), chapters 1 and 2.

6. Ibid., chapters 5 and 7.

7. See George A. Lindbeck, *The Nature of Doctrine: Religion and Theology in a Post Liberal Age* (Philadelphia: Westminster, 1984).

8. Clyde Manschreck, *A History of Christianity*, 2 vols. (Grand Rapids: Baker, 1990 [earlier ed. 1962, 1981]).

9. See Harvie M. Conn, ed., *Inerrancy and Hermeneutic: A Tradition, a Challenge, a Debate* (Grand Rapids: Eerdmans, 1988).

10. See Charles J. Scalise, *From Scripture to Theology* (Downers Grove, Ill.: InterVarsity, 1996).

11. See Arthur C. Cochrane, ed., *Reformed Confessions of the Sixteenth Century* (Philadelphia: Westminster, 1966).

12. See F. F. Bruce, *Tradition: Old and New* (Grand Rapids: Zondervan, 1970).

13. Tertullian, *De Praescriptione Haereticorum;* in *Ante-Nicene Fathers* as "The Prescription against Heretics" (Grand Rapids: Eerdmans, 1978), III, 243–65.

14. Athanasius, *Ad Serap;* in *Nicene and Post-Nicene Fathers* (see above), IV, 564–66.

15. See Birger Gerhardsson, *Tradition and Transmission in the Early Church* (Grand Rapids: Eerdmans, 1998).

16. Eusebius, *Ecclesiastical History*, book III, XXII; in *Nicene and Post-Nicene Fathers*, second series, as "Church History," I, 149.

17. See Lindbeck, *Nature of Doctrine*, 18.

18. For a study of gnosticism, see P. Perkins, *The Gnostic Dialogue: The Early Church and the Crisis of Gnosticism* (New York: Paulist, 1980).

19. *Tertullian, Adversus Praxean,* in *Ante-Nicene Fathers,* as "Against Praxeas" (Grand Rapids: Eerdmans, 1978), III, 597–627.

20. *Irenaeus, Against Heresies,* ch. 4 in *Ante-Nicene Fathers* (Grand Rapids: Eerdmans, 1978), I, 320–22.

21. Lindbeck, *Nature of Doctrine,* 18.

22. Ibid., 112–38.

23. Ibid.

24. *Dialogue,* 80, 3.

25. *Ad Serap* I, 28.

26. See George Tavard, *Holy Writ on Holy Church* (London: Burns & Oates, 1959; Westport, Conn.: Greenwood, 1978) chapter 1.

27. See W. Foerster, *Gnosis,* 2 vols. (Oxford: Clarendon, 1972–74).

28. Irenaeus, *Against Heresies,* in *Ante-Nicene Fathers* (Grand Rapids: Eerdmans, 1978), I, 315ff.

29. *Epistle of Barnabas,* 5, 1.

30. Gerald F. Hawthorne, ed., "A New English Translation of Melito's Paschal Homily," *Current Issues in Biblical and Patristic Interpretation* (Grand Rapids: Eerdmans, 1975), 147.

31. *Dialogue,* 80, 3.

32. Irenaeus, *Against Heresies,* in *Ante-Nicene Fathers* (Grand Rapids: Eerdmans, 1978), I, 315ff.

33. See F. F. Bruce, *The Canon of Scripture* (Downers Grove, Ill.: InterVarsity, 1988).

34. Kelly, *Early Christian Doctrine,* 60.

35. *The First Letter of Clement to the Corinthians,* XLII, 1, 2; in *Ante-Nicene Fathers* (Grand Rapids: Eerdmans, 1978), I, 16; X, 241f.

36. Irenaeus, *Against Heresies;* in *Ante-Nicene Fathers* (Grand Rapids: Eerdmans, 1978), I, 315f.

37. John Chrysostom, Colossians, Homily IX; in *Nicene and Post-Nicene Fathers,* first series (Grand Rapids: Eerdmans, 1979), XIII, 300–303.

38. George Tavard, *Holy Writ on Holy Church* (London: Burns & Oates, 1959; Westport, Conn.: Greenwood, 1978), chapter 1.

39. Hans-Georg Gadamer, *Truth and Method* (New York: Crossroads, 1991).

40. Ibid.

41. Charles J. Scalise, *From Scripture to Theology* (Downers Grove, Ill.: InterVarsity, 1996), 64.

42. For a discussion of Christianity and pluralism see S. Mark Heim, *Grounds for Understanding: Ecumenical Resources for Responses to Religious Pluralism* (Grand Rapids: Eerdmans, 1998); and Lesslie Newbigin, *The Gospel in a Pluralistic Society* (Grand Rapids: Eerdmans, 1989).

43. See Lindbeck, *Nature of Doctrine,* 74.

44. Ibid., 32–41.

45. Irenaeus, *Against Heresies,* book III, *Ante-Nicene Fathers* (Grand Rapids: Eerdmans, 1885, 1956, 1973, 1986), 4.

46. See Dennis L. Okholm and Timothy D. Phillips, eds., *More Than One Way? Four Views on Salvation in a Pluralistic World* (Grand Rapids: Zondervan, 1995).

47. *Commonitory,* II.

48. See the jacket flap.

49. Helmut Thielicke, *Evangelical Faith* (Grand Rapids: Eerdmans, 1974).

50. Ibid., 38.

51. Ibid.

52. *The Chalcedon Creed.*

RECOMMENDED READING

Part 1

Postmodernism

Berquist, William. *The Post Modern Organization: Mastering the Art of Irreversible Change.* San Francisco: Jossey Bass, 1993.

Cahoone, Lawrence, ed. *From Modernism to Postmodernism.* Oxford: Blackwell, 1995.

Clayton, Philip D. *God and Contemporary Science.* Grand Rapids: Eerdmans, 1998.

Connor, Steven. *Post Modernist Culture: An Introduction to Theories of the Contemporary.* Oxford: Blackwell, 1996.

Eco, Umberto. *Semiotics and the Philosophy of Language.* Bloomington: Indiana University Press, 1984.

———. *Philosophical Hermeneutics.* Translated by David Line. Berkely: University of California Press, 1976.

Gadamer, Hans-Georg. *Truth and Method.* Edited by Garrett Barden and John Cumming. New York: Seabury, 1975.

Gregerson, Niels Henrick, and J. Wentzel Van Huyssteen. *Rethinking Theology of Science: Six Models for the Current Dialogue.* Grand Rapids: Eerdmans, 1998.

Jencks, Charles. *The Postmodern Reader.* New York: St. Martin's, 1992.

Ward, Graham. *The Postmodern God: A Theological Reader.* Oxford: Blackwell, 1997.

Zuckert, Catherine H. *Postmodern Platos: Nietzsche, Heidegger, Gadamer, Strauss, Derrida.* Chicago: University of Chicago Press, 1996.

General Responses to Postmodernism

Allen, Diogenes. *Christian Belief in a Postmodern World: The Full Wealth of Conviction.* Oxford: Blackwell, 1997.

Anderson, Walter Truett. *Reality Isn't What It Used to Be.* San Francisco: Harper, 1990.

———. *The Truth about Truth: De-Confusing and Re-Constructing the Postmodern World.* New York: Putman's Sons, 1995.

Beaudoin, Tom. *Virtual Faith: The Irreverent Spiritual Quest of Generation X.* San Francisco: Jossey-Bass, 1998.

Bellah, Robert, Richard Maken, William Sullivan, Ann Swidler, and Steve Tipton. *Habits of the Heart: Individualism and Commitment in American Life.* Berkeley: University of California Press, 1985.

Burnham, Frederic B., ed. *Postmodern Theology: Christian Faith in a Pluralist World.* San Francisco: Harper, 1989.

Carter, Stephen L. *The Culture of Disbelief: How American Law and Politics Trivialize Religious Devotion.* New York: Basic Books, 1993.

Eagleton, Terry. *The Illusions of Postmodernism.* Oxford: Blackwell, 1996.

Grant, C. David. *Thinking through Our Faith: Theology for Twenty-First-Century Christians.* Nashville: Abingdon, 1988.

Griffin, David Ray, William A. Beardslee, and Joe Holland. *Varieties of Postmodern Theology.* Albany: State University of New York Press, 1989.

Hampshire, Stuart, ed. *The Age of Reason: Basic Writings of Bacon, Pascal, Hobbes, Galileo, Descartes, Spinoza, Leibniz.* New York: A Mentor Book, 1956.

Harvey, David. *The Condition of Postmodernity: An Enquiry into the Origins of Cultural Change.* Oxford: Blackwell, 1989.

Hassen, Ihab. *The Postmodern Turn: Essays in Postmodern Theology and Culture.* Athens: Ohio University Press, 1987.

Lakeland, Paul. *Postmodernity: Christian Identity in a Fragmented Age.* Minneapolis: Fortress, 1997.

Lernert, Charles, ed. *Social Theory: The Multicultural and Classical Readings.* Oxford: Westview, 1993.

Lindbeck, George A. *The Nature of Doctrine: Religion and Theology in a Post Liberal Age.* Philadelphia: Westminster, 1984.

Tickle, Phyllis A. *God-Talk in America.* New York: Crossroad, 1998.

Young, Pamela Dickey. *Christ in a Post-Christian World.* Minneapolis: Fortress, 1995.

Evangelical Responses to Postmodernism

Beckwith, Francis J., and Greg Koukl. *Relativism: Feet Firmly Planted in Mid Air.* Grand Rapids: Baker, 1996.

Clapp, Rodney. *Families at the Crossroads: Beyond Traditional and Modern Options.* Downers Grove, Ill.: InterVarsity, 1993.

Clouse, Robert G., Robert N. Hosack, and Richard V. Pierard. *The New Millennial Manual: A Once and Future Guide.* Grand Rapids: Baker, 1999.

Dockery, David S., ed. *The Challenge of Postmodernism: An Evangelical Engagement.* Wheaton: Victor/BridgePoint, 1995.

Dorrien, Gary. *The Remaking of Evangelical Theology.* Louisville: Westminster John Knox, 1998.

Erickson, Millard J. *The Evangelical Left: Encountering Postconservative Evangelical Theology.* Grand Rapids: Baker, 1997.

―――. *Postmodernizing the Faith: Evangelical Responses to the Challenge of Postmodernism.* Grand Rapids: Baker, 1998.

Grenz, Stanley. *A Primer on Postmodernism.* Grand Rapids: Eerdmans, 1996.

Hahn, Todd, and David Verhaagen. *Genxers after God: Helping a Generation Pursue Jesus.* Grand Rapids: Baker, 1997.

Henderson, David W. *Culture Shift: Communicating God's Truth to Our Changing World.* Grand Rapids: Baker, 1997.

Knight, Henry H., III. *The Future for Truth: Evangelical Theology in a Postmodern World.* Nashville: Abingdon, 1997.

Lundin, Roger. *The Culture of Interpretation: The Christian Faith and the Postmodern World.* Grand Rapids: Eerdmans, 1993.

McGrath, Alister. *A Passion for Truth: The Intellectual Coherence of Evangelism.* Downers Grove, Ill.: InterVarsity, 1996.

Middleton, J. Richard, and Brian J. Walsh. *Truth Is Stranger Than It Used to Be: Biblical Faith in a Postmodern World.* Downers Grove, Ill.: InterVarsity, 1995.

Murphy, Nancey. *Beyond Liberalism and Fundamentalism.* Valley Forge, Pa.: Trinity Press International, 1996.

Oden, Thomas C. *After Modernity . . . What? Agenda for Theology*. Grand Rapids: Zondervan, 1990.

Phillips, Timothy R., and Dennis L. Okholm. *Christian Apologetics in the Postmodern World*. Downers Grove, Ill.: InterVarsity, 1995.

Phillips, Timothy, and Dennis Okholm, eds. *The Nature of Confession: Evangelicals and Post Liberals in Conversation*. Downers Grove, Ill.: InterVarsity, 1996.

Sweet, Leonard. *Faith Quakers*. Nashville: Abingdon, 1994.

Thiselton, Anthony C. *Interpreting God and the Post Modern Self*. Grand Rapids: Eerdmans, 1995.

Tomlinson, Dave. *The Post-Evangelical*. London: S.P.C.K., 1995.

Veith, Gene Edward, Jr. *Postmodern Times*. Wheaton: Crossway, 1994.

Wells, David. *Losing Our Virtue: Why the Church Must Recover Its Moral Vision*. Grand Rapids: Eerdmans, 1998.

Classical Christianity

Arnold, Eberhard. *The Early Christians in Their Own Words*. Farmington, Pa.: Plough, 1997.

Athanasius. *On The Incarnation*. Crestwood, N.J.: St. Vladimir's Orthodox Theological Seminary.

Bettenson, Henry. *The Early Church Fathers*. Oxford: Oxford University Press, 1956.

———. *The Later Christian Fathers*. London: Oxford University Press, 1970.

Chadwick, Henry. *Alexandrian Christianity*. Philadelphia: Westminster, 1964.

———. *Early Christian Thought and the Classical Tradition*. Oxford: Clarendon, 1966.

Cochrane, Charles Norris. *Christianity and Classical Culture*. New York: Oxford University Press, 1964.

Cullmann, Oscar. *The Early Church: Studies in Early Christian History and Theology*. Philadelphia: Westminster, 1956.

Ellis, Earle E. *The Old Testament in Early Christianity*. Tübingen, Germany: J. C. B. Mohr/Paul Siebeck, 1991.

Eusebius' Ecclesiastical History. Grand Rapids: Baker, 1962.

The Faith of the Early Church Fathers. Vol. 5. Minneapolis: Liturgical, 1978.

Ferguson, Everett. *Early Christians Speak: Faith and Life in the First Three Centures*. Abilene, Tex.: Acu, 1981.

———. *Encyclopedia of Early Christianity*. New York: Garland, 1990.

Greenslade, S. L. *Early Latin Theology*. Philadelphia: Westminster, 1996.

Hazlett, Ian, ed. *Early Christianity Origins and Evolution to A.D. 600*. Nashville: Abingdon, 1991.

Kee, Howard Clark, et al. *Christianity: A Social and Cultural History*. New York: Macmillan, 1991.

Kelly, J. N. D. *Early Christian Creeds*. New York: David McKay, 1976.

———. *Early Christian Doctrine*. New York: Harper, 1958.

Kelly, Joseph F. *The Concise Dictionary of Early Christianity*. Collegeville, Minn.: Liturgical, 1992.

Lightfoot, J. B., J. R. Harmer, and Michael W. Holmes, eds. *The Apostolic Fathers*. 2nd ed. Grand Rapids: Baker, 1997.

Murphy, Francis X. *The Christian Way of Life: Message of the Fathers of the Church*. Wilmington, Del.: Michael Glazier, 1986.

Nassif, Bradley. *New Perspectives on Historical Theology: Essays in Memory of John Meyendorff*. Grand Rapids: Eerdmans, 1996.

Norris, R. A. *God and World in Early Christian Theology.* New York: Seabury, 1965.

Pelikan, Jaraslov. *The Emergence of the Catholic Tradition.* Chicago: University of Chicago Press, 1971.

———. *The Spirit of Eastern Christendom (600–1700).* Chicago: University of Chicago Press, 1974.

Prestige, G. L. *Fathers and Heretics.* London: S.P.C.K., 1968.

Quastnen, Johannes. *Patrology.* Vols. 1–3. Westminster, Md.: Christian Classics, 1986.

Ramsey, Boniface. *Beginning to Read the Fathers.* New York: Paulist, 1985.

Studer, Basil. *Trinity and Incarnation: The Faith of the Early Church.* Collegeville, Minn.: Liturgical, 1993.

Wiles, Maurice, and Mark Santer. *Documents in Early Christian Thought.* New York: Cambridge University Press, 1975.

Williams, Robert R. *A Guide to the Teachings of the Early Church Fathers.* Grand Rapids: Eerdmans, 1960.

Wolterstorff, Nicholas. *Divine Discourse.* Cambridge: Cambridge University Press, 1995.

Part 2

Primary Sources

Irenaeus, *Against Heresies,* and Tertullian, *Against Praexeus.* In *The Ante-Nicene Fathers.* Vols. 1, 3, 4. Grand Rapids: Eerdmans, 1973.

Jasper, R. C. D., and G. J. Cummings, eds. *Prayers of the Eucharist: Early and Reformed.* 2nd ed. New York: Oxford University Press, 1980 (contains the liturgies of the early church).

von Balthasar, Hans Urs. *The Scandal of the Incarnation: Irenaeus Against the Heresies.* San Francisco: Ignatius, 1981 (contains a study of Irenaeus's work).

Secondary Studies of Christus Victor

Aulen, Gustav. *Christus Victor.* New York: Macmillan, 1969.

Berkhof, Hendrikus. *Christ and the Powers.* Scottsdale, Pa.: Herald, 1977.

Boyd, Gregory. *God at War.* Downers Grove, Ill.: InterVarsity, 1997.

Florovskii, Georgii. *Creation and Redemption.* Belmont, Mass.: Nordland, 1976.

Frei, Hans W. *The Identity of Jesus Christ.* Eugene, Ore.: WIPF and Stock, 1998.

Fries, Paul R., and Tiran Nersoyan, eds. *Christ in East and West.* Atlanta: Mercer, 1987.

Grenz, Stanley J. *Revisioning Evangelical Theology.* Downers Grove, Ill.: InterVarsity, 1993.

Gunton, C. E. *Christ and Creation.* Grand Rapids: Eerdmans, 1992.

Kelly, J. N. D. *Early Christian Creeds.* New York: David McKay, 1976.

Lane, Dermot A. *Christ at the Centre.* Mahwah, N.J.: Paulist, 1991.

Marthaler, Berard. *The Creed: The Apostolic Faith in Contemporary Theology.* Mystic, Conn.: Twenty Third Publication, 1993.

Norris, Richard A., Jr. *The Christological Controversy.* Philadelphia: Fortress, 1980.

Peters, Ted. *Sin: Radical Evil in Soul and Society.* Grand Rapids: Eerdmans, 1994.

Rusch, William G. *The Trinitarian Controversy.* Philadelphia: Fortress, 1980.

Schönborn, Christoph. *The Mystery of the Incarnation.* San Francisco: Ignatius, 1992.

Wainwright, Geoffrey. *For Our Salvation: Two Approaches to the Work of Christ.* Grand Rapids: Eerdmans, 1997.

Wink, Walter. *Engaging the Powers.* Philadelphia: Fortress, 1992.

———. *Naming the Powers: The Language of Power in the New Testament.* Philadelphia: Fortress, 1984.

———. *Unmasking the Powers: The Invisible Forces That Determine Human Existence.* Philadelphia: Fortress, 1986.

Ware, Kallistos. *The Orthodox Way.* Crestwood, N.Y.: St. Vladimir's Orthodox Theological Seminary Press, 1980.

von Balthasar, Hans Urs. *Mysterium Paschale.* Grand Rapids: Eerdmans, 1990.

Centrality of Christ to the Christian Faith

Athanasius. *On the Incarnation.* Crestwood, N.Y.: St. Vladimir's Orthodox Theological Seminary, 1993.

Interpretation of Nicene and Chalcedon Thought

Studer, Basil. *Trinity and Incarnation: The Faith of the Early Church.* Collegeville, Minn.: Liturgical, 1993.

Part 3

Primary Sources of Ignatius and Cyprian

Dogmatic Constitution on the Church in the Documents of Vatican II, available in numerous publications.

Richardson, Cyril. *Early Christian Fathers.* Philadelphia: Westminster, 1963.

Cyprian of Carthage. *On the Unity of the Catholic Church.* St. Louis: Herder, 1924.

Cyprian of Carthage, The Lapsed. *The Unity of the Church.* Translated by Maurice Bevenot, S.J. Westminster, Md.. Newman, 1957, London. Longmans, Green and Co., 1957.

Secondary Sources

Azevedo, Marcelo del. *Basic Ecclesial Communities in Brazil: The Challenge of a New Way of Being Church.* Translated by John Drury. Washington, D.C.: Georgetown University Press, 1987.

Banks, Robert. *Paul's Idea of Community: The Early House Churches in Their Historical Setting.* Grand Rapids: Eerdmans, 1980.

Bonhoeffer, Dietrich. *Life Together.* San Francisco: Harper, 1954.

Braaten, Carl E. *Mother Church: Ecclesiology and Ecumenism.* Minneapolis: Fortress, 1998.

Carmody, Denise Lardner, and John Tully Carmody. *Bonded in Christ Love: Being a Member of the Church, An Introduction to Ecclesiology.* Oxford: Blackwell, 1996.

Clapp, Rodney. *A Peculiar People: The Church as Culture in a Post-Christian Society.* Downers Grove, Ill.: InterVarsity, 1996.

Dulles, Avery. *Models of the Church.* New York: Image Books, 1978.

Fournier, Keith, with William D. Watkins. *House United? Evangelicals and Catholics Together.* Colorado Springs: NavPress, 1994.

Gorman, Julie. *Community That Is Christian: A Handbook on Small Groups.* Wheaton, Ill.: Victor Books, 1993.

Hanson, Paul D. *The People Called: The Growth and Community in the Bible.* San Francisco: Harper & Row, 1987.

Hauerwas, Stanley. *A Community of Character: Toward a Constructive Christian Social Ethic.* Notre Dame, Ind.: University of Notre Dame Press, 1981.

223

Himes, Michael J. *Ongoing Incarnation: Johann Adam Möhler and the Beginnings of Modern Ecclesiology.* New York: Crossroad, 1997.

Hinchtiff, Peter. *Cyprian of Carthage and The Unity of the Christian Church.* London: Geoffrey Capman, 1974.

Hodgson, Peter C. *Revisioning the Church: Ecclesial Freedom in the New Paradigm.* Philadelphia: Fortress, 1988.

Küng, Hans. *Structures of the Church.* New York: Nelson, 1964.

Meyendorff, John. *Catholicity and the Church.* Crestwood, N.Y.: St. Vladimir's Orthodox Theological Seminary Press, 1983.

Ogden, Greg. *The New Reformation: Returning the Ministry to the People of God.* Grand Rapids: Zondervan, 1990.

Radner, Ephraim. *The End of the Church: A Pneumatology of Christian Division in the West.* Grand Rapids: Eerdmans, 1999 (sets forth an "ecclesiology of division").

Sullivan, Francis A. *The Church We Believe In: One, Holy, Catholic and Apostolic.* New York: Paulist, 1988.

Tavard, George H. *The Church, Community of Salvation: An Ecumenical Ecclesiology.* Collegeville, Minn.: Liturgical, 1992.

Volf, Miroslav. *After Our Likeness: The Church as the Image of the Trinity.* Grand Rapids: Eerdmans, 1988.

Wuthnow, Robert. *Sharing the Journey: Support Groups and Americas New Quest for Community.* New York: Macmillan, 1994.

Part 4

Adam, Adolf. *The Liturgical Year: Its History and Its Meaning after the Reform of the Liturgy.* New York: Pueblo, 1981.

Adams, Doug. *Meeting House to Camp Meeting: Toward a History of American Free Church Worship from 1620 to 1835.* Austin: The Sharing Company, 1981.

Bouyer, Louis. *Eucharist: Theology and Spirituality of the Eucharistic Prayer.* Notre Dame, Ind.: University of Notre Dame Press, 1968.

———. *Rite and Man: Natural Sacredness and Christian Liturgy.* Notre Dame, Ind.: University of Notre Dame Press, 1967.

Brueggemann, Walter. *Israel's Praise: Doxology Against Idolatry and Ideology.* Philadelphia: Fortress, 1988.

Dawn, Marva J. *Reaching Out without Dumbing Down: A Theological Worship for the Turn of the Century Culture.* Grand Rapids: Eerdmans, 1995.

———. *A Royal Waste of Time: The Splendor of Worshiping God and Being Church for the World.* Grand Rapids: Eerdmans, 1999.

Duffy, Eamon. *The Stripping of the Altars: Traditional Religion in England 1400–1500.* New Haven, Conn.: Yale University Press, 1992.

Dupré, Louis. *Religious Mystery and Rational Reflection.* Grand Rapids: Eerdmans, 1998.

Hill, Andrew. *Enter His Courts with Praise: Old Testament Worship for a New Testament Church.* Grand Rapids: Baker, 1996.

Hustad, Donald P. *Jubilate II: Church Music in Worship and Renewal.* Carol Stream, Ill.: Hope, 1993.

Jasper, R. C. D., and G. J. Cummings. *Prayers of the Eucharist: Early and Reformed.* New York: Oxford University Press, 1980.

Jones, Cheslyn, Geoffrey Wainwright, and Edward Yarnold, eds. *The Study of Liturgy.* New York: Oxford University Press, 1978.

Kavanagh, Aidan. *On Liturgical Theology.* New York: Pueblo, 1984.

La Verdiere, Eugene. *The Breaking of the Bread: The Development of the Eucharist according to Acts.* Chicago: Liturgical Training Publications, 1998.

Mascall, E. L. *Theology and Images.* London: A. R. Mowbray, 1963.

Morgenthaler, Sally. *Worship Evangelism.* Grand Rapids: Zondervan, 1995.

Nevin, John W. *The Mystical Presence and Other Writings on the Eucharist.* Edited by Bard Thompson and George Bricker. Philadelphia: United Church Press, 1966.

Nichols, Aiden. *The Art of God Incarnate: Theology and Symbol from Genesis to the Twentieth Century.* New York: Paulist, 1980.

O'Conner, James T. *The Hidden Manna: A Theology of the Eucharist.* San Francisco: Ignatius, 1988.

Otto, Rudolf. *The Idea of the Holy.* New York: Oxford University Press, 1950.

Old, Hughes Oliphant. *The Reading and Preaching of the Scriptures.* Vol. 2, *The Patristic Age.* Grand Rapids: Eerdmans, 1998.

Peterson, David. *Engaging with God: A Biblical Theology of Worship.* Grand Rapids: Eerdmans, 1992.

Prestor, Geoffrey. *Hallowing the Time: Meditations on the Cycle of the Christian Liturgy.* New York: Paulist, 1980.

Root, Michael, and Risto Saarinen. *Baptism and the Unity of the Church.* Grand Rapids; Eerdmans, 1999.

Rordorf, Willy, et al. *The Eucharist of the Early Christians.* New York: Pueblo, 1978.

Schmemann, Alexander. *The Eucharist.* Crestwood, N.Y.: St. Vladimir's Orthodox Theological Seminary Press, 1987.

Scott, Steve. *Like a House on Fire: Renewal of the Arts in a Postmodern Culture.* Chicago: Cornerstone, 1997.

Senn, Frank. *Christian Liturgy: Catholic and Evangelical.* Minneapolis: Fortress, 1997.

Shaughnessy, James D. *The Roots of Ritual.* Grand Rapids: Eerdmans, 1973.

Sykes, Stephen. *The Identity of Christianity: Theologians and the Essence of Christianity from Schleiermacher to Barth.* Philadelphia: Fortress, 1976.

Talley, Thomas J. *The Origins of the Liturgical Year.* New York: Pueblo, 1986.

Thurian, Max, and Geoffrey Wainwright, eds. *Baptism and Eucharist: Ecumenical Convergence in Celebration.* Grand Rapids: Eerdmans, 1983.

Trubetskoi, Eugene N. *Icons: Theology in Color.* Crestwood, N.Y.: St. Vladimir's Orthodox Theological Seminary Press, 1973.

Underhill, Evelyn. *Worship.* New York: Crossroad, 1989.

Webber, Robert. *Blended Worship: Achieving Substance and Relevance in Worship.* Peabody, Mass.: Hendrickson, 1996.

———. *Planning Blended Worship: The Creative Mixture of the Old and New.* Nashville: Abingdon, 1998.

———. *Worship Old and New.* 2nd ed. Grand Rapids: Zondervan, 1994.

White, James F. *A Brief History of Christian Worship.* Nashville: Abingdon, 1993.

———. *Documents of Christian Worship: Descriptive and Interpretive Sources.* Louisville: Westminster/John Knox, 1992.

———. *Protestant Worship: Traditions in Transition.* Louisville: Westminster/John Knox, 1989.

Willimon, William H. *The Service of God: How Worship and Ethics Are Related.* Nashville: Abingdon, 1983.

Introduction to Worship

Webber, Robert. *Worship Old and New.* Grand Rapids: Zondervan, 1994.

White, James F. *An Introduction to Christian Worship.* Nashville: Abingdon, 1980.

Jewish Roots of Christian Worship

DiSante, Carmine. *Jewish Prayer: The Origins of Christian Liturgy.* New York: Paulist, 1985.

Fisher, Eugene J. *The Jewish Roots of Christian Liturgy.* New York: Paulist, 1990.

Hill, Andrew. *Enter His Courts with Praise: Old Testament Worship for the New Testament Church.* Grand Rapids: Baker, 1997.

Theology of Worship

Dawn, Marva J., *Reaching Out without the Dumbing Down: A Theological Worship for the Turn of the Century Culture.* Grand Rapids: Eerdmans, 1995.

Kavanagh, Aiden. *Liturgical Theology.* New York: Pueblo, 1964.

Torrance, T. F. *Worship, Community, and the Triune God of Grace.* Downers Grove: Inter-Varsity, 1996; Carlisle, U.K.: Parternoster, 1996.

History of Worship

The Complete Library of Christian. Vol. 2, *Twenty Centuries of Christian Worship.* Peabody, Mass.: Hendrickson, 1993.

Folwy, Edward. *From Age to Age.* Chicago: Liturgy Training Publication, 1991.

Senn, Frank C. *Christian Liturgy: Catholic and Evangelical.* Minneapolis: Fortress, 1997.

White, James F. *Documents of Christian Worship.* Louisville: Westminster/John Knox, 1992.

Space

Bouyer, Louis. *Liturgy and Architecture.* Notre Dame, Ind.: University of Notre Dame Press, 1967.

Eucharist

O'Conner, James T. *The Hidden Manna: A Theology of the Eucharist.* San Francisco: Ignatius, 1988.

Rordaore, Willy, et al. *The Eucharist of the Early Christians.* Collegeville, Minn.: Liturgical, 1978.

Music in Worship

Hustad, Donald P. *Jubilate II: Church Music in Worship and Renewal.* Carol Stream, Ill.: Hope, 1993.

Part 5

Spirituality

Allen, Joseph S. *Inner Way: Toward a Rebirth of Eastern Christian Spiritual Direction.* Grand Rapids: Eerdmans, 1994.

Balentine, Samuel E. *Prayer in the Hebrew Bible: The Drama of Divine-Human Dialogue.* Minneapolis: Fortress, 1993.

Bauman, Zygmlit. *Post Modern Ethics.* Oxford: Blackwell, 1993.

Blumhardt, Christopher. *Action in Waiting.* Farmington, Pa.: Plough, 1998.

Bouyer, Louis. *Liturgical Piety.* Notre Dame, Ind.: University of Notre Dame Press, 1955.

Braso, Gabriel M. *Liturgy and Spirituality.* Collegeville, Minn.: Liturgical, 1971.

Clark, David K., and Robert V. Rakestraw, eds. *Readings in Christian Ethics.* Vol. 2, *Issues and Applications.* Grand Rapids: Baker, 1997.

———. *Readings in Christian Ethics.* Vol. 1, *Theory and Method.* Grand Rapids: Baker, 1997.

Colliander, Tito. *Way of the Ascetics: The Ancient Tradition of Discipline and Inner Growth.* Crestwood, N.Y.: St. Vladimir's Orthodox Theological Seminary Press, 1994.

Farley, B. W. *In Praise of Virtue: An Exploration of the Biblical Virtues in a Christian Context.* Grand Rapids: Eerdmans, 1995.

Fee, Gordon D. *God's Empowering Presence: The Holy Spirit in the Letter of Paul.* Peabody, Mass.: Hendrickson, 1994.

Fénelon, Francois. *Talking with God.* Brewster, Mass.: Paraclete, 1997.

Foster, Richard J. *Celebration of Discipline.* San Francisco: Harper San Francisco, 1978.

———. *Finding the Heart's True Home.* San Francisco: Harper San Francisco, 1992.

———. *Streams of Living Waters: Celebrating the Great Traditions of Christian Faith.* San Francisco: Harper San Francisco, 1998.

Foster, Richard J., and James Bryan Smith. *Devotional Classics: Selected Readings for Individuals and Groups.* San Francisco: Harper San Francisco, 1993.

Fowl, Stephen E., and L. Gregory Jones. *Reading in Communion: Scripture and Ethics in Christian Life.* Grand Rapids: Eerdmans, 1991.

French, R. M., trans. *The Pilgrim Continues His Journey.* New York: Seabury, 1965.

———. *The Way of a Pilgrim.* New York: Seabury, 1965.

Gangel, Kenneth O., and James C. Wilhoit, eds. *The Christian Educator's Handbook on Spiritual Formation.* Wheaton, Ill.: Victor Books, 1994.

Guroian, Vigen. *Ethics after Christendom.* Grand Rapids: Eerdmans, 1994.

Harkness, Georgia. *Mysticism: Its Meaning and Message.* Nashville: Abingdon, 1973.

Hauerwas, Stanley. *A Community of Christian Character.* Notre Dame, Ind.: University of Notre Dame Press, 1983.

———. *The Peaceable Kingdom.* Notre Dame, Ind.: University of Notre Dame Press, 1983.

———. *Remembering and Reforming: Toward a Constructive Christian Moral Philosophy.* Notre Dame, Ind.: University of Notre Dame Press, 1985.

Hourlier, Dom Jacques. *Reflection on the Spirituality of Gregorian Chant.* Orleans, Mass.: Paraclete, 1995.

Irwin, Kevin W. *Liturgy, Prayer and Spirituality.* New York: Paulist, 1984.

Jones, Cheslyn, and Geoffrey Wainfight, eds. *The Story of Spirituality.* Oxford: Oxford University Press, 1986.

Jones, L. Gregory. *Embodying Forgiveness.* Grand Rapids: Eerdmans, 1995.

Kelsey, Morton T. *Healing and Christianity: In Ancient Thought and Modern Times.* San Francisco: Harper & Row, 1973.

Leech, Kenneth. *Experiencing God: Theology as Spirituality.* San Francisco: Harper & Row, 1985.

Lossky, Vladimir. *The Mystical Theology of the Eastern Church.* London: James Clarke, 1973.

———. *The Vision of God.* Leighton Buzzard, Bedfordshire, U.K.: The Faith Press, 1973; also London: Faith Press, 1964.

Maas, Robin, and Gabriel O'Donnell, O.P. *Spiritual Traditions for the Contemporary Church.* Nashville: Abingdon, 1990.

MacIntyre, Alisdair. *After Virtue.* Notre Dame, Ind.: University of Notre Dame Press, 1984.

Maloney, George A. *Prayer of the Heart.* Notre Dame, Ind.: Ave Maria, 1983.

McGinn, Bernard. *The Presence of God: A History of Western Mysticism.* 4 vols. New York: Crossroad/Herder, 1994.

Meyendorff, John. *St. Gregory Palamas and Orthodox Spirituality.* Crestwood, N.Y.: St. Vladimir's Orthodox Theological Seminary Press, 1974.

Moreau, Scott. *Essentials of Spiritual Warfare.* Wheaton, Ill.: Harold Shaw, 1997.

Muto, Susan Annette. *A Practical Guide to Spiritual Reading.* Petersham, Mass.: St. Bedes, 1994.

Nelson, S. T. Thayer. *Spirituality and Pastoral Care.* Philadelphia: Fortress, 1985.

Nemeck, Francis Kelly, and Marie Theresa Coombs. *Contemplation.* Collegeville, Minn.: Liturgical, 1982.

Nicodemus of the Holy Mountain. *Unseen Warfare,* rev. by Theophan the Recluse. Crestwood, N.Y.: St. Vladimir's Orthodox Theological Seminary Press, 1995.

O'Donavan, O. *Resurrection and the Moral Order: An Outline for Evangelical Ethics.* Grand Rapids: Eerdmans, 1994.

Packer, J. I., and Loren Wilkinson, eds. *Alive to God: Studies in Spirituality.* Downers Grove, Ill.: InterVarsity, 1992.

Pearson, Mark. *Christian Healing.* Grand Rapids: Baker, 1995.

Pennington, M. Basil. *Lectio Divine: Renewing the Ancient Practice of Praying the Scripture.* New York: Crossroads, 1998.

Pfatteicher, Philip H. *Liturgical Spirituality.* Valley Forge, Pa.: Trinity Press International, 1997.

Ratzinger, Joseph Cardinal. *A New Song for the Lord: Faith in Christ and Liturgy Today.* New York: Crossroads, 1997.

Schreiter, Robert J. *In Water and in the Blood: A Spirituality of Solidarity and Hope.* New York: Crossroads, 1988.

Sliers, Don E. *Worship and Spirituality.* Philadelphia: Westminster, 1984.

Squire, Aelred. *Asking the Fathers: A Lively Look at the Oldest and Longest Christian Tradition of Spiritual Living.* Westminster, Md.: Christian Classics, 1993.

Underhill, Evelyn. *The Spiritual Life.* Wilton, Conn.: Morehouse Barlow, 1955.

Wells, David. *Losing Our Virtue: Why the Church Must Recover Its Moral Vision.* Grand Rapids: Eerdmans, 1998.

Willard, Dallas. *The Spirit of the Disciplines: Understanding How God Changes Lives.* San Francisco: Harper San Francisco, 1988.

Part 6

Mission of Evangelism

Bosch, David J. *Believing in the Future: Toward a Missiology of Western Culture.* Valley Forge, Pa.: Trinity Press International, 1995.

———. *Transforming Mission: Paradigm Shifts in Theology of Mission.* Maryknoll, N.Y.: Orbis, 1994.

Christian Initiation Resource Reader. Vol. 1, *Precatechumenate;* Vol. 2, *Catechumenate;* Vol. 3, *Purification and Enlightenment;* Vol. 4, *Mystagogis and Ministries.* New York: William Sadier, 1994.

Field, Anne. *From Darkness to Light.* Ben Lomond, Calif.: Conciliar, 1997.

Guder, Darrell. *Missional Church: A Vision for the Sending of the Church in North America.* Grand Rapids: Eerdmans, 1998.

Guroian, Vigen. *Ethics after Christendom: Toward an Ecclesial Christian Ethic.* Grand Rapids: Eerdmans, 1994.

Hunsberger, George R., and Craig Van Gelder. *The Church between Gospel and Culture.* Grand Rapids: Eerdmans, 1996.

Keifert, Patrick R. *Welcoming the Stranger: A Public Theology of Worship and Evangelism.* Minneapolis: Fortress, 1992.

The Murphy Center for Liturgical Research. *Made Not Born: New Perspectives on Christian Initiation and the Catechumenate.* Notre Dame, Ind.: University of Notre Dame Press, 1976.

Schmemann, Alexander. *Of Water and the Spirit.* Crestwood, N.Y.: St. Vladimir's Orthodox Theological Seminary Press, 1974.

Webber, Robert. *Liturgical Evangelism.* Harrisburg, Pa.: Morehouse, 1994.

Mission of Education

Bushnell, Horace. *Christian Nurture.* Cleveland: Pilgrim, 1994.

Dupré, Louis. *Religious Mystery and Rational Reflection.* Grand Rapids: Eerdmans, 1997.

Estes, Daniel J. *Hear, My Son: Teaching and Learning in Proverbs 1–9.* Grand Rapids: Eerdmans, 1998.

Green, Michael. *Evangelism in the Early Church.* Grand Rapids: Eerdmans, 1975.

Groome, Thomas H. *Christian Religious Education: Sharing Our Story and Our Vision.* San Francisco: Harper San Francisco, 1980.

Matsagouras, Elias. *The Early Church Fathers as Educators.* Minneapolis: Light and Life, 1977.

Palmer, Parker J. *To Know as We Are Known: Education as a Spiritual Journey.* San Francisco: Harper San Francisco, 1993.

Van Der Ven, Johannes A. *Formation of the Moral Self.* Grand Rapids: Eerdmans, 1997.

Westerhoff, John H., III, and William H. Willimon. *Liturgy and Learning through the Life Cycle.* Akron, Ohio: OSL Publications, 1994.

Mission to the World

Bosch, David J. *Transforming Mission: Paradigm Shifts in Theology of Mission.* Maryknoll, N.Y.: Orbis, 1994.

Hauerwas, Stanley. *After Christendom? How the Church Is to Behave If Freedom, Justice and a Christian Nation Are Bad Ideas.* Nashville: Abingdon, 1951.

Hauerwas, Stanley, and William H. Willimon. *Resident Aliens.* Nashville: Abingdon, 1989.

Kraus, C. Norman. *The Community of the Spirit: How the Church Is in the World.* Scottdale, Pa.: Herald, 1993.

Lingenfelter, Sherwood. *Transforming Culture: A Challenge for Christian Mission.* Grand Rapids: Baker, 1997.

Lingenfelter, Sherwood G., and Marvin K. Mayers. *Ministering Cross-Culturally: An Incarnational Model for Personal Relationships.* Grand Rapids: Baker, 1995.

Phillips, Timothy R., and Dennis L. Okholm. *Welcome to the Family: An Introduction to Evangelical Christianity.* Wheaton, Ill.: Victor/BridgePoint, 1996.

Van Engen, Charles. *Mission on the Way: Issues in Modern Theology.* Grand Rapids: Baker, 1997.

Yoder, John Howard. *The Politics of Jesus.* Grand Rapids: Eerdmans, 1972.

Evangelism

Christian Initiation Resources Reader. 4 vols. New York: Sadlier, 1984.

Green, Michael. *Evangelism in the Early Church.* Grand Rapids: Eerdmans, 1970.

Hippolytus, The Treatise on *The "Apostolic Tradition."* 2nd ed. London: SPCK, 1968.

Webber, Robert. *Liturgical Evangelism.* Harrisburg, Pa.: Morehouse, 1992.

Education and Nurture

Babin, Pierre, and Mercedes Iannone. *The New Era in Religious Communication.* Minneapolis: Fortress, 1991.

Duffy, Eamon. *The Stripping of the Altars.* New Haven, Conn.: Yale University Press, 1992.

Groame, Thomas H. *Christian Religious Education.* San Francisco: Harper & Row, 1980.

Matsagouras, Elias. *The Early Church Fathers as Educators.* Minneapolis: Light and Life, 1977.

Palmer, Parker J. *To Know as We Are Known: Education as a Spiritual Journey.* San Francisco: Harper & Row, 1993.

The Church in the World

Guder, Darrell L. *Missional Church.* Grand Rapids: Eerdmans, 1998.

Hauerwas, Stanley. *A Community of Character.* Notre Dame, Ind.: University of Notre Dame Press, 1981.

Yoder, John Howard. *The Politics of Jesus.* Grand Rapids: Eerdmans, 1972.

Part 7

Authority

Adam, A. K. M. *What Is Post Modern Criticism?* Minneapolis: Fortress, 1995.

Allen, Diogenes. *Philosophy for Understanding Theology.* Atlanta: John Knox, 1985.

Augustine. *On Christian Doctrine.* Translated by D. W. Robertson Jr. New York: Liberal Arts, 1958.

Beegle, D. *Scripture, Tradition, and Infallibility.* Grand Rapids: Eerdmans, 1963, 1973; 2nd ed., Ann Arbor: Pettengill, 1979.

Braaten, Carl E., and Robert W. Jenson, eds. *Reclaiming the Bible for the Church.* Grand Rapids: Eerdmans, 1995.

Bruce, F. F. *Tradition Old and New.* Grand Rapids: Zondervan, 1970.

Brueggemann, Walter. *Texts under Negotiation: The Bible and Postmodern Imagination.* Minneapolis: Fortress, 1993.

The Challenge of Religious Pluralism: An Evangelical Analysis and Response. Wheaton College, Wheaton Theological Conference, 1992.

Childs, Brevard S. *Introduction to the Old Testament as Scripture.* Philadelphia: Fortress, 1979.

———. *The New Testament as Canon: An Introduction.* Philadelphia: Fortress, 1985.

Davis, Leo Donald. *The First Seven Ecumenical Councils* (325–787) *Their History and Theology.* Collegeville, Minn.: Liturgical, 1983.

Demson, David E. *Hans Frie and Karl Barth: Different Ways of Reading Scripture.* Grand Rapids: Eerdmans, 1997.

Dulles, Avery. *Models of Revelation.* New York: Doubleday, 1985.

Eco, Umberto. *Interpretation and Overinterpretation.* Cambridge: Cambridge University Press, 1992.

Fackre, Gabriel. *The Christian Story.* Grand Rapids: Eerdmans, 1988.

———. *Ecumenical Faith in Evangelical Perspective.* Grand Rapids: Eerdmans, 1993.

Farrar, Frederic W. *History of Interpretation.* Grand Rapids: Baker, 1961.

Fowl, Stephen E. *The Theological Interpretation of Scripture.* Oxford: Blackwell, 1997.

Frei, Hans W. *The Eclipse of Biblical Narrative: A Study in Eighteenth and Nineteenth Century Hermeneutics.* New Haven, Conn.: Yale University Press, 1974.

———. *Types of Christian Theology*. New Haven, Conn.: Yale University Press, 1992.

Gerhardsson, Binger. *Tradition and Transmission in Early Christianity*. Grand Rapids: Eerdmans, 1998.

Grenz, Stanley J. *Created for Community*. Wheaton, Ill.: Victor/BridgePoint, 1996.

———. *Theology for the Community of God*. Nashville: Broadman, 1994.

Groupe des Dombes, For the Conversion of the Churches. Geneva: WCC Publications, 1993.

Heim, S. Mark. *Grounds for Understanding: Ecumenical Resources for Responses to Religious Pluralism*. Grand Rapids: Eerdmans, 1998.

———. *Salvations: Truth and Difference in Religions*. New York: Orbis, 1995.

Hick, John, and Paul F. Knitter, eds. *The Myth of Christian Uniqueness: Toward a Pluralistic Theology of Religions*. New York: Orbis, 1987.

Hunsberger, George R. *Lesslie Newbigin's Theology of Cultural Plurality*. Grand Rapids: Eerdmans, 1998.

Ingraffia, Brian D. *Postmodern Theory and Biblical Theology*. Cambridge: Cambridge University Press, 1995.

Lodahl, Michael. *The Story of God: Wesleyan Theology and Biblical Narrative*. Kansas City: Beacon Hill, 1994.

Longenecker, Richard N. *Biblical Exegesis in the Apostolic Period*. Grand Rapids: Eerdmans, 1987.

Marsden, George. *Reforming Fundamentalism: Fuller Seminary and the New Evangelicalism*. Grand Rapids: Eerdmans, 1987.

McKim, Donald K. *Theological Turning Points: Major Issues in Christian Thought*. Atlanta: John Knox, 1988.

McKnight, Edgar. *Postmodern Use of the Bible: The Emergence of Reader-Oriented Criticism*. (Nashville: Abingdon, 1988).

Meeks, Wayne A., ed. *Early Biblical Interpretation*. Philadelphia: Westminster, 1986.

Netland, Harold A. *Dissonant Voices: Religious Pluralism and the Question of Truth*. Grand Rapids: Eerdmans, 1991.

Newbigin, Lesslie. *Truth and Authority in Modernity*. Valley Forge, Pa.: Trinity Press International, 1996.

Okholm, Dennis L., and Timothy R. Phillips, eds. *Four Views on Salvation in a Pluralistic World*. Grand Rapids: Zondervan, 1997.

Pinnock, Clark H. *Scripture Principle*. San Francisco: Harper & Row, 1984.

Pinnock, Clark H., and Robert C. Brow. *Unbounded Love: A Good News Theology for the Twenty-First Century*. Downers Grove, Ill.: InterVarsity, 1994.

von Campenhausen, Hans. *Tradition and the Life of the Church*. Philadelphia: Fortress, 1968.

William, C[arl] Peachen. *Narratives of a Vulnerable God: Christ, Theology and Scripture*. Louisville: Westminster/John Knox, 1994.

Faith

Newbigin, Lesslie. *Foolishness to the Greeks: The Gospel and Western Culture*. Grand Rapids: Eerdmans, 1986.

———. *The Gospel in a Pluralistic Society*. Grand Rapids: Eerdmans, 1989.

———. *Proper Confidence: Faith, Doubt and Certainty in Christian Discipleship*. Grand Rapids: Eerdmans, 1995.

Origen. *Origen on First Principles*. Translated by G. W. Butterworth. London: S.P.C.K., 1936.

Pinnock, Clark H. *A Wideness in God's Mercy: The Finality of Jesus Christ in a World of Religions.* Grand Rapids: Zondervan, 1992.

Pinnock, Clark H., et al. *The Openness of God: A Biblical Challenge to the Traditional Understanding of God.* Downers Grove, Ill.: InterVarsity, 1994.

Ricoeur, Paul. *The Conflict of Interpretation: Essays in Hermeneutics.* Evanston, Ill.: Northwestern University Press, 1974.

Radner, Ephraim. *The End of the Church.* Grand Rapids: Eerdmans, 1998.

Sanders, James A. *Canon and Community: A Guide to Canonical Criticism.* Philadelphia: Fortress, 1984.

Scalise, Charles J. *From Scripture into Theology: A Canonical Journey into Hermeneutics.* Downers Grove, Ill.: InterVarsity, 1996.

Schroeder, H. J. *Canons and Decrees of the Council of Trent.* St. Louis: B. Herder, 1960.

Smith, Wilfred Cantwell. *Towards a World Theology: Faith and the Comparative History of Religion.* New York: Maryknoll, 1981.

Strauropoules, Archimandrite Christophorus. *Partakers of the Divine Nature.* Minneapolis: Light and Life, 1976.

Tavard, George H. *Holy Writ or Holy Church.* New York: Harper & Brothers, 1959.

Thiel, John E. *Nonfoundationalism.* Minneapolis: Augsburg, 1994.

Thiemann, Ronald F. *Revelation and Theology: The Gospel as Narrated Promise.* Notre Dame Ind.: University of Notre Dame Press, 1985.

Thiselton, Anthony C. *Interpreting God and the Postmodern Self: On Meaning, Manipulation and Promise.* Grand Rapids: Eerdmans, 1955.

———. *New Horizons in Hermeneutics.* Grand Rapids: Zondervan, 1992.

Tracy, David. *Plurality and Ambiguity: Hermeneutics Religion, Hope.* San Francisco: Harper San Francisco, 1987, 1994.

———. *The Analogical Imagination: Christian Theology and the Culture of Pluralism.* New York: Crossroads, 1995.

Ward, Timothy. *The Orthodox Church.* England: Penguin Books, 1964.

Wilson, Marvin R. *Our Father Abraham: Jewish Roots of the Christian Faith.* Grand Rapids: Eerdmans, 1989.

von Campenhausen, H. *The Formation of the Christian Bible.* (London: Black, 1972; Mifflintown, Pa.: Sigler, 1972, 1997; Philadelphia: Fortress, 1977)

C. S. Lewis said, "The true literary person is not the one that reads many books, it is the one who reads those books again and again." In this spirit I wish to suggest ten books that are worth reading again and again.

Postmodern Thought

Gadamer, Hans-Georg. *Truth and Method.* New York: Crossroad, 1991.

Jencks, Charles. *The Postmodern Reader.* New York: St. Martin's, 1992.

Paradigms in History

Allen, Diogenes. *Philosophy for Understanding Theology.* Atlanta: John Knox, 1985.

Christ

Aulen, Gustav. *Christus Victor.* New York: Macmillan, 1969.

Florovskii, Georgii. *Creation and Redemption.* Belmont, Mass.: Nordland, 1976.

Church

Dulles, Avery. *Models of the Church.* New York: Image Books, 1978.

Worship

Senn, Frank. *Christian Liturgy: Evangelical and Catholic.* Minneapolis: Fortress, 1997.

Spirituality

Jones, Cheslyn, Geoffrey Wainwright, and Edward Yarnold. *The Study of Spirituality.* New York: Oxford University Press, 1986.

Mission

Bosch, David J. *Transforming Mission: Paradigm Shifts in Theology of Mission.* New York: Orbis, 1994.

Theology

Lindbeck, George. *The Nature of Doctrine: Religion and Theology in a Post Liberal Age.* Philadelphia: Westminster, 1984.

Read, mark, learn, and inwardly devour these books and you will attain an integrated knowledge of the primary material you need to consider for an effective ministry that is rooted in Scripture, embraces history, and is deeply committed to contemporary relevance.

INDEX